the dissolve

the dissolve

EIGHTH INTERNATIONAL BIENNIAL EXHIBITION 2010

SARAH LEWIS AND **DANIEL BELASCO**, CURATORS
DAVID ADJAYE, **ADJAYE ASSOCIATES**, EXHIBITION DESIGN

SITE SANTA FE

the dissolve

biennial artists

ROBERT **BREER**

PAUL **CHAN**

MARTHA **COLBURN**

THOMAS **DEMAND**

BRENT **GREEN**

GEORGE **GRIFFIN**

EZRA **JOHNSON**

BILL T. **JONES** AND **OPENENDED GROUP**

WILLIAM **KENTRIDGE**

AVISH **KHEBREHZADEH**

LALEH **KHORRAMIAN**

MARIA **LASSNIG**

JENNIFER AND KEVIN **McCOY**

JOSHUA **MOSLEY**

OSCAR **MUÑOZ**

JACCO **OLIVIER**

RAYMOND **PETTIBON**

ROBERT **PRUITT**

CHRISTINE **REBET**

MARY **REID KELLEY**

ROBIN **RHODE**

HIRAKI **SAWA**

BERNI **SEARLE**

CINDY **SHERMAN**

FEDERICO **SOLMI**

KARA **WALKER**

with historical works by

EDISON MANUFACTURING COMPANY

FLEISCHER STUDIOS

LOTTE **REINIGER**

DZIGA **VERTOV**

the dissolve

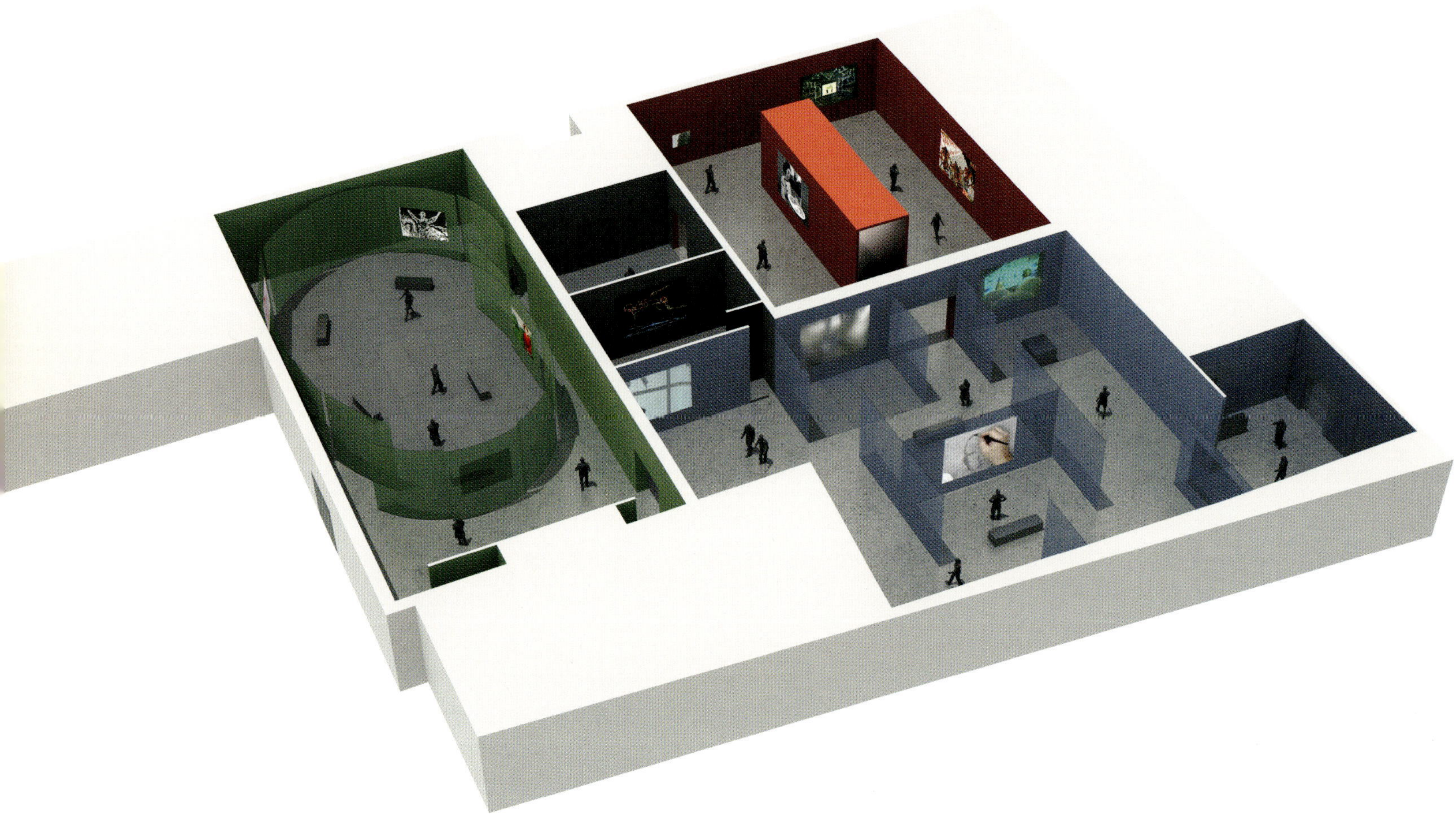

— AERIAL VIEW OF EXHIBITION DESIGN
Courtesy of Adjaye Associates

contents

foreword

SINCE SITE SANTA FE PRODUCED ITS FIRST BIENNIAL in 1995, the world has seen a proliferation of international biennials. These periodic exhibitions vary in almost every imaginable way, as they attempt to convey something singular and true about the particular moment of their production. SITE's Biennial is no exception. In fact, its relatively small scale in comparison to some of the behemoths of the biennial circuit empowers its curators to speak even more directly and personally about our cultural moment.

This is certainly what Sarah Lewis and Daniel Belasco have achieved with *The Dissolve*, SITE's Eighth International Biennial, a groundbreaking presentation of work by individuals who use moving-image art in a broad range of styles and with a remarkable arc of intentions. *The Dissolve* features a cross-generational balance of emerging and established artists who use animation as their visual organizing principle of choice, but with vastly different outcomes.

A striking development in contemporary art is rare and hard to recognize at its inception, but that is what Lewis and Belasco have demonstrated in *The Dissolve*. They present a new sensibility in the art of our time, a mingling of contemporary technologies and traditional visual arts—painting, drawing, and sculpture along with dance, music, and film. The fundamental form this work assumes is in the guise of animation, which unites the technological with the handmade.

These curators have found that what is most contemporary in this exhibition is its responsiveness to ancient, if not timeless desires for a direct empathetic connection to the artist through compelling narratives and the visual traces of the artist's individual process. Lewis and Belasco have found this connection in animated art, though the term implies a narrower history than the one they examine here. The works in the exhibition are almost all presented in the format of video and yet, all originate in something the artists quite obviously made by hand: drawings, paintings, or sculptures, most of which are figurative. These source materials are then animated using a variety of methods. The medium of moving-image art, like a novel or a play, allows an artist to create a narrative that unfolds over time. In this sense, the exhibition draws on the best of two worlds: the ability of drawings and paintings to show us the clear use of the artist's hand and the ability of moving images to tell stories with characters to whom we can relate in a personal way.

What can art do in the face of challenging times? Lewis and Belasco, along with the exhibition designer David Adjaye and all the artists in this Biennial, prove that the art of our time, while continuing to carry forward vanguard critical, intellectual, and technological trajectories, can also attend to the human and enduring need for a sustained and deep emotional connection. This connection is deepened in the Biennial through work that embeds itself within the entire history of film while expanding film's parameters into the moving-image technologies of today. For these reasons, SITE Santa Fe is extraordinarily proud to present *The Dissolve*, an unusually provocative, coherent, and far-reaching exhibition.

— LAURA STEWARD
Phillips Director, SITE Santa Fe

introduction

THE DISSOLVE, SITE SANTA FE'S EIGHTH INTERNATIONAL BIENNIAL, not only takes the pulse of contemporary moving-image art—whether designated as film, video, animation, or any other technology—but this exhibition also makes visible the *history* of the medium as a dynamic subtext for today's artists and audiences. The selection of works and their careful cinematic presentation in this exhibition produce an interaction between current and historical practices that is consistent with the merging of artistic media or "in-betweenness" that the curators have taken as their theme.

The Dissolve's emphasis on time, both in the sense of time-based media and in the sense of self-consciousness about history, makes it logical to review the original interrelationship between art and film technologies and, furthermore, to investigate how moving pictures got into art museums in the first place. My research in this area of late-nineteenth-century visual studies led to the exhibition and book, *Moving Pictures: American Art and Early Film, 1880-1910* (2005), which linked moving and still images on the spectrum of visual culture—and placed them side by side in museum galleries.

The nineteenth-century technologies that made moving pictures possible—improved photographic, mechanical, and electrical inventions—were so dramatic that history has typically defined early film as a scientific enterprise. But a closer look at the pivotal figures in the development of this medium shows that their goals were more artistic than technological. Eadweard Muybridge, Thomas Edison, William Dickson, and J. Stuart Blackton in the United States, as well as Étienne-Jules Marey, Georges Demeny, and the Lumière brothers in France (to name just a few of the international contributors to the effort) were keenly interested in fine art applications of moving images. The creation of this medium involved a complex merging of art forms: drawing, painting, photography, as well as, music and other performance arts involving the highly trained body.

Muybridge, for instance, was a fine art landscape photographer of the American West before being tapped to create stop-action photographs of Leland Stanford's race horses. From 1880 on, Muybridge had his photographs redrawn and colored on what he called "zoopraxiscope" discs which revolved in a projector to create moving art. Thomas Edison, inspired by Muybridge, believed that he could adapt his phonograph-cylinder technology to the recording of images so that the great musicians, rhetoricians, and performers could be preserved for history. Edison charged William Dickson, a company photographer, graphic designer, and electrical engineer, with the perfection of the medium. Dickson led the team which developed the standard technology of celluloid film strips, which were first shown in the cabinet viewer (the kinetoscope) and were later projected. But Dickson's illustrations for the cover of his book, *History of the Kinetograph, Kinetoscope, and Kineto-phonograph* (1895) show that he thought of those films as delicate colored drawings fluttering in the breeze. Both Edison and Lumière films were available in hand-painted versions for those who wanted the colorful, "artistic" effect rather than the standard black and white.

Films about artists creating drawings, paintings, sculpture, photographs, and even films themselves were plentiful in the era around 1900. Echoing the self-reflexive mood of the post-impressionist and modernist schools, filmmakers such as J. Stuart Blackton examined fundamental issues of creativity and the art-and-nature relationship in short, amusing skits. Blackton was trained as a painter but worked as a cartoonist for the *New York World* and switched to filmmaking for the Edison Manufacturing Company in 1896. His films about artists, such as *The Enchanted Drawing* (1900) and *The Artist's Dilemma* (1900), as well as other examples from that time, such as Edwin S. Porter's *The Animated Painting* (1904), examine the mysteries of the creative process and the power of the work of art to take on a life of its own.

the dissolve

For the *Moving Pictures* exhibition, I wanted to show films as art, playing continuously on monitors on the museum walls alongside related "still" works. Facing the skepticism of both art and film historians about whether monitors and movies belonged in such a setting, I found unexpected support for this installation in the exhibition history of early film. The kinetoscope, for example, was first demonstrated by the Edison team at the Brooklyn Institute of Arts and Sciences (now the Brooklyn Museum) in 1893. The first film audiences watched these moving pictures in museum spaces, such as the Eden Musée in New York, or in specialized art galleries called kinetoscope parlors. Going from cabinet to cabinet, the viewing experience was directly based on the centuries-old practice of the museum or art exhibition. After 1896, when projection became the dominant form of film presentation, and performance spaces such as vaudeville theaters were adapted for this purpose, films were separated from the live acts by the presence of an ornate gold frame around the screen—imitating once again museum or fine art exhibition practice.

As film viewing moved to dedicated spaces for projection, such as storefront nickelodeons and, later, movie theaters, it departed from the art exhibition tradition and became associated in the larger public's mind with theater rather than art. But the smaller art-going public never let go entirely of moving pictures in galleries. Artists as diverse as Charles Sheeler and Rube Goldberg made films throughout the teens, and avant-garde movements like Dada, Surrealism, and the Bauhaus always made space in their exhibitions for the showing of artists' films. Some outspoken writers, such as Vachel Lindsay in his 1915 book *The Art of the Moving Picture*, argued that films belonged in the permanent collections of museums, and, conversely, that the museum experience was by definition a cinematic one. In 1935, The Museum of Modern Art in New York established its own film library, later called the Department of Film and Media.

In recent years, the rise of video art has re-energized the art/film relationship within traditional art exhibition spaces. For museums with historical collections, such as the Brooklyn Museum, Whitney Museum of American Art, The Museum of Modern Art, and even The Metropolitan Museum of Art, films have made an appearance in special exhibitions and permanent collection installations, as all visual media are re-integrated into the framework of art history. For contemporary artists, such as those featured in *The Dissolve*, the elision of all artistic media shown within an enduring tradition of museums and galleries is an essential precondition of thinking about art in 2010.

— NANCY MOWLL MATHEWS
Eugénie Prendergast Senior Curator of Nineteenth and Twentieth Century Art,
Williams College Museum of Art

the dissolve

inventing the in-between

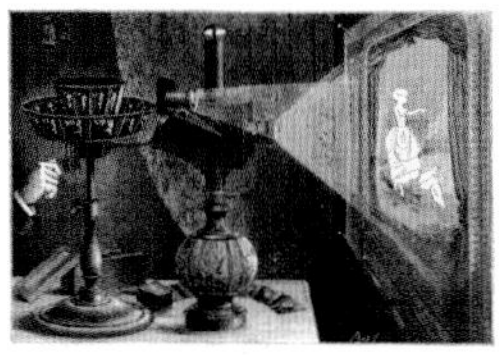

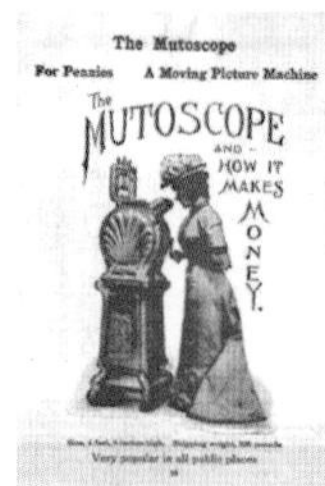

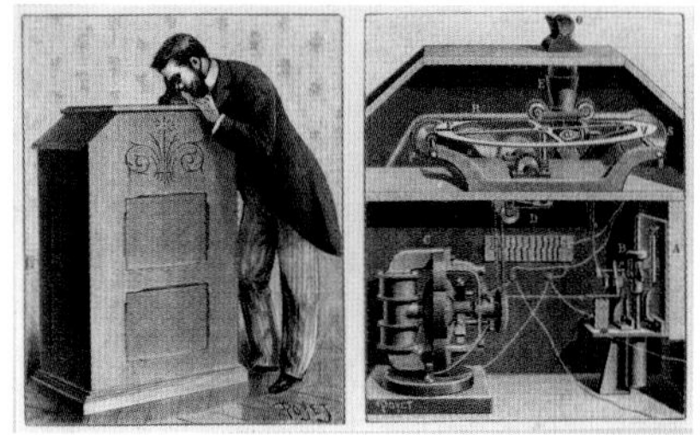

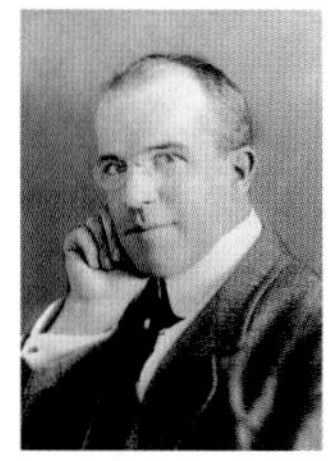

1833 Zoetrope, a device that produces an illusion of movement from spinning a succession of static images, is invented by British mathematician William Horner.

1872 Eadweard Muybridge begins his study of animals in motion, photographing a galloping horse.

1877 Émile Reynaud patents the praxinoscope, a device similar to the zoetrope that incorporates mirrors to create more complex illusions.

1885 Muybridge publishes *Animal Locomotion*: an eleven-volume electro-photographic investigation of consecutive phases of animal movements (1872-85).

1892 Reynaud debuts the *Pantomimes Lumineuses*, the first animation shown publicly at the Musée Grévin in Paris. The film is screened using a Théâtre Optique, a device combining the praxinoscope and a projector.

1894 Herman Casler develops the mutoscope, a motion-picture viewing device using a spinning sequence of cards.

1894 Holland Brothers opens the first kinetoscope parlor in New York. The kinetoscope, invented by Thomas Edison, is a device with a peephole used to view motion pictures.

1896 Georges Méliès invents stop-motion animation. He is also a lightning-sketch cartoonist.

1896 J. Stuart Blackton is hired by the Edison Manufactoring Company to perform lightning-sketch drawings for three short films: *Edison Drawn by World Artist, Humorous Cartoon,* and *Political Cartoon.*

1900 Léon Gaumont is awarded a French patent for stop-motion techniques.

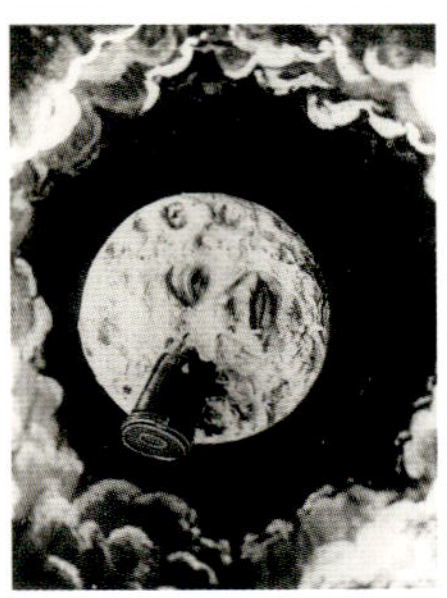

1902 Méliès creates stop-motion film, *A Trip to the Moon.*

1906 Blackton creates *Humorous Phases of Funny Faces.* Often considered first animated cartoon, the film depicts the faces of a man and woman, drawn in chalk, interacting with lifelike emotion and expression.

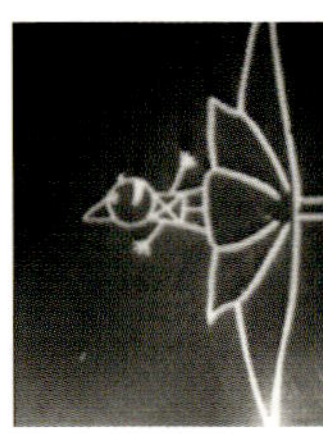

1908 Émile Cohl, French cartoonist and member of the Incoherents movement, makes *Fantasmagorie* for Gaumont Studios. The film depicts stick figures drawn in black on white paper, then photographed and shown in reverse to create a black background with white figures.

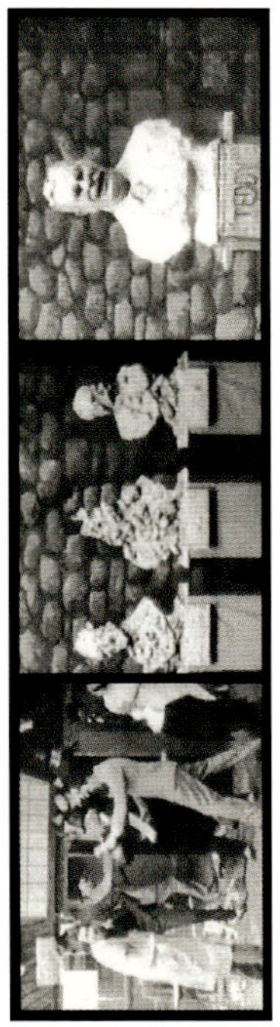

1908 Billy Bitzer pioneers "claymation" with *The Sculptor's Nightmare*, in which plasticene sculptures are brought to life using stop-motion techniques.

1910 Cohl creates the first paper cut-out animation, *En Route.*

1910 Ladislas Starewitch, pioneer in puppet animation, first uses insects in mating ritual "documentary," *Battle of the Stag-Beetles.* He continues to use insects in his fiction films.

1910 Together with his brother, Bruno Carro, Arnaldo Ginna, Futurist filmmaker, pioneers painting directly on film.

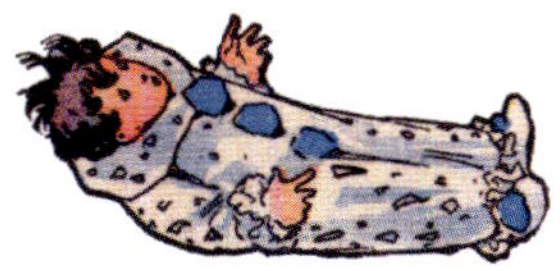

1911 Winsor McCay and Blackton create a short film titled *Little Nemo* based on the comic strip, the first animated film to use established newspaper cartoon characters. The film is presented in the vaudeville circuit with other films and live performers.

1913 Raoul Barré creates what is considered the world's first animation studio. John Bray sets up a similar studio in the U.S. in 1914.

1914 McCay premieres *Gertie the Dinosaur*, with Blackton credited as working on live-action sequences. McCay toured with the film, appeared at the opening to explain how the film was made, that Gertie was the only dinosaur in captivity, and then cracked his whip and the film began.

1915 Bray-Hurd process of using celluloid overlays is patented and enjoys a monopoly on licenses for seventeen years, starting the industrialization of animation cartoons.

1917 Max Fleischer invents the rotoscope to give more realistic movement to animated drawings by projecting live-action film movement on an easel to be traced over and redrawn. First used for KoKo the Clown character in cartoon series, *Out of the Inkwell.*

the dissolve

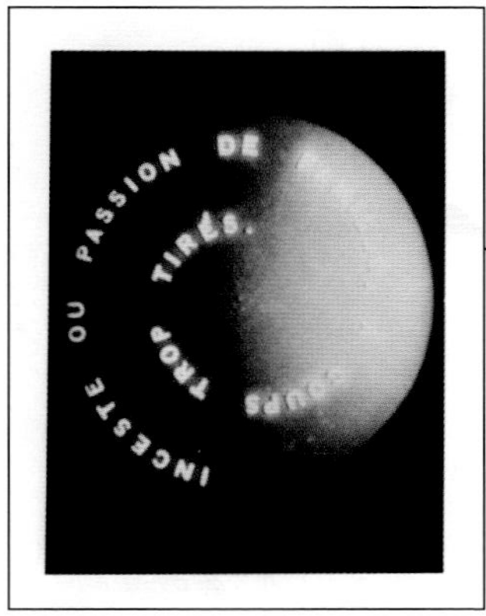

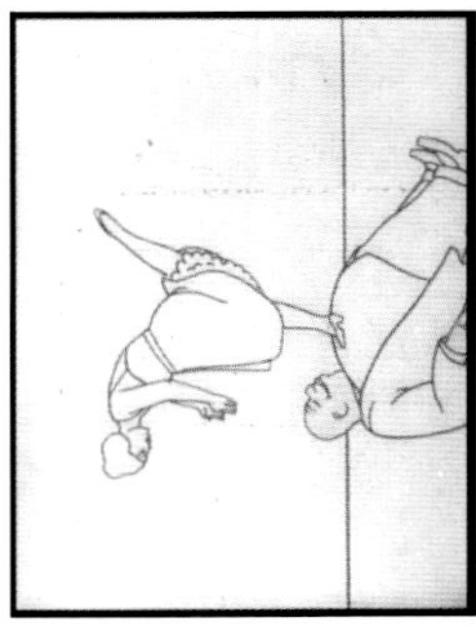

1928 Disney creates *Steamboat Willie*, the first sound-synched cartoon.

1926 Lotte Reiniger completes her feature-length silhouette animation film, *The Adventures of Prince Achmed.*

1925 Marcel Duchamp makes *Anemic Cinema*, with Man Ray and Marc Allégret. The experimental animation features a rotating disc motif as well as verbal and visual puns.

1925 Special effects artist Willis O'Brien does stop-motion animation of dinosaurs for *The Lost World.*

1924 Fernand Léger creates *Ballet Mécanique* combining frame-by-frame animation with paper cut-outs, painting on film, stop-motion, and live-action.

1924 Dziga Vertov directs his first artistic animation, *Soviet Toys*. This crudely drawn propaganda cartoon is shown in conjunction with his newsreels.

1921 Walt Disney's first cartoons featuring his own drawings, *Newman Laugh-O-Grams*, premiere at the Newman Theater in Kansas City.

1921 Walter Ruttmann shows *Lightplay Opus 1* in Frankfurt, Germany, thought to be the first screening of an abstract animated film in the world. Hans Richter begins to dedicate his film work to abstraction with his first film *Rhythm 21.*

1921 Viking Eggeling begins the first abstract film in animation, *Diagonal Symphony*. Completed in 1924, the film is an early attempt to link animation and sound.

1919 Lotte Reiniger creates her first film, *The Ornament of the Heart in Love.*

1917 Oten Shimokawa makes *Mukuzo Imokawa the Doorman*, a short animation often considered the first anime.

1917 *El Apóstol,* written and directed by Quirino Cristiani, considered by some to be the first feature-length animated film, is created. All known copies are destroyed in a fire in 1926.

1940 Whitney brothers, John and James, create their first animation, the abstract *24 Variations on a Theme*, in 8mm film.

1940 Disney releases *Fantasia*.

1940 John Halas and Joy Batchelor establish an animation studio in London, creating work influenced by the Bauhaus movement.

1940 The Museum of Modern Art, New York mounts their first animation exhibition, *A Short History of Animation: The Cartoon 1879-1933*.

1937 Disney's first feature, *Snow White and the Seven Dwarfs,* premieres and is a great success. In anticipation of its popularity, merchandising is prepared in advance of the opening. The film is an early example of the use of multidimensional effects, using six planes of glass to achieve a realistic perspective.

1935 Norman McLaren makes *Color Cocktail*, an animation combining images and jazz music, utilizing paint-on-film techniques.

1935 Fischinger wins a prize for *Composition in Blue* at the Venice Film Festival. The notoriety he gains from this film brings him to Hollywood. Fischinger's practice of synching images with classical music would inspire Disney's *Fantasia*.

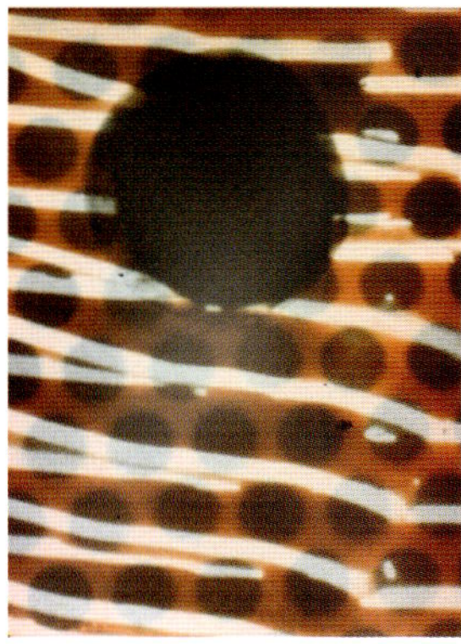

1935 Len Lye's, *A Colour Box,* is the first direct paint-on-film animation shown to a general audience.

1934 Ub Iwerks, chief animator at Disney, creates the multiplane camera. Capable of filming multiple cels simultaneously moving at varying speeds, the device achieves a 3-D effect.

1933 Warner Bros. creates its animation division, known as the Leon Schlesinger Productions.

1932 Creating what is perhaps the first computer animation, Mary Ellen Bute and Leon Thurmin make *The Perimeters of Light and Sound and Their Possible Synchronisation*, an abstraction created by drawing with electronically determined codes.

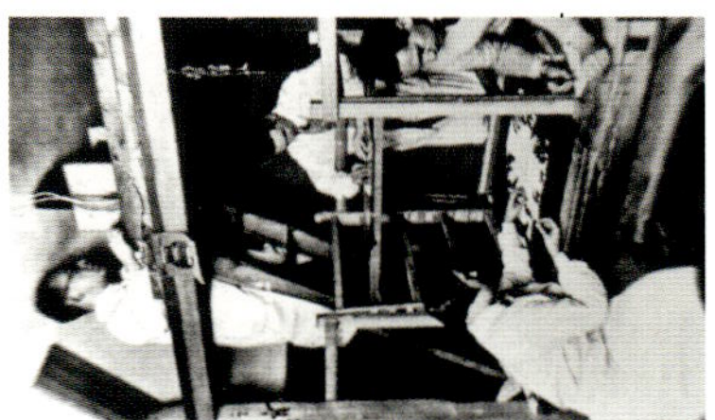

1930 Oskar Fischinger creates *Studie Nr. 2*. A landmark in abstract film, the animation incorporates sound and is created using negatives.

the dissolve

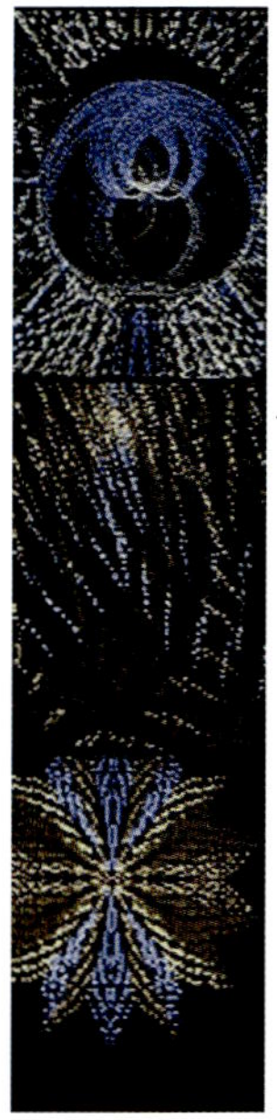

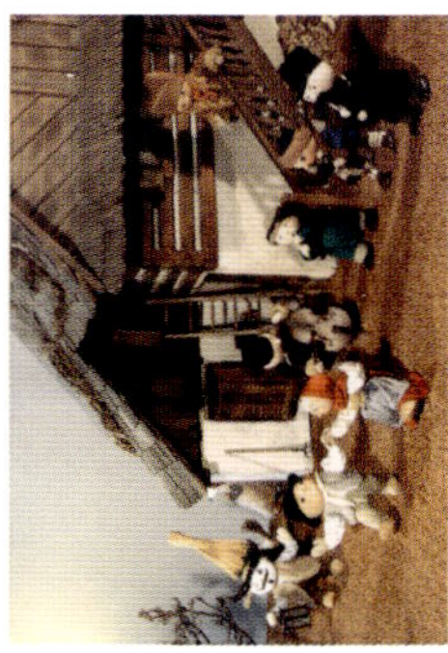

1960 Annecy International Animation Festival in Annecy, France is founded, and remains first biennial of its kind until 1998.

1959 John Whitney experiments with simple analog computer to produce visual effects.

1956 Robert Breer presents his animation, *Recreation*.

1956 Toei Doega, the first major Japanese animation studio, is created. Its goal is to be the Disney of the East, featuring cute animals in adapted folk tales.

1954 Disney's *Donald Duck* cartoon appears in Cinemascope.

1950 Jay Ward and Alex Anderson's *Crusader Rabbit*, first television-only cartoon, airs.

1947 Hans Richter and Duchamp create *Dreams that Money Can Buy* (other contributors to this film include Max Ernst, Van Ray, Alexander Calder, Darius Milhaud, and Fernand Léger).

1947 Jiří Trnka creates first puppet animation, *The Czech Year*, which marks the rise of a new Eastern European animation tradition.

1943 Mitsuyo Seo makes *Momotaro, the Brave Sailor*, a propaganda cartoon.

1943 Bob Clampett, director at Warner Bros., produces *Black Coal and de Sebben Dwarfs*, a parody of *Snow White* with voices lent by all black cast (aside from Mel Blanc). Despite racially volatile content is regarded as an animation masterpiece.

1941 McLaren is hired by National Film Board of Canada to start in-house animation unit in 1942.

1940 Bugs Bunny makes definitive appearance in *A Wild Hare*, directed by Tex Avery for Warner Bros.

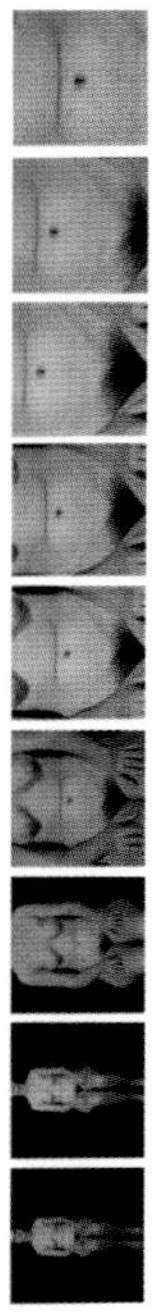

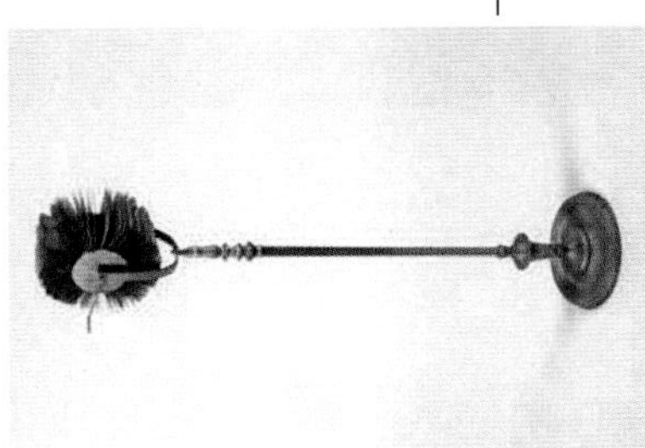

1964 Sol LeWitt creates *Muybridge*, a long box with ten identical apertures revealing an increasingly detailed view of a nude in a photograph. This serial sculpture—as well as that of Breer's—signals the phenomenological return of early animation in a sculptural and conceptual mode that prefigures the work explored by the artists in *The Dissolve*.

1963 Stan Brakhage creates *Mothlight* using handmade techniques including scratching and painting.

1963 Breer creates *Homage to John Cage*, a freestanding, hand-cranked mutoscope.

1963 *Gigantor* and *Astro Boy* premiere on Japanese TV, the latter is the first to appear on U.S. TV.

1962 Chris Marker creates *La Jetée*, a stop-motion film constructed using still photos.

1961 Lye exhibits kinetic sculptures.

1960 Harry Smith creates *Heaven and Earth Magic*, a masterpiece of esoteric imagery and collaged stop-motion annimation.

1960 *The Flintstones*, by Hanna-Barbera, is the first prime-time network cartoon series.

the dissolve

the dissolve

A NEW HISTORICALLY ROOTED IMPULSE IS PERMEATING contemporary art practice. Emerging and established artists working in many mediums, from painting and sculpture to film and mixed-media installation, are mining techniques of early animation and moving-image technologies to create hybrid forms where the homespun meets the high-tech. Consider three examples: the vaudevillian lightning sketch and the stop-motion animation of early Edison Manufacturing Company films appear as the foundation of recent works by Oscar Muñoz, Robin Rhode, and William Kentridge. Shadow puppetry in the moving image, popularized by Lotte Reiniger's 1926 film, *The Adventures of Prince Achmed*, offers Kara Walker's silhouette technique a powerful historical antecedent. Hiraki Sawa's *Airliner* (2003) uses the model of the flip book as the template for the action of his video. These artists are among many others who have activated their work by borrowing from earlier moving-image technology. With drawn lines, brush-strokes, and hand-manipulated objects, each artist decisively leaves an organic trace, insisting on the primacy of the body and the human imagination.

The title of SITE Santa Fe's Eighth International Biennial: *The Dissolve*, describes the essence of the new development that these artists exemplify—an alchemical quality inherent to the deliberate merger of historical models, advanced digital technologies, and a self-conscious foregrounding of gestures, marks, and materials that indicate the physical occasion of their production. A visceral, handmade quality unites these 16 and 35mm films, stop-motion animations, video, sculptural, and digital works by a diverse, international, and multigenerational roster of artists. While there have been exhibitions about discrete aspects of this practice—the intersection of animated art and drawing, flip books, painting, slides, drawing on film, and puppets, to name a few—*The Dissolve* is distinct in that, motivated by a desire to understand the meaning behind this collective, yet uncoordinated aesthetic, it gathers the extreme diversity of expression that shares the impulse to activate static media.[1]

In his seminal text, *The Shape of Time*, art historian George Kubler astutely points out that every work of art across the field of time represents the hard-won solution to a specific line of inquiry.[2] This Biennial is motivated by a foundational consideration: does this handmade/high-tech hybridity question the limits of technology in the face of the renewable fount of the creative process, the human imagination? Or is there another more urgent question behind this new approach? In other words, why is this collective, yet uncoordinated aesthetic emerging among so many artists?

The Dissolve has a deliberately bifocal lens, organized with an eye to both cultural history and contemporary aesthetics, connected to the technical developments of the moving image. It showcases a laboratory of works that combine past and present technologies and visual schema. It occasions the rare move of presenting the historical context of the artist's work to the viewer's retinal mind through the Biennial's installation itself, executed through a commission by architect David Adjaye. As such, the exhibition displays works by thirty contemporary artists juxtaposed with four historical animations, dating back to the early twentieth century.

It is tempting to ascribe the term "animation" to the works in the Biennial. The techniques of animation are clearly defined, yet, as Paul Wells and other historians have argued, it has an inexact aesthetic, making it possible to designate anything that moves, including drawn lines, shadows, clay, and collage as animation.[3] However, only a few of the artists in the exhibition claim the title of animator; others resist the category completely, while some see animation not as an end but a means for narrative opportunity. George Griffin describes himself as an animator, though even he says that he "ran truant into an experimental zone." Christine Rebet trained in traditional animation techniques while working in a studio in Berlin with political animators. Yet, others refute the term animation as an accurate descriptor of their work and will tell you clearly that they are opposed to it. "I don't want to be considered an animator," states Martha Colburn.[4]

For other artists, the integrative device to meld diverse forms inspired their practice. Avish Khebrehzadeh, who also trained in animation, uses it as "a tool."[5] Ezra Johnson claims, "My first animation came directly out of my painting, motivated by a state of frustration with painting. I was looking for a way to push the medium."[6] Jacco Olivier wanted "to get away from the realm of cinema."[7] Laleh Khorramian asserts that her "twisted process" resists conventional approaches to the linear assembly of narrative.[8] For these artists, and others in the Biennial, the turn toward setting their work in motion and exploring the unexpected developments became a satisfying, if laborious, instrument to integrate diverse media and include the element of time. For many, their strategies, too, are deployed to counteract the tendency toward seamless naturalistic animation originated by Walt Disney and brought to the highest technological achievement to date in popular culture by Pixar and James Cameron. For others, it is to insist that we are living in a moment when, more than ever, the slow media of the past seem increasingly relevant to counterbalance the digital convergence of the present.

Jasper Johns's axiom of art— "Take an object. Do something to it. Do something else to it."[9]— also guides many of the artists in the show unwittingly or not. That "doing" is the difference. This is the attitude that these artists have in common—a willingness to insert themselves into the construction of the moving image.

There is a veritable goldmine of disused, archaic, and obsolete technologies that artists have breathed life back into over the last fifteen years. With a renewed focus on process, these artists recall the earliest stages of motion pictures. *The Dissolve* recognizes a collective, fleeting wish to recapture some of the wonder and mystery of early film and animation, when the moving image exerted a magical power upon its viewer. Though many artists are not consciously working with century-old forms, the unexpected similarity between past and present reiterates that we are in an aesthetic and cultural moment that prizes authenticity over theory and improvisation over formula.

One revival has been interest in direct-manipulation animation once popular in vaudeville circuit acts where quick-sketch artists would amaze audiences with their on-the-spot inventions, performing and interacting with a drawing or other animation.[10] *The Enchanted Drawing* (1900), produced by J. Stuart Blackton in collaboration with Edison Manufacturing Company, exemplifies this early method with its frame-by-frame alteration of one single drawing and filmic capture of the variations on the images. Blackton draws a man's face, endowing it with expressive responses to his gags—giving him a glass of wine, taking away his cigarette—he foregrounds surface with his own expert representational forms. This multilayered approach in direct-manipulation animation was one of the signature developments in early film and was one of the earliest examples of what we now call stop-motion animation. Thomas Demand's *Rain* (2008) is one of the most subtle examples of the genre. With repeated photographic sequences that record a series of slight alterations to glass, candy wrappers, and other media placed on an already wet surface, Demand achieves a mesmerizing, all-over image of rain splashing on the ground.

In *Re/trato* (2003), Oscar Muñoz creates his own lightning sketch by painting self-portraits with water on a hot sidewalk. As the heat evaporates the water, the portrait vanishes before Muñoz can complete the facial line; he never fully manages to show us the portrait in its entirety. The deft use of the lightning-sketch approach allows Muñoz to replace the materiality of obvious forms of memorial with ephemerality.

The playful early form of cameraless animation, the flip book—first patented in 1868 by John Barns Linnet as a kineograph—is embedded into contemporary animated art, specifically in work by George Griffin, Robin Rhode, Hiraki Sawa, and Cindy Sherman. In Sherman's 16mm film, *Doll Clothes* (1975), the flip book becomes a template through which she expands her concept of character changes through sartorial transformations.

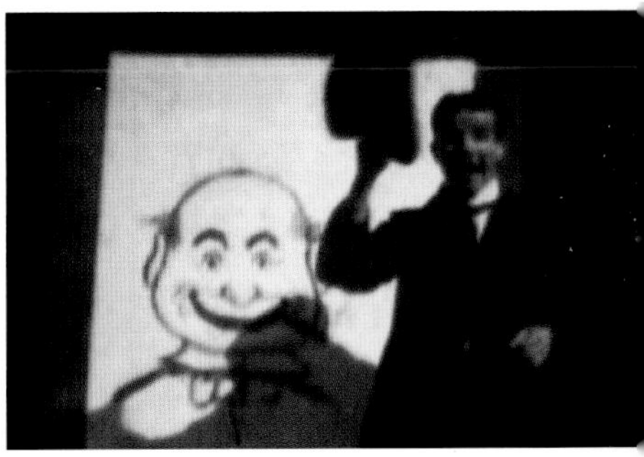

EDISON MANUFACTURING COMPANY
Still from *The Enchanted Drawing,* 1900

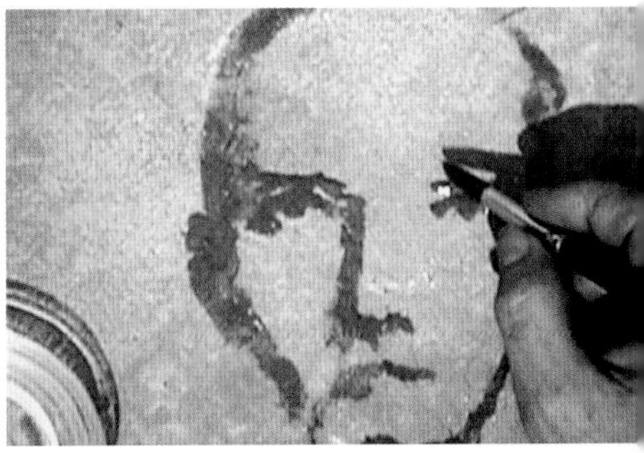

OSCAR MUÑOZ
Still from *Re/trato, 2003*

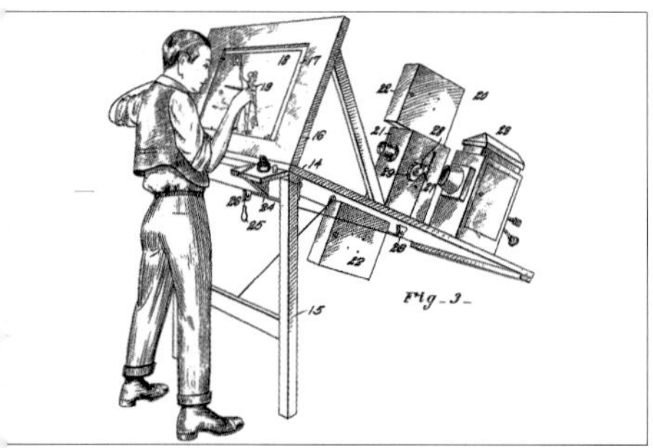

Patent drawing for Fleischer's original rotoscope, 1914

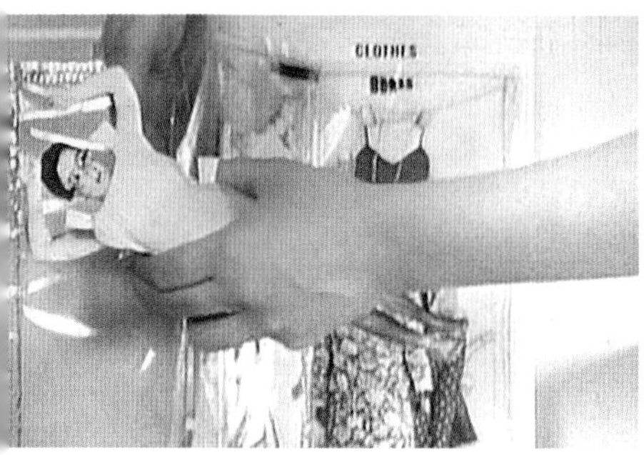

CINDY SHERMAN
Still from *Doll Clothes,* 1975

This technique is akin to her skillful mining of conventional performance in popular movies—the bodily position and style that represent her signature photographic aesthetic. With *Doll Clothes*, Sherman participated in the feminist intervention in film during the 1970s, when "female characters in animated films were given female psyches."[11] Many other women as well, including Maria Lassnig, Eleanor Antin, and Ida Applebroog, found new freedom in presenting personal, and often very satiric stories through the animation of sequential pictures. The flip-book technique, dematerialized and transmuted, was also revived by George Griffin in the burgeoning development of alternative and postmodernist self-reflexive animations of the 1970s.[12] The flip book has long delivered an intimate experience of the moving image. Robin Rhode's early photographic practice—sequential shots of the artist's engagement with objects rendered through oil-stick, chalk, or spray paint forms— splayed out the pages of a flip book imaging a twenty-first century lightning sketch in the round.

Other artists have found the rotoscope, whether in practice or in metaphor, to be a salient tool for investigating the placement of the body within the space of film. Invented by Max Fleischer in 1914, rotoscoping is the technique whereby film strips of live-action figures are outlined to create cartoons and then taken to hilarious, if politically incorrect, directions in shorts like *"Big Chief" Ko-Ko* (1924).[13] Animator Robert Breer employed rotoscoping—one could say revived it—with his landmark film, *Bang!* (1986). Along with the truncated sense of what could comprise a "shot," he emphasized the body by tracing single frames of crowds taken from television and home movies and projecting them in rapid succession.

In the revelatory eight-minute dance/video work *Ghostcatching* (1999), Bill T. Jones's movements in time and space are rendered as expressive and often contiguous marks through his collaboration with new-media artists Shelley Eshkar and Paul Kaiser. As Jones moves, we perceive a world described as if by afterimages, human movement traced through the gestural aid of Eshkar's hand-drawn lines. Otherworldly and futuristic as this work appears, there is a vernacular vocabulary throughout, which emerges in its aural qualities. Jones's voice begins the piece as if going back to bodily basics: he intones "A" and we see that a figure moves into a position that mimics that letter; then "B" and the figure moves again; then "C," and so on. As Jones's outlined body moves in space, new lines and shapes are created by his gestures such that his body operates as an organic technology, fashioning the structures that he ultimately inhabits. *Ghostcatching* ends with an insistence on the body—its perfection and failure. Jones's voice directs dancers who move expertly yet just out of synch with one another to grasp their fallibility, their humanity.

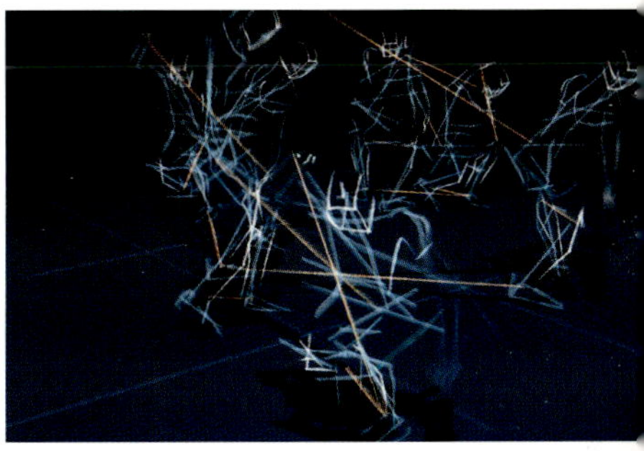

BILL T. JONES AND OPENENDED GROUP
Still from *Ghostcatching,* 1999

The updated version of this piece, *After Ghostcatching*, commissioned for the Biennial, allowed Jones and OpenEnded Group (Marc Downie, Eshkar, and Kaiser) to expand upon the motion-capture data in *Ghostcatching* and to take advantage of new three-dimensional, resolution-independent technology that was unavailable for the 1999 piece. This new technology has enabled them to realize one of many initial goals: "to enter a drawing as if entering 3-D space."[14] Despite its reliance on motion-capture technology, the impulse behind *Ghostcatching* and the new commission thematizes turn of the last century moments in the moving image when there was a focus on the human form. This was prominently manifested, for instance, through the physical-culture movement and visual art such as Loie Fuller's skirt dance and influenced by Thomas Eakins's anatomical studies from the nineteenth-century that once dominated the pedagogy at the Pennsylvania Academy of the Fine Arts.

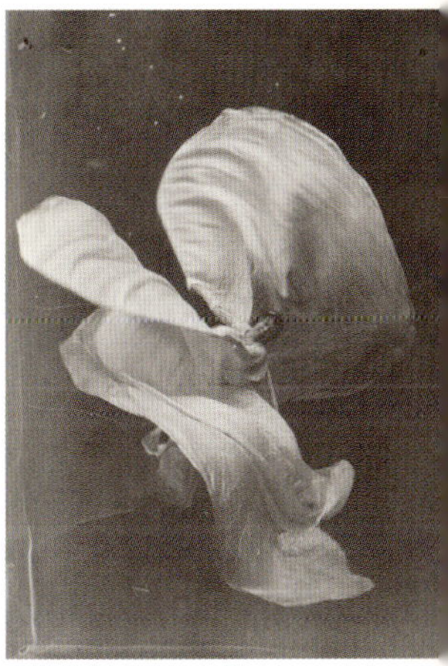

ISAIAH WEST TABER
Loie Fuller dancing, circa 1900

From the foundational moments in moving-image art, the focus on technology and the body—its capacities and limitations—has been a central issue. When Eadweard Muybridge fashioned a device to capture the imperceptible movement of a horse, and subsequently those of men and women, he inaugurated a technique to freeze physical

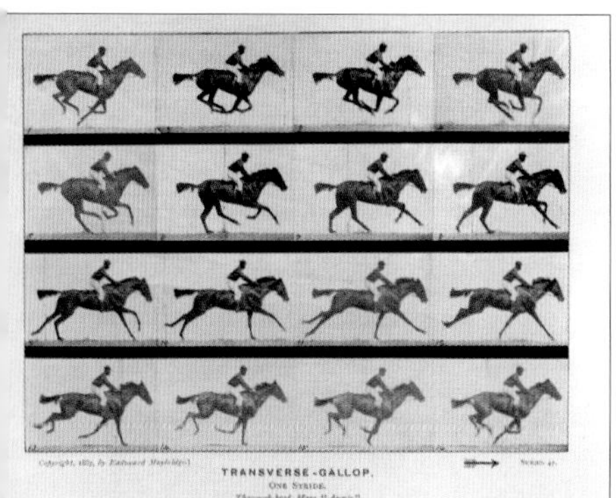

EADWEARD MUYBRIDGE
The Transverse-Gallop: one stride. From "Animals in Motion," 1887

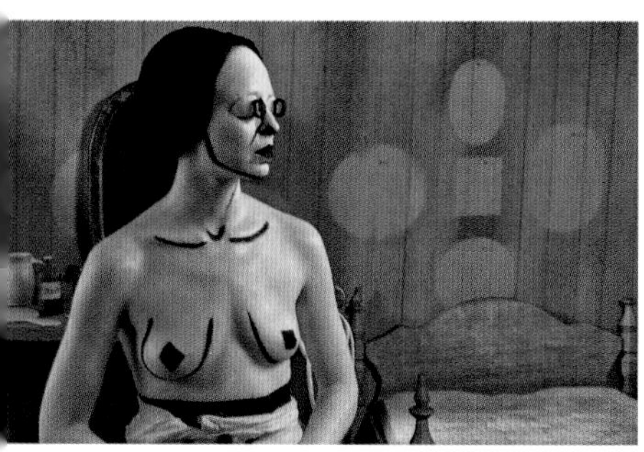

MARY REID KELLEY
Still from *You Make Me Iliad*, 2010

motion. In 1872, Muybridge had been hired by California tycoon Leland Stanford to challenge the standards of European academic art and determine whether all four legs of a running horse leave the ground at the same point. Muybridge tested this device—comprising twenty-four cameras, twelve inches apart—on Stanford's 8,000 acre estate in Palo Alto. They went off at 1/1,000 of a second, triggered by the horse galloping on the track. On the third day, he finally got the adjustment right, proving that "unsupported transit" did in fact take place.[15] He would later publish his project, *Animal Locomotion* (1872-85) to show the other physical movements that human vision can not capture—and it fascinated the public. Étienne-Jules Marey gave the name chronophotography to the new stop-action photography Muybridge pioneered. Meanwhile, Edison aimed to devise an instrument that would "do for the eye what the phonograph does for the ear."[16] Edison and Marey developed new versions of Muybridge's zoopraxiscope (1890), capitalizing on the international interest aroused in Muybridge's lecture tour to further deconstruct the image of natural movement.

Mary Reid Kelley uses a version of rotoscoping to revisit wartime's psychological and physical impact on civilians and non-civilians in the early twentieth century. In her films—influenced by German Expressionism—Reid Kelley attempts to mask her body so that it can "fit" into the illusionistic space of constructed sets and props. Accepting the three-dimensionality of her own given form, she ironically flattens a sense of her volume through the standard tricks of theatrical art—painting herself with line and shadow as if she were a drawing. As she embodies her assiduously archived and researched characters—men and women working as sailors, soldiers, nurses, prostitutes, and factory laborers in World War I-era Europe—her elaborate mise-en-scène, complete with her own poetry, performance, and song, turns the notion of rotoscoped animation inside out. Federico Solmi's work is also a contemporary rotoscope, in this case, for computer animation. He first models the action of his characters in a 3-D program, prints out stills that serve as animation frames, and then works from the images to enhance the extreme zooms and pans that allow him to easily construct spatially complex scenes he would otherwise be unable to render with pen and paper alone. His new work for the Biennial, *Douche Bag City* (2010), a satire of the corporate financial misdeeds that resulted in the recent economic meltdown, takes the classic immersive first-person-shooter video game, namely *Doom*, as a formal and narrative inspiration. A sequence of vignettes presents abject capitalist antiheros attempting—and always failing—to defeat the henchmen. Solmi's method of working backwards, that is taking the 3-D model, flattening it into its constituent profiles, and drawing it, so that an evil spider looks like a squashed abstraction—just as a human face looks rolled out in Jasper Johns's charcoal drawing *Study for "Skin" I* (1962)—takes the moving image full circle back to Cubism.

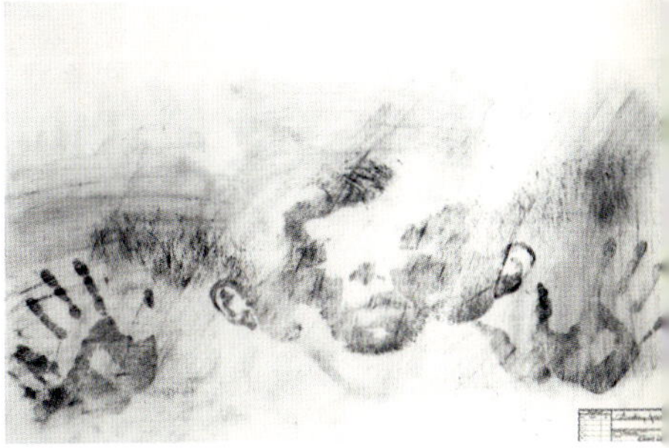

JASPER JOHNS
Study For *"Skin" 1*, 1962

The potent emotional and historical resonance of shadows, part of the grammar of early animation, also have been deployed in diverse ways. Berni Searle's three-channel video projection, *About to Forget* (2005), lingers over the bleeding from wet crimson crêpe paper silhouettes of her mother and grandmother cut-out from her mother's family photographs. This metaphoric action unifies two generations of a family that were estranged due to religious differences, one Muslim, one Catholic. Blood ties endured despite divisive religious beliefs. In artist activist Paul Chan's *4th ~~Light~~* (2006), a lighter-than-air shadow projection, the artist floats visual signifiers of twenty-first century religious, cultural, and military conflicts through the form of a faux window, suggesting, but ultimately failing, to deliver a way out.

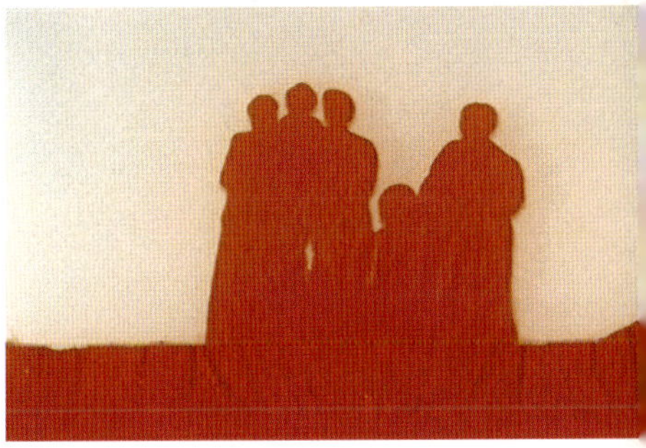

BERNI SEARLE
Still from *About to Forget*, 2005

Shadow puppetry became a staple of the European avant-garde interested in the capacity for humble materials to embody human gesture and inspire imagination. For example, Picasso's first move away from drawing was into this format when he created shadow puppets for the Barcelona cabarets in the late 1890s. Lotte Reiniger's 1926 film, *The Adventures of Prince Achmed*, brought the shadow puppet into the

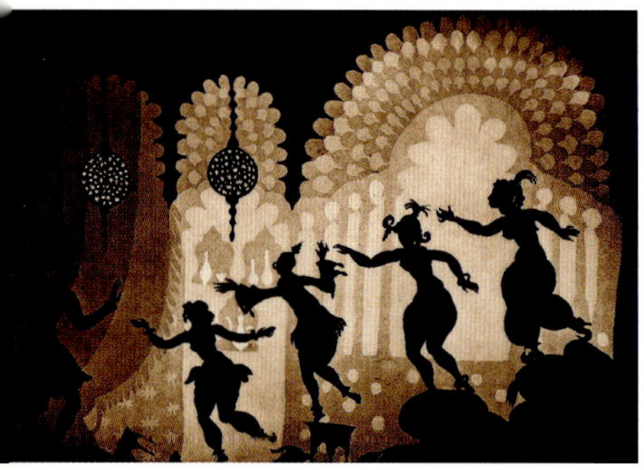

LOTTE REINIGER
Still from *The Adventures of Prince Achmed*, 1926

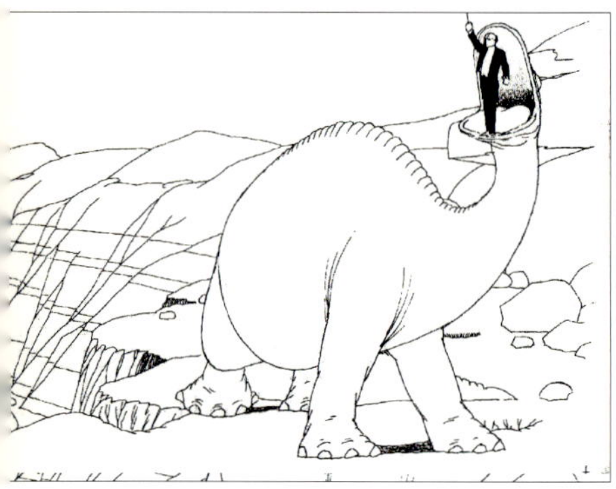

WINSOR McCAY
Gertie the Dinosaur carrying animated version of Winsor McCay, 1913

realm of film and mythic narration. This piece, with its dream-like background by Walter Ruttmann and a symphonic score by Wolfgang Zeller, is the oldest surviving-animated feature. Reiniger used animation to offer us seamless sequences from the *Arabian Nights* that belong to the realm of reverie and imagination. Today, Kara Walker unflinchingly roots the action of her shadow-puppet animation in the realm of a Faulknerian sense of history —"The past is never dead. It's not even past"—often instantiating her own body in the works by showing the actions of her hand.[17]

Avish Khebrehzadeh's reference to the techniques invented in the heyday of animation in the early twentieth century is achieved through an approach honed by her initial work as an "in-betweener," the job that consists of drawing the frames that connect the key frames in cartoon animation. The key frame embodies the genius of "good" animation, as originated by Winsor McCay and other pioneering cartoonists at the beginning of the twentieth century. McCay drew the frames that contained the most extreme poses, then had others fill in the gaps. But for Khebrehzadeh, the real creative work manifests itself in the moody, meandering in-between spaces. Often working from literature and poetry from her native Iran, she is innovative in the space between mediums, employing animation to combine distinct disciplines.

Among all the artists in the Biennial, William Kentridge's work serves as a fulcrum between past and present. His *Drawings for Projection*, a series of nine films begun in 1989, brought the pre-modernist world of early animation into the environment of the white cube and beyond—into performance spaces like the Metropolitan Opera. His works use lightning-sketch and stop-motion animation to interrogate the history of Apartheid in South Africa, yet are mediated through an exploration of the process of perception, observation, and monitoring. The imperfect erasures in Kentridge's charcoal drawing animations are of critical importance. "One had to look backwards—

even if quaintness was the price one paid," Kentridge explained in a conversation with curator Neal Benezra.[18]

The emergence of Kentridge at the same time that popular animations in America like the *Simpsons* (1987) and *Who Framed Roger Rabbit?* (1988) appeared, not only reintroduced the concept of animation as an essential form of creative freedom, but signified a cultural shift towards a growing interest in process. With process comes a play between authority and chance. The fate of the human body is embedded in every instance of the work, which displays its dependence on the hand and mind for its existence. In this case, process is not free from, or distinct from, technology. Raymond Pettibon, when transforming his drawings of anarchic California sublime into a sequence of interrelated vignettes, turned to Flash animation. The artist's familiar line, brushy yet penetrating, comes to life in the digital video *Sunday Night and Saturday Morning* (2005), representing the unexpected irony that new technologies deliver an enhanced experience of the handmade. Laleh Khorramian, too, engages in a meta- and creatively self-referential practice. She often starts by building up a stop-motion animation environment through a series of monotypes, studies them for narrative and formal ideas, and then creates drawings, collages, and models to create each scene. At this stage, "there are no rules to the process," she continues—"If I need to blow dust on a piece of paper and shake that paper to make it look like a flock of birds, or use the computer to make a minor effect, I will."[19]

The painstaking, laborious process of animating drawings, sculptures, or paintings inherently asserts the *presentness* of the artist, and with *presentness* comes a new awareness of the ethical value of maintaining subjectivity, even when the political situation defeats conceptual clarity—or one wants to say—especially in those situations similar to what Kentridge experienced growing up in a liberal Jewish family under

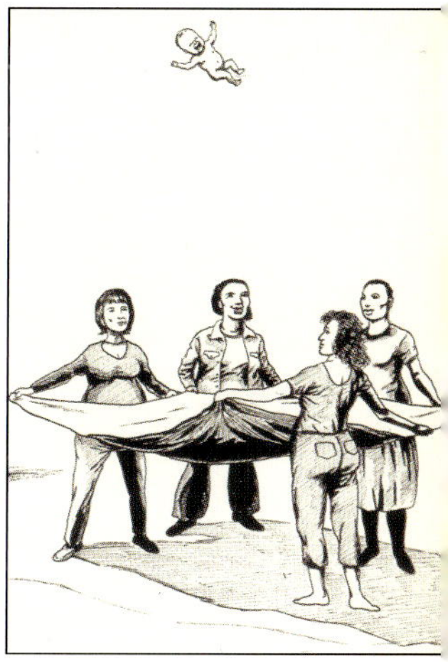

RAYMOND PETTIBON
Drawing from *Sunday Night and Saturday Morning*, 2005

the dissolve

Apartheid in South Africa. The results, like *History of the Main Complaint* (1996), have been a pioneering poetics of an animated handiwork, one that anticipated the mood of a younger generation both enamored with and wary of the digitization of our vision. Kentridge's oeuvre, imbued with its imperfections and laden with history, became a springboard for artists born in the 1970s: pivotal work for a number of younger artists in the Biennial, like Johnson and Solmi, who were inspired by his example to activate their art and produce their first films.

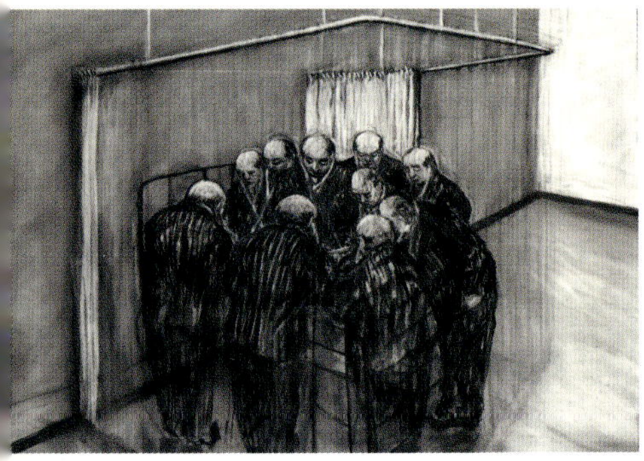

WILLIAM KENTRIDGE
Still from *History of the Main Complaint*, 1996

One large group of artists in this Biennial takes inspiration from pre-filmic animation technologies and early film animation techniques, while another cohort works more squarely through the history of painting. What would it be like to enter a painting in the way that you enter a three-dimensional space? Dutch painter Jacco Olivier's narrative video *Almost* (2009), just under two minutes long, shows us the answer. He compiles a luminous sequence of paint strokes and washes set to ambient and environmental sounds—birds chirping, doors closing—to give the viewer an experience of the painting as if you had been invited to step inside it. He achieves this by painting on several overlapping planes of glass which, when photographed sequentially and then filmed, renders the space of painting as a volume, not a surface. This glass painting technique is one part of the arsenal of classic animated features—a method perfected by Disney in *Snow White and the Seven Dwarfs* (1937)—to show animated dream sequences with persuasive vitality. *Almost* is representative of Olivier's achievement, offering vignettes of quotidian moments with extraordinary beauty. Each frame of Olivier's work is loaded with incident and the palimpsest of the process is visible in every frame. The all-over quality of painting, where the nature of the medium pushes the artist to cover the entire surface, allows for the filming of painting without worry about final resolution in a single frame because there is always the next sequence to make it right.

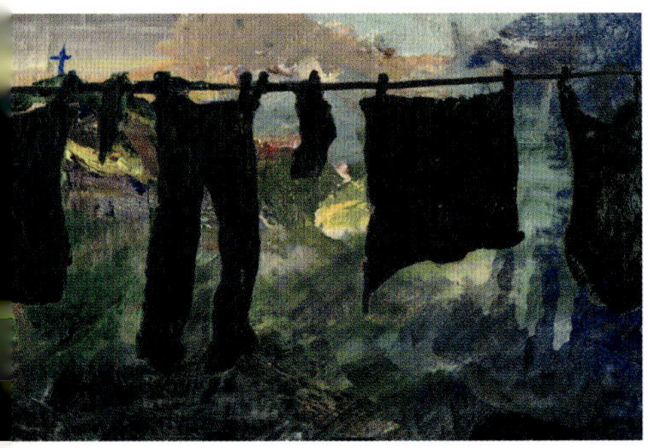

JACCO OLIVIER
Still from *Almost*, 2009

Ezra Johnson's first video, *What Visions Burn* (2006) is a twenty-two-minute, twenty-six-second, meta-narrative about painting itself. Johnson has said that he began to animate his paintings to allow himself "to paint badly," to not worry about achieving a finished or resolved work. The choice of the word "badly" is debatable; what his work undoubtedly offers is a process of painting in which the "finished" piece is ironically one that is always in a constant state of becoming, always on the verge of revelatory clarity, but never quite getting there for fear of sacrificing the full range of experience.

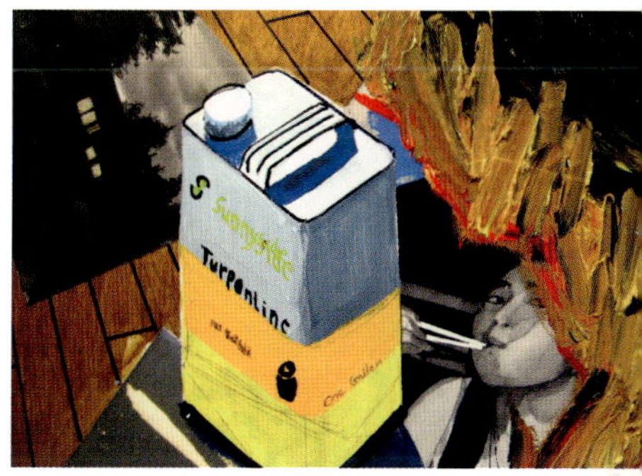

EZRA JOHNSON
Still from *What Visions Burn,* 2006

In focusing on landscape, Olivier and Johnson revisit nineteenth-century Romanticism as well as the turn of the twentieth century moving-picture panoramas first explored and popularized within environments like the Vitascope, which debuted in New York in 1896. Artists such as Frederic Church in paintings like *Niagara* (1857) aimed to duplicate the psychological experience of *being there*, which Nancy Mowll Mathews in her landmark 2005 exhibition *Moving Pictures: American Art and Early Film, 1880-1910*, demonstrates. Edison also investigated this experience in his film, *American Falls from Above, American Side* (1896). The result was a sense of immediacy and the thematization of a "New World sublime" through film.[20]

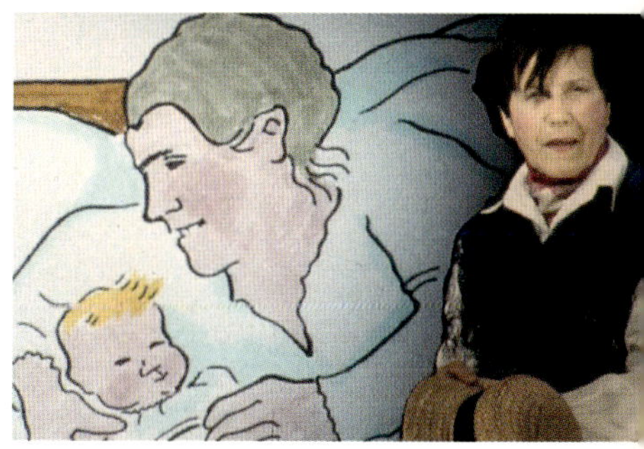

MARIA LASSNIG
Still from *Maria Lassnig Kantate,* 1992

Maria Lassnig's video piece *Maria Lassnig Kantate* (1992) records her singing narration of her life before the painted scenes that bear out the stories. Though the artist does not play with illusionism to the same extent as does Reid Kelley, she similarly unfolds a visual debate between the artist and her painted living creations, much as Winsor McCay interacted with his project animated cartoon *Gertie the Dinosaur* nearly a hundred years ago.

Russian film director and theorist Sergei Eisenstein's definition of animation asserted long ago this spirit as an essential animating desire to mix media, enjoy free play, and revel in an inventive process concerned more with means than ends. Eisenstein thought the elastic creatures in early *Silly Symphonies* cartoons were the epitome of

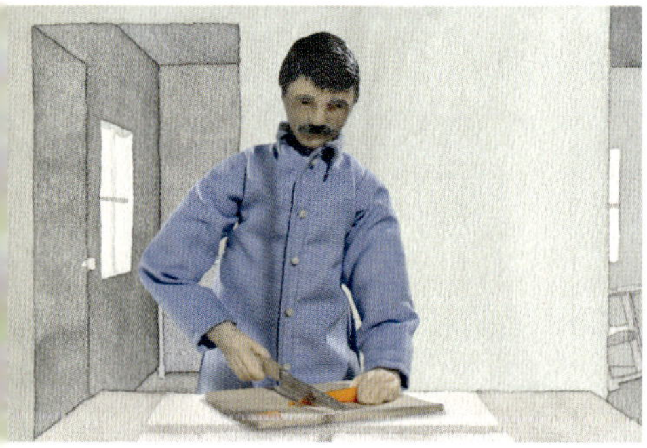

JOSHUA MOSLEY
Still from *A Vue*, 2004

"plasmaticness,"[21] which he defined as "a rejection of once-and-forever allotted form, freedom from ossification, the ability to dynamically assume any form."[22] The urge to animate every possible medium and substance, from scotch tape to oil paint to clay, extends far beyond the conventional, if stereotypical, association of animation with drawing and cartooning. This compulsion is apparent in Brent Green's handmade stop-motion films of his Appalachian-inspired story lines featuring isolated and often gothic characters.

By showing his work in art galleries, in addition to film festivals, Joshua Mosley, a professor of animation, became more aware of, and concerned with, how the horizon line in the gallery asserts itself, positioning his work as a landscape painting. The purposeful awkwardness of Mosley's characters defies the formulaic naturalistic schemas that are imposed on professional animators. Thus, Mosley may more overtly conjure his admiration for the work of painter Philip Guston whose plasmatic forms, staggering across a desolate landscape, resonate with Mosley's own claymation avatars in *A Vue* (2004). Indeed, for all the Biennial artists, the digital image dates quickly and shows its age, but the hand-drawn or painted line is timeless. From cave painting to this moment and into the future, the handmade has an eternal present that the computer-rendered image does not.[23]

That these works push painting to engage with the earlier phases of the moving image is, in fact, not as inter-media as it seems. The historical moments of codevelopment and convergence between art, animation, and the museum space was the subject of extensive study by Mathews in her *Moving Pictures* exhibition. Following empirical triumphs like Muybridge's, wonder shifted from nature to the body as rendered through technology, expanding the possibilities of realism through photographic technologies.[24] Eakins's *A May Morning in the Park (The Fairman Rogers Four-in-Hand)* (1879-80) exemplifies the work of a painter who consciously explored the visual insights made possible by the use of machinery and photographic motion studies.[25] If film took on the role of showing what the eye could not, the contemporary artists in the Biennial prove that painting and other media too have answers worthy of our rapt attention.

The Biennial focuses on works from two periods, from 1900-1930 and 1975 to the present, and little from the period between 1930-1975. Nor is there any work that can be defined as abstract or non-representational. These two facts are related, for the connective tissue of all of the Biennial works is narrative. For many artists, the attraction to animation was its narrative possibilities, an opportunity offered by expanding into time. Above all, it is the turn to painting, a medium abandoned en masse by the Conceptual avant-garde in the 1960s and '70s, that signals the way that animating leads to revitalizing the neglected, discarded, and overlooked—an embracing position toward the past and its subjects that resonates today.

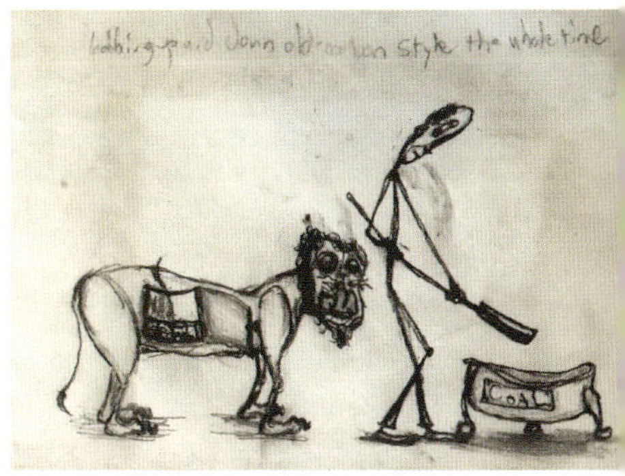

BRENT GREEN
Still from *Paulina Hollers*, 2006

Storytelling is of course a notion anathema to the formalism that came to dominate avant-garde filmmaking and cinema in the mid-twentieth century. With the exception of Surrealist-inspired film, this era was defined by structuralist cinema, which emphasized formal experimentation, the setting of technical limitations, repetition, abstraction, and anti-narrative. Artists strove for a blunt, plain aesthetic, emphasizing the concrete, cold and hard facts of the camera, the film, and the projector. The creative impulses ran toward stripping actions to the essentials and single gestures. These deconstructions, from Ken Jacobs's projected images of his "nervous system" to Richard Serra's highly deliberate and narrowly focused video performances, skewed toward the conceptual and away from the surrealist and the narrative. These individual, studio-based experimentations were strong reactions against the commercialism, kitsch, and collectivism of Disney's animated features, not to mention the mythic and highly subjective claims of Abstract Expressionism. However, a work like Dziga Vertov's *Soviet Toys* (1924) represents a crossroads, where an archaistic aesthetic and political position could be fused in an image-based, animated narrative film.[26] His work

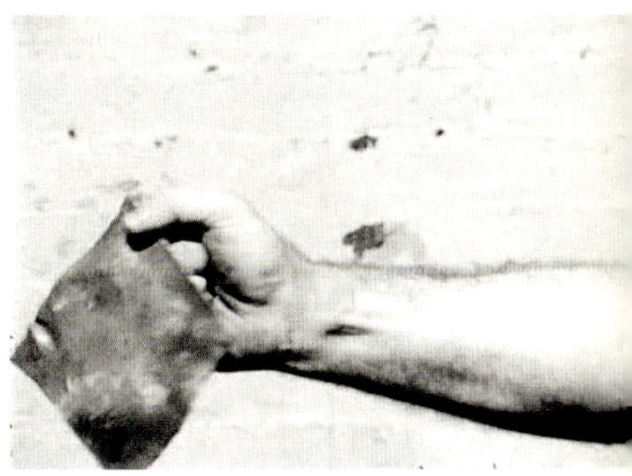

RICHARD SERRA
Still from *Hand Catching Lead*, 1968

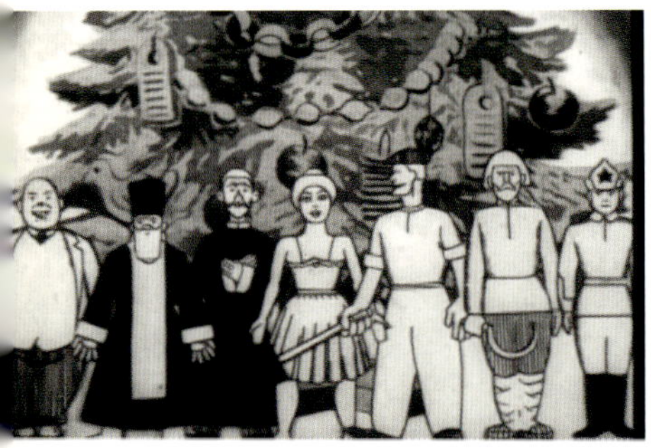

DZIGA VERTOV
Still from *Soviet Toys*, 1924

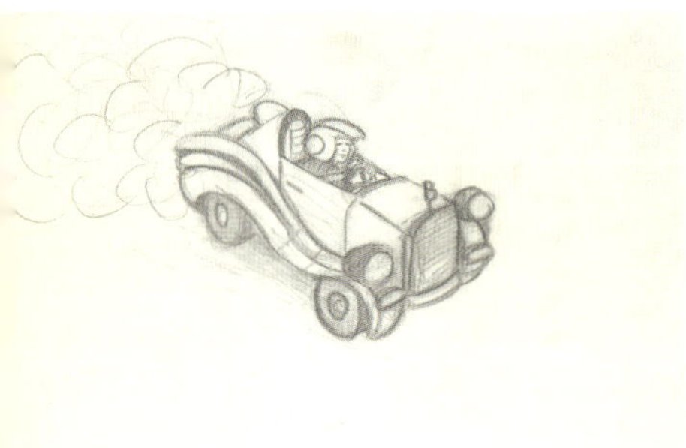

ROBERT PRUITT
Still from *Black Stuntman (Volumes 1 and 2)*, 2004

fused agitational journalism, advertisement, and animation, influenced by cartoonist Viktor Deni, whose work often appeared in *Pravda*, the Communist party daily.[27]

Many of the works in the Biennial make emotional claims that constitute a move away from the non-representational animation of the 1930s and '40s—pioneered by Oskar Fischinger, Len Lye, and Mary Ellen Bute—and the structural and formalist film and video of the 1960s and '70s. (The range of recent and past creativity in such work was explored in *The Abstract Dissolve*, a film program presented on the opening weekend of the Biennial.) Martha Colburn's work sets in motion puppets, cutouts, puzzles, random pictures scanned from magazines, and hand-painted imagery. *Myth Labs* (2008), like some of her recent works, is a rambunctious send-up of American politics, particularly the struggles evinced by religious zealots, the military, as well as by early settlers' encounters with Native Americans. Unlike the stereotyping within Fleischer Studios' *"Big Chief" Ko-Ko*, Colburn addresses the myths regarding Western expansion with a direct confrontation. In her hands, this original struggle is materialized as a poison in the form of the drug, crystal meth, that is taking over the nation. The autodidactic artist claims that she strives to achieve a dematerialized quality of expressive poetry with her film. Colburn shoots in 16mm film, with frame-by-frame, stop-motion animation, recalling the funky collaged films of 1960s animation, from Larry Jordan to Terry Gilliam, which drew liberally from Victorian-era visual culture.

Artists such as Colburn and Johnson use animating techniques to tell stories about lived realities fully felt, but rarely seen. As Wells reminds us, animation's narrative expression was often characterized by this "desire to express *difference* and *otherness*."[28] The distinctly hand-drawn animations and voice-overs by Robert Pruitt in *Black Stuntman (Volumes 1 and 2)* (2004)—which recall the low-tech productions of 1970s Hanna-Barbera and *Speed Racer* cartoons—offer short narratives that delve into African Americans' consciousness at this point in time. Pruitt's technique of "smuggling" in perspectives not often seen reinforces how the rudimentary forces of identity-formation are played out amid the diffuse background of pop cultural entertainment. It also offers a revision to the first stereotype-ridden black-themed cartoons, like *Fat Albert*, which also first appeared on television in the 1970s.[29]

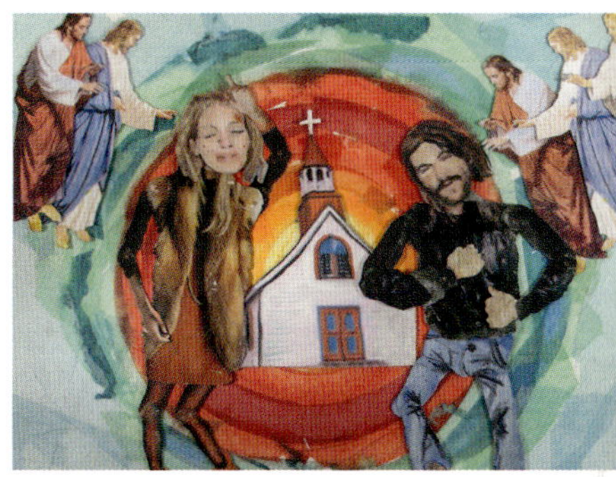

MARTHA COLBURN
Still from *Myth Labs*, 2008

Labor in much of these contemporary works is not veiled, but is transparent, as it was in the earliest animations. In her films, Kara Walker shows the hand—implicating the body as present in her films—moving her puppets with expert care. When Lotte Reiniger began work in 1923 on *The Adventures of Prince Achmed*, she used a four-poster bed contraption to film under the low ceiling of the attic roof of her studio in Potsdam, and a bicycle pump to create the stop-motion with her left hand as she kept her right hand steady on the figures on the glass plate. Unlike experiencing a painting or sculpture as finished, we can visualize in animation how artists work. For example, see Muñoz's hand drawing water portraits in *Re/trato*. The more artists reveal of their process, the more the amazement amplifies, as the viewer is more easily able to imagine him or herself embedded in the action. The labor-intensive quality of the work is common in the Biennial. Many artists themselves are exhausted at the thought of the literally thousands of drawings or minute alterations that had to be made to produce a minute or two of film, yet they feel compelled to remain committed to the process. There are no limits to the amount of times they are willing to "do something, and do it again."

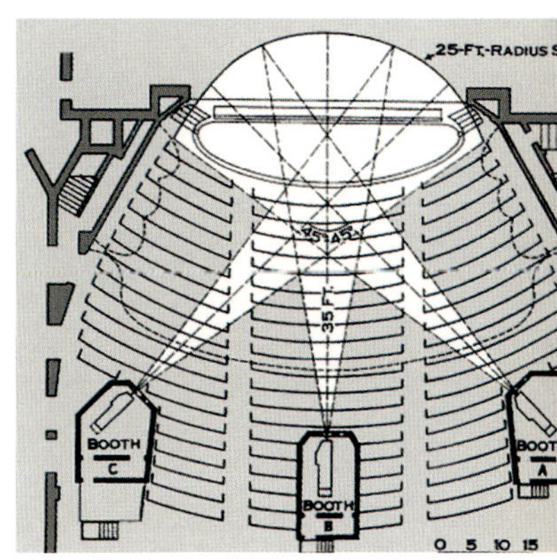

Diagram of how Cinerama is projected

The Dissolve exhibition design by David Adjaye has recapitulated the diverse viewing environments of the twentieth century. The viewer is first taken to the shadow-infused situations offered by the nickelodeon, mutoscope, and flip book in the first section of the exhibition. The second section evokes the shared arena-like space of Cinerama. The postwar popularization of Cinemascope, Panavision, 3-D, and other technologies expanded the visual experience to the point of becoming all encompassing. The viewing experience in these places was fundamentally communal, and the audience observed

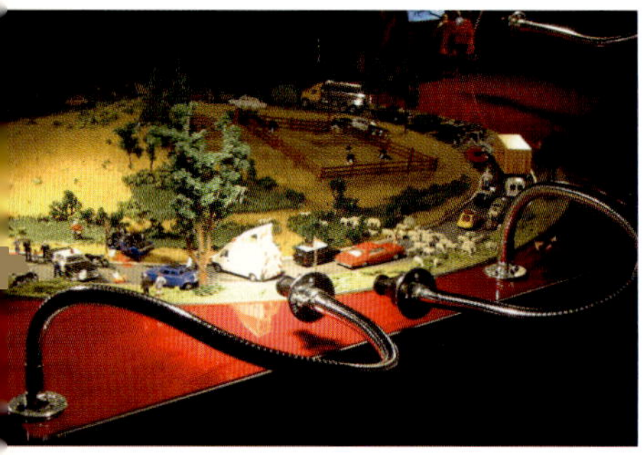

JENNIFER AND KEVIN McCOY
Traffic #1: Our Second Date, 2004

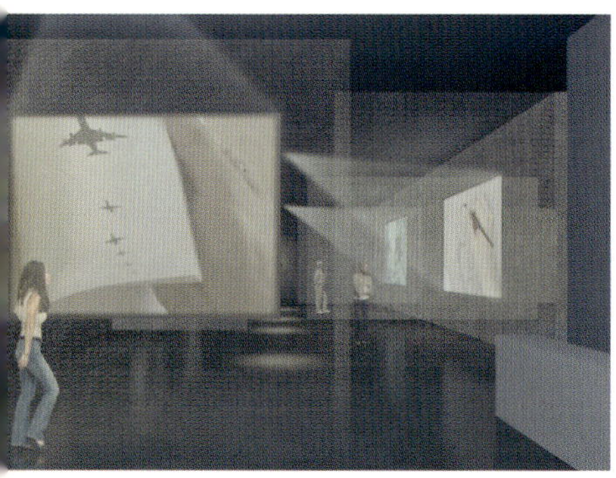

Image from David Adjaye's design proposal for *The Dissolve*.

others watching films as much as they experienced their own spectatorship, an experience akin to the cyclorama—the old-fashioned circular space, which presented painted panoramas in a sequence of events, so that the nineteenth-century viewer would feel a sense of historical progression. Adjaye has structured a cyclorama space, which, too, allows film and video to be read as painting.

The development of "expanded cinema" relocated the moving image to the three-dimensional place of the museum gallery with the development of video and multi-channel film installation in the 1960s.[30] What is new today is that artists are seemingly condensing cinema, combining their diverse media within the frame of the projection, while making us aware of the objecthood of the technologies behind projections. This new exhibition style correlates to the move of artists seeking to lend a new physicality to the visual field of the film or video through various animating processes. All of these maneuvers create a heightened self-consciousness on the part of the viewer, of the constructedness of the imagination itself, and of its various expressions in myth, dreams, and storytelling.

Jennifer and Kevin McCoy stage personal viewing experiences of cinema in their motorized diorama *Traffic #1: Our Second Date* (2004). The anti-climactic traffic jam of Godard's *Week-End* (1967) rotates in miniature on a disk, the well-known scene coming to life in a sequence of programmed cuts projected in live video. By offering both the source of the animation (the miniature models) and the filmic product, the artists bring us, the viewers, into the center of the cognitive experience of the *in-between* space of animation. Between the image and the object lies the emotional life of the body.

Adjaye's design route cycles us through to the third space which affirms the twenty-first century personal mode of viewing through the dominance of digital platforms and self-enclosed spaces. Yet, the works in this section hearken back to the requisite intimacy of the earliest stage of moving images. Christine Rebet's hand-drawn and painted work, exploring the admixture of early modernism and late magic, requires display in a claustrophobic setting in tune with the subject of her film, *The Black Cabinet* (2007), a two-channel cartoon depicting a turn-of-the-century Coney Island séance. In short, the Biennial's design requires that we engage with the temporal changes in the development of moving images, that we recall an anterior time. The design telegraphically communicates the message about the historical actions through the structure of the rooms themselves. Adjaye takes space as a material susceptible to animating, in the same spirit as the Biennial artists bring to painting and collage.

The show leaves us with the paradigmatic moving-image interface of today—the Web-based video—which offers metaphorical insight into the visual operations of contemporary art. More intimate and personalized, individual experiences on YouTube and iPhone bring us back to the mutoscope, zoetrope, and other pre-filmic animations. George Griffin's digital mutoscope, essentially a computer with a hand-cranked interface, reinvents his landmark cartoon *Viewmaster* (1976), itself a satirical homage to Muybridge's zoopraxiscope, by literalizing the ongoing stream of unexpected fusions and corollaries that characterize contemporary culture. While the scale of presentation and the range of materials vary greatly, one element remains constant: the remixing and recombining of the familiar and the strange which revitalizes old media, creating compelling new stories that probe social histories and private narratives.

In addition to Jasper Johns's adage, bricolage, or creation through the use of materials and concepts at hand, provides a compelling analogy for the multifaceted artistic practice explored in the Biennial. Claude Lévi-Strauss, when advancing his theory of the bricoleur in *The Savage Mind*, identified the stage sets of Georges Méliès, the inventor of stop-motion "trick films"—most famously *A Trip to the Moon* (1902)—as an archetypical example of how "mythical reflection can reach brilliant unforeseen results on the intellectual plane."[31] Méliès here represents a model of the tinkerer

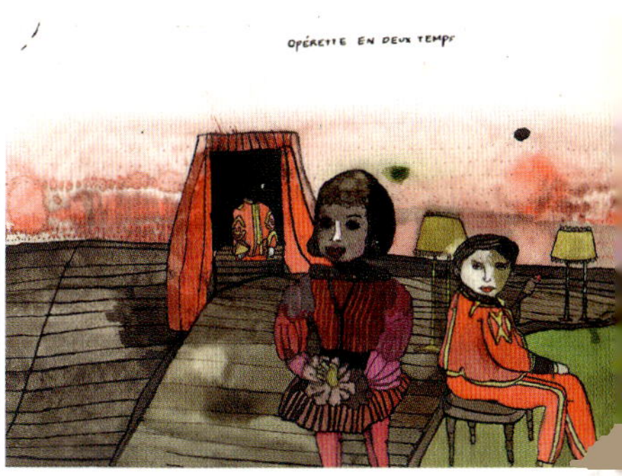

CHRISTINE REBET
Still from *The Black Cabinet*, 2007

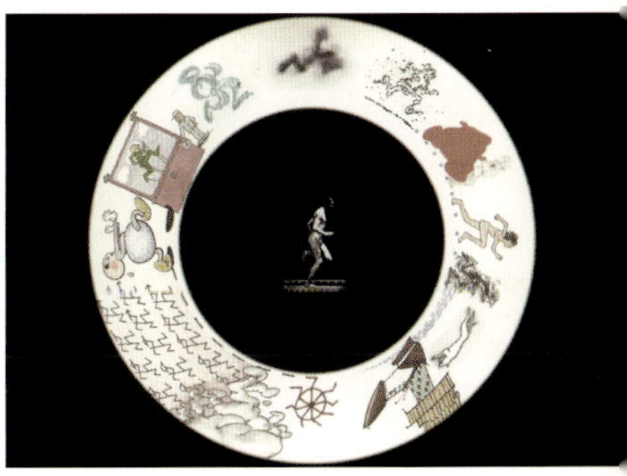

GEORGE GRIFFIN
Still from *Viewmaster, a digital mutoscope*, 1976/2007

the dissolve

who uses "devious means" to achieve mythical thought through a labor-intensive, heterogeneous repertoire. The artists in the Biennial, for the most part not formally trained in filmmaking or animation techniques, are free to act the part of the bricoleur and craft magic and myth wherever they find it, making all discoveries through the continual play and manipulation of materials. The moments of conjoining effect the dissolve and the dissolve is analogous to the space of the *in-between*.

This practice of animating as an expository process of the *in-between* has proven to be a way to expand the possibilities of each of the Biennial artists' chosen medium. Following postmodernism's demolition of disciplinary boundaries, artists remain intrigued by the potential for animating to invest emotion, narrative, empathy, and improvisation into otherwise static media and perspective. Perhaps it is the search for a personal voice in the image overload of the internet and the hand-held that has brought these artists back to an earlier day, when new technology asserted its challenge to the subjective experience of the body. Whatever the impulse, the result is that technology becomes not an end, but, even more to the point, a means to more effectively enhance the sense of the authentic, the handmade.

— SARAH LEWIS AND DANIEL BELASCO
Curators, SITE Santa Fe's Eighth International Biennial

NOTES

[1] See *Drawing on Film*, Drawing Center, New York, 2008; *Animated Painting*, San Diego Museum of Art, 2007; *Momentary Momentum: Animated Drawings*, Parasol Unit, London, 2007; *Daumenkino (The Flip Book Show)*, Kunsthalle Düsseldorf, 2005; and *Slide Show*, Baltimore Museum of Art, 2005. *Animations* at P.S.1 Contemporary Art Center, 2001, signaled the first exhibition to survey this new focus on animating imagery.

[2] George Kubler, *The Shape of Time* (New Haven: Yale University Press, 1962), 33.

[3] Paul Wells, *Animation and America* (Edinburgh: Edinburgh University Press, 2002), 8.

[4] All preceding quotes in this paragraph from transcript of SITE Santa Fe's 2010 Biennial Artists Roundtable, Long Island City, N.Y., October 5, 2009.

[5] Ibid.

[6] Ibid.

[7] Jacco Olivier, email to authors, September 2, 2009.

[8] Laleh Khorramian, email to authors, August 27, 2009.

[9] From Jasper Johns's notebooks. Our thanks go to Robert Storr for calling our attention to this quote.

[10] Contemporary comedians such as Demetri Martin have revived drawing as prop in live performance, as well as television commentator Glenn Beck.

[11] Cecile Starr and Robert Russett, *Experimental Animation: An Illustrated Anthology* (New York: Van Nostrand Reinhold, 1976), 21.

[12] See George Griffin, *Frames: A Selection of Drawings and Statements by Independent American Animators* (Montpelier, Vt.: Capital City Press, 1978).

[13] Rotoscoping and its various technological followers is still a staple of contemporary animation, though CGI [Computer Generated Imagery] in Hollywood has moved from stop-motion animation to more digital techniques, employed in *Star Wars* (1977), *Tron* (1982), *Forrest Gump* (1994), and recently with the production of James Cameron's *Avatar* (2009).

[14] Paul Kaiser, "Steps," in *Ghostcatching: A Virtual Dance Installation* (New York: The Cooper Union School of Art, 1999), 43.

[15] It took until 1878 to create a more refined system. Muybridge later revisited Palo Alto to replicate the test, the result of which is the artist's famous photograph, *The Horse in Motion*, 1878.

[16] Nancy Mowll Mathews, "Early Film and American Artistic Traditions," in *Moving Pictures: American Art and Early Film, 1880-1910* (Manchester, Vt.: Hudson Hills Press for Williams College Museum of Art, 2005), 53n.4.

[17] William Faulkner, *Requiem for a Nun: A Play*. Based on the novel by William Faulkner, (New York: Random House, 1959), 33.

[18] Kentridge quoted in "William Kentridge: Drawings for Projection" in *William Kentridge* (New York: Harry N. Abrams, 2001), 6.

[19] Laleh Khorramian. Email to authors. February 14, 2010.

[20] Katherine Manthorne, "Experience Nature in Early Film: Dialogues with Church's Niagara and Homer's Seascapes," in *Moving Pictures: American Art and Early Film, 1880-1910* (Manchester, Vt.: Hudson Hills Press for Williams College Museum of Art, 2005), 55.

[21] Paul Wells, *Animation: Genre and Authorship* (London; New York: Wallflower, 2002), 39.

[22] Ibid.

[23] Walt Disney's television program "The Story of the Animated Drawing" (1955) began by proposing that cave paintings were the first animations, set in motion through the flickering of fire light and sequence of images. Wells, *Animation: Genre and Authorship*, 33.

[24] See Neil Harris, *Humbug: The Art of P.T. Barnum* (Boston: Little Brown, 1973) and Michael Leja, *Looking Askance: Skepticism and American Art from Eakins to Duchamp* (Berkeley: University of California Press, 2004).

[25] Charles Musser, "A Cornucopia of Images: Comparison and Judgment across Theater, Film, and the Visual Arts during the Late Nineteenth Century," in *Moving Pictures: American Art and Early Film, 1880-1910* (Manchester, Vt.: Hudson Hills Press for Williams College Museum of Art, 2005).

[26] Lora Wheeler Mjolsness, "Dziga Vertov's *Soviet Toys*: Commerce, Commercialization and Cartoons," *Studies in Russian and Soviet Cinema* 2, n. 3 (2008), 247-266.

[27] John MacKay. Interview with Sarah Lewis. March 15, 2010.

[28] Wells, *Animation: Genre and Authorship* (London; New York: Wallflower, 2002), 1.

[29] Christopher Lehman, *The Colored Cartoon: Black Representation in American Animated Short Films, 1907-1954* (Amherst, Mass.: University of Massachusetts Press), 2007, 121.

[30] See Gene Youngblood, *Expanded Cinema* (New York: Dutton, 1970); and *Beyond Cinema: The Art of Projection: Films, Videos and Installations from 1965 to 2005*, eds. Anette Hüsch, Joachim Jäger, and Gabriele Knapsteinn, (Berlin: Hatje Cantz, 2005).

[31] Claude Lévi-Strauss, *The Savage Mind* (Chicago: University of Chicago Press, 1966), 17.

the dissolve

artists' pages

the dissolve

ROBERT **BREER**

BORN IN 1926, LIVES AND WORKS IN TUCSON, ARIZONA

Bang!, 1986

In *Bang!*, Robert Breer deftly combines drawing, painting, found photographs, and found film footage to create a montage of rapidly changing images. A rotoscoped drawing of a baseball player at bat morphs into film footage of the same subject, creating linkages through line and form. *Bang!*'s soundtrack provides a compelling counterpoint to its imagery. Sometimes the sound is synchronized with the visual action, at other times it is deliberately at odds with it, as when the sound of roosters crowing accompanies the image of roaring crowds.

ROBERT BREER
Stills from *Bang!*, 1986
16mm film transferred to DVD
Images courtesy of the artist and gb agency, Paris

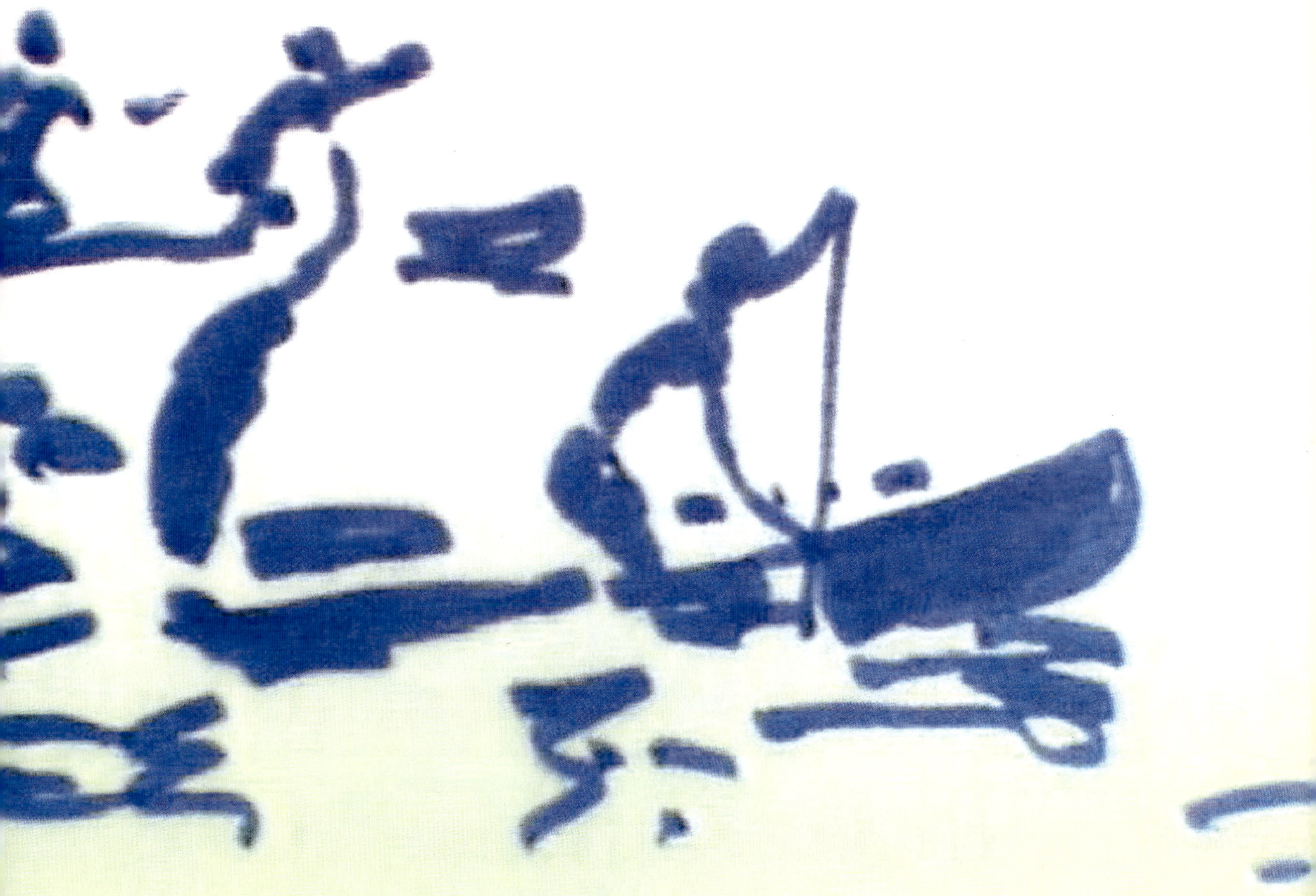

the dissolve

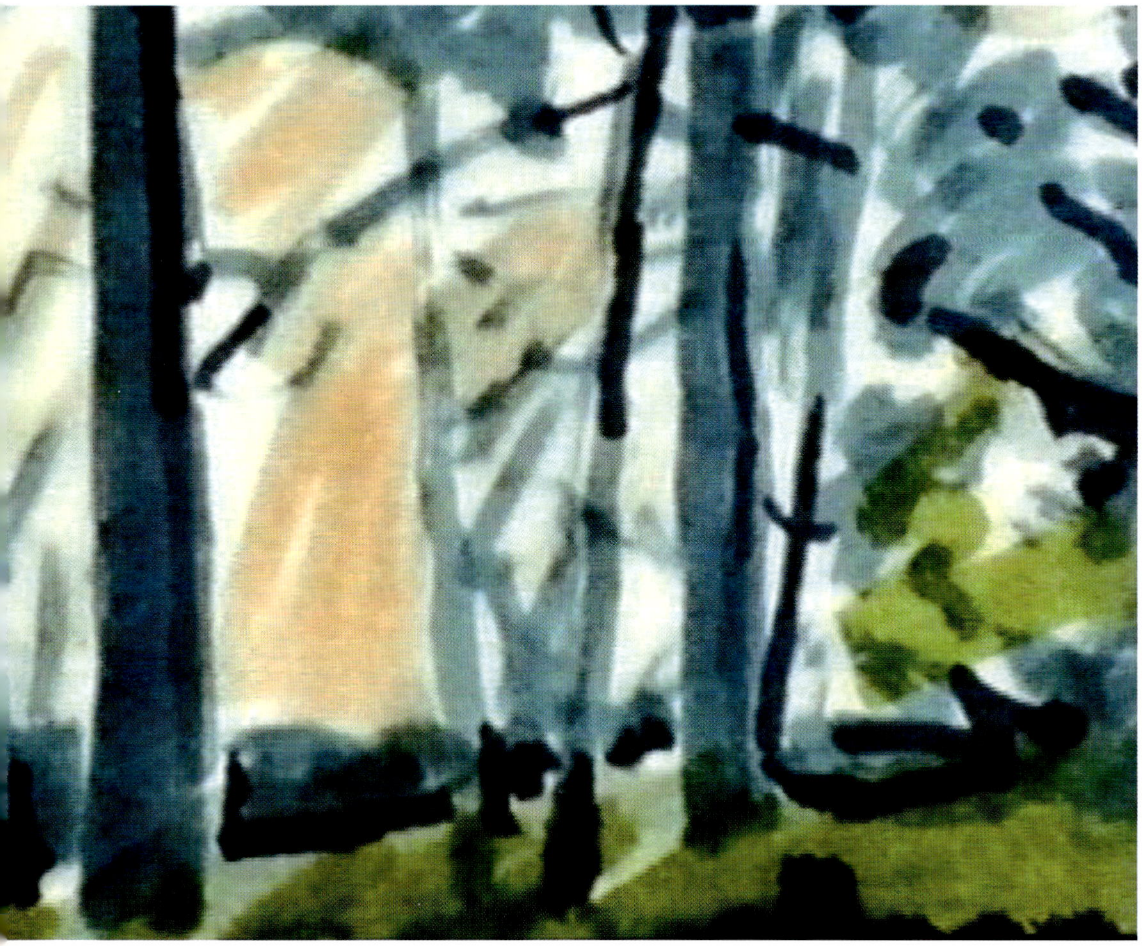

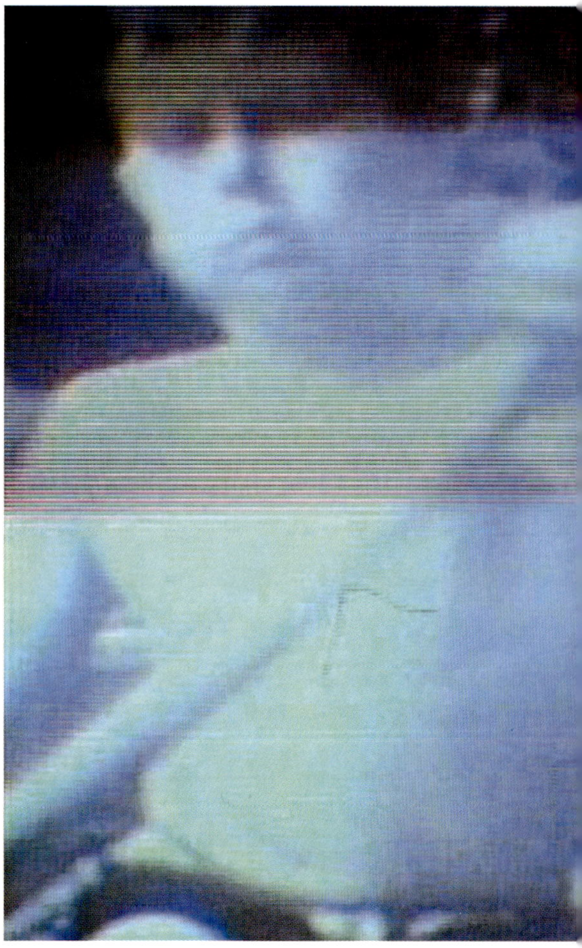

"Don't take anyone else's advice including this." — RB

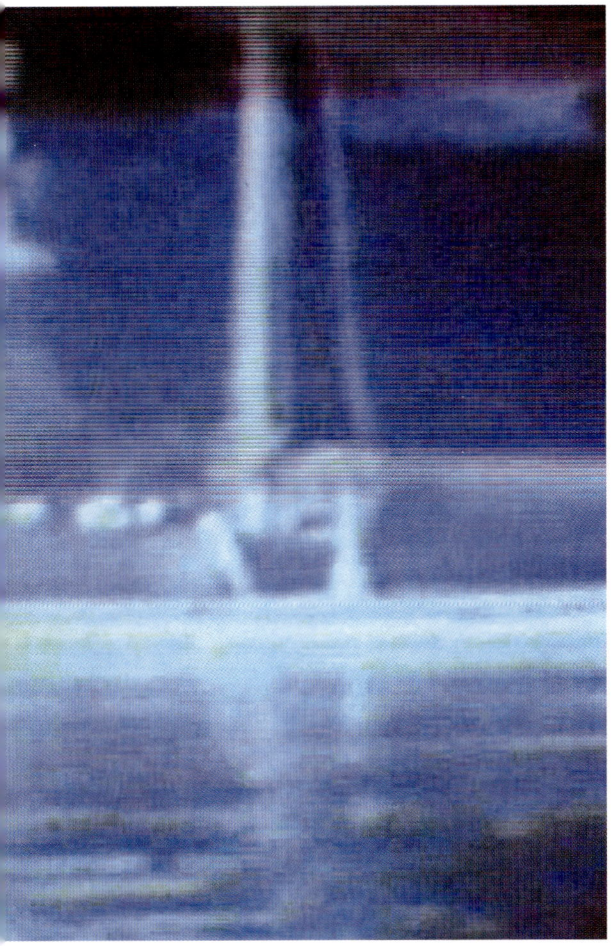

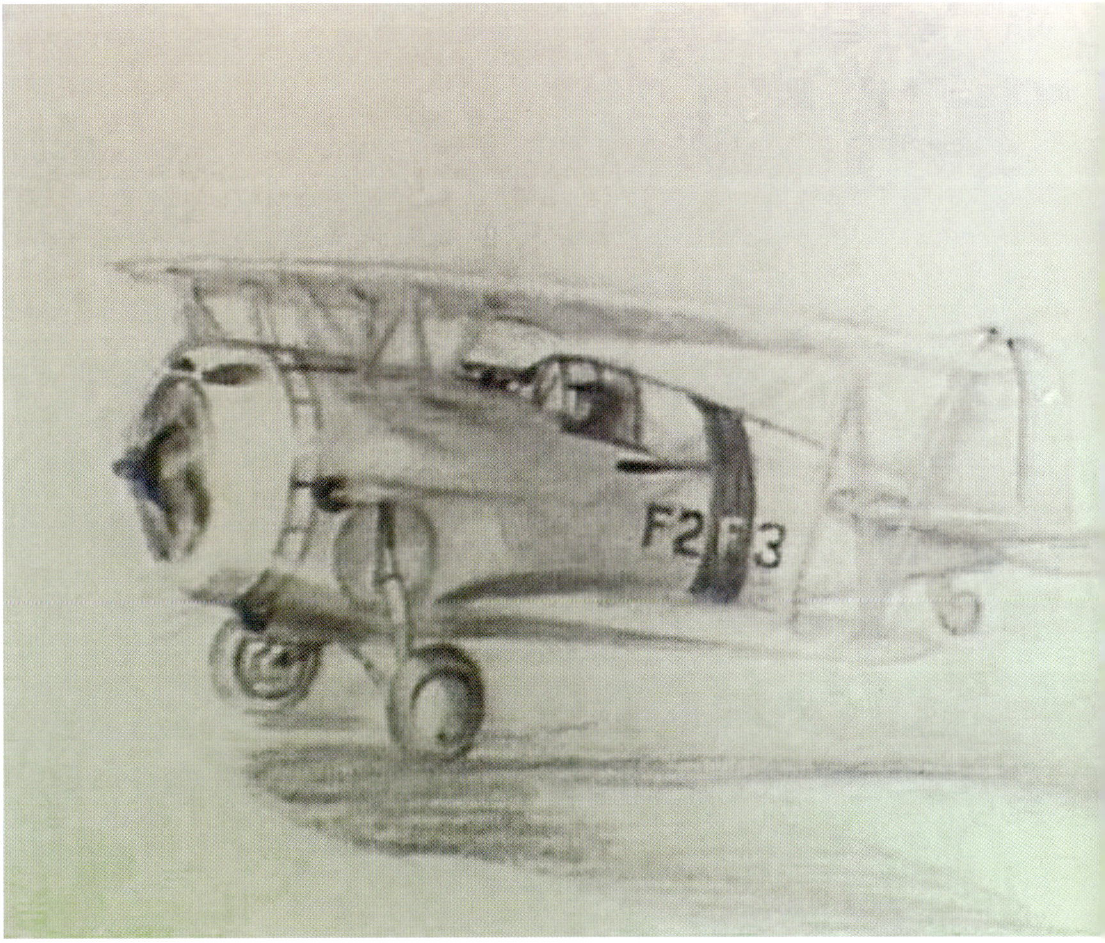

PAUL **CHAN**

BORN IN 1973, LIVES AND WORKS IN NEW YORK

4th ~~Light~~, 2006

Paul Chan's *4th ~~Light~~* is part of the *7 ~~Lights~~* series that Chan created between 2005 and 2008. In these works Chan uses computer technology to create a black-and-white universe of shadow play. *4th ~~Light~~* presents a window onto an alternate realm where human bodies free-fall toward the ground, while a disparate assortment of objects, including guns, public telephones, hammers, and building exteriors float effortlessly upward. With *4th ~~Light~~* Chan may offer a subtle, poetic critique of a world turned upside down.

PAUL CHAN
Stills from *4th ~~Light~~*, 2006
Digital projection
Images courtesy of the artist and Greene Naftali Gallery, New York

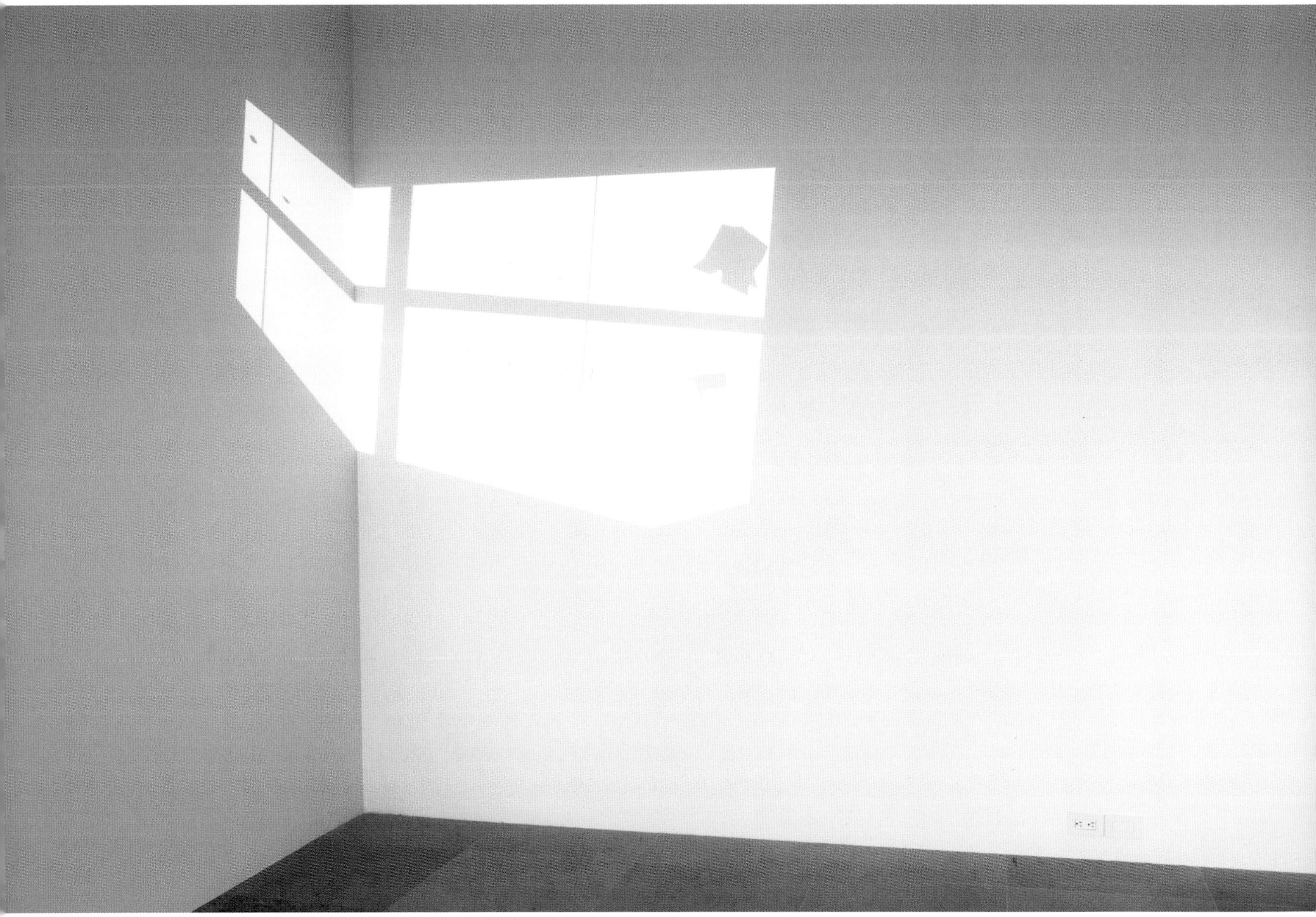

the dissolve

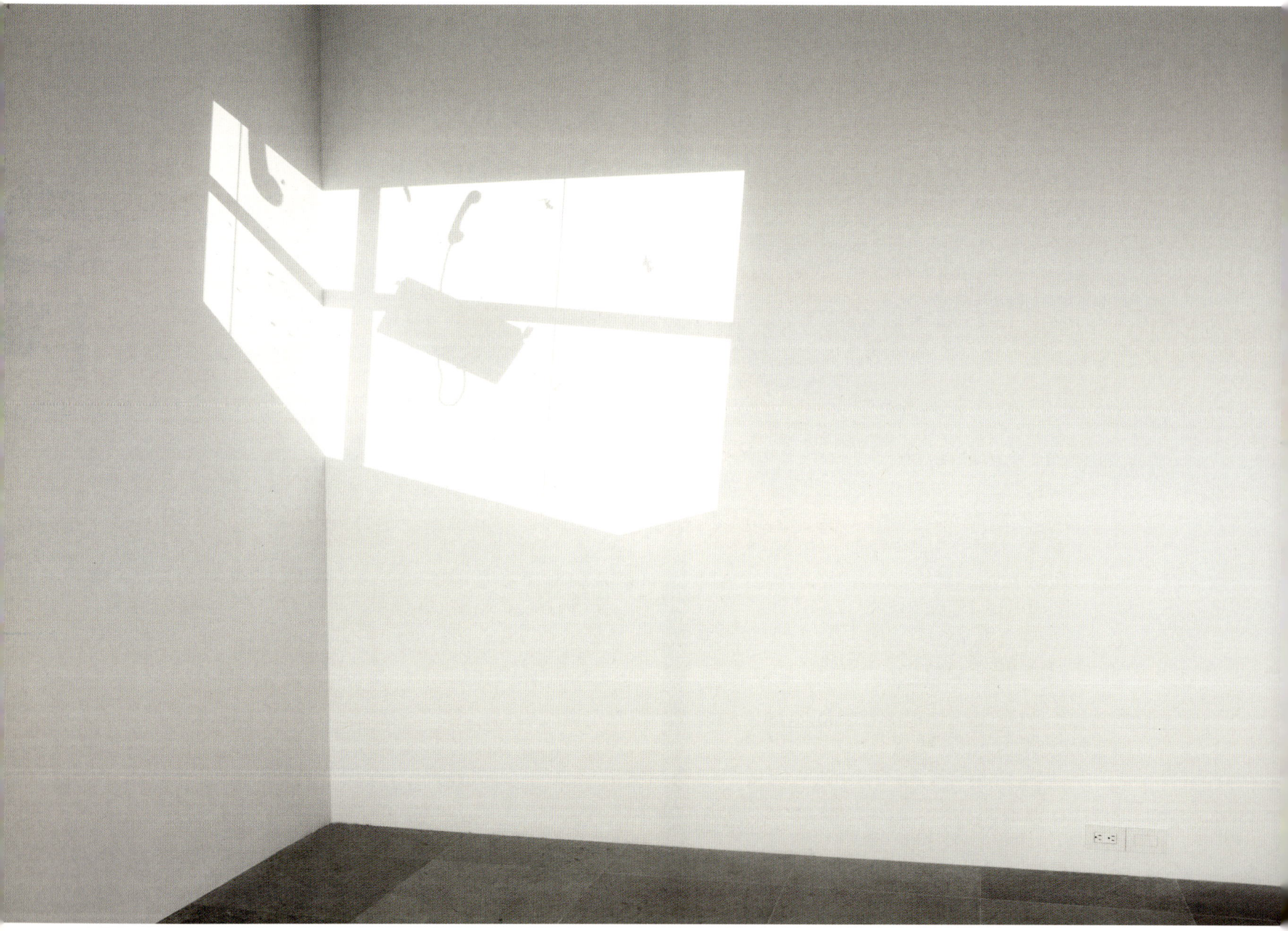

"Installations using multiple projections and screens transform the architectural into the archi-luminal... Brightness becomes not only an attribute of the image but also a luminous value in the space, carving out of the darkness an environment that engulfs the body of the viewer in the cold radiance of recorded light." — PC

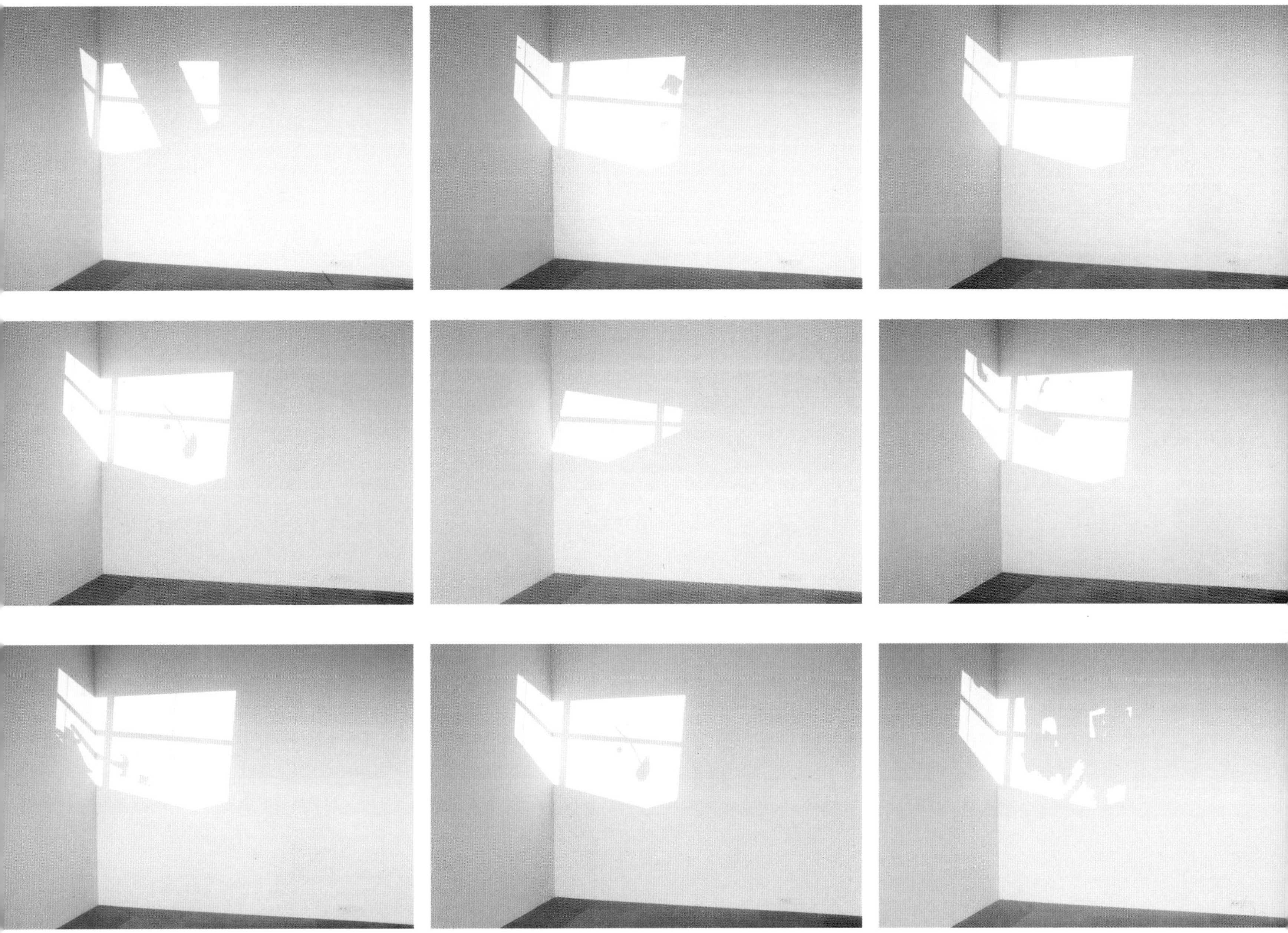

MARTHA **COLBURN**

BORN IN 1971, LIVES AND WORKS IN AMSTERDAM AND NEW YORK

Myth Labs, 2008

Martha Colburn's *Myth Labs* presents an extended metaphor in which America's founding myths are likened to so many unstable elements as if cooked up in a methamphetamine lab. Colburn posits drug use, violence, and religious indoctrination as interconnected elements in American history. Through clever juxtapositions, Colburn conflates past and present, linking contemporary social issues with the first contact between Pilgrims and Native Americans. The pulsing musical soundtrack is an integral aspect of this work and it appears as if the music is the catalyst that drives the narrative forward.

MARTHA COLBURN
Stills from *Myth Labs*, 2008
16mm film transferred to DVD
Images courtesy of the artist and James Cohan Gallery, New York

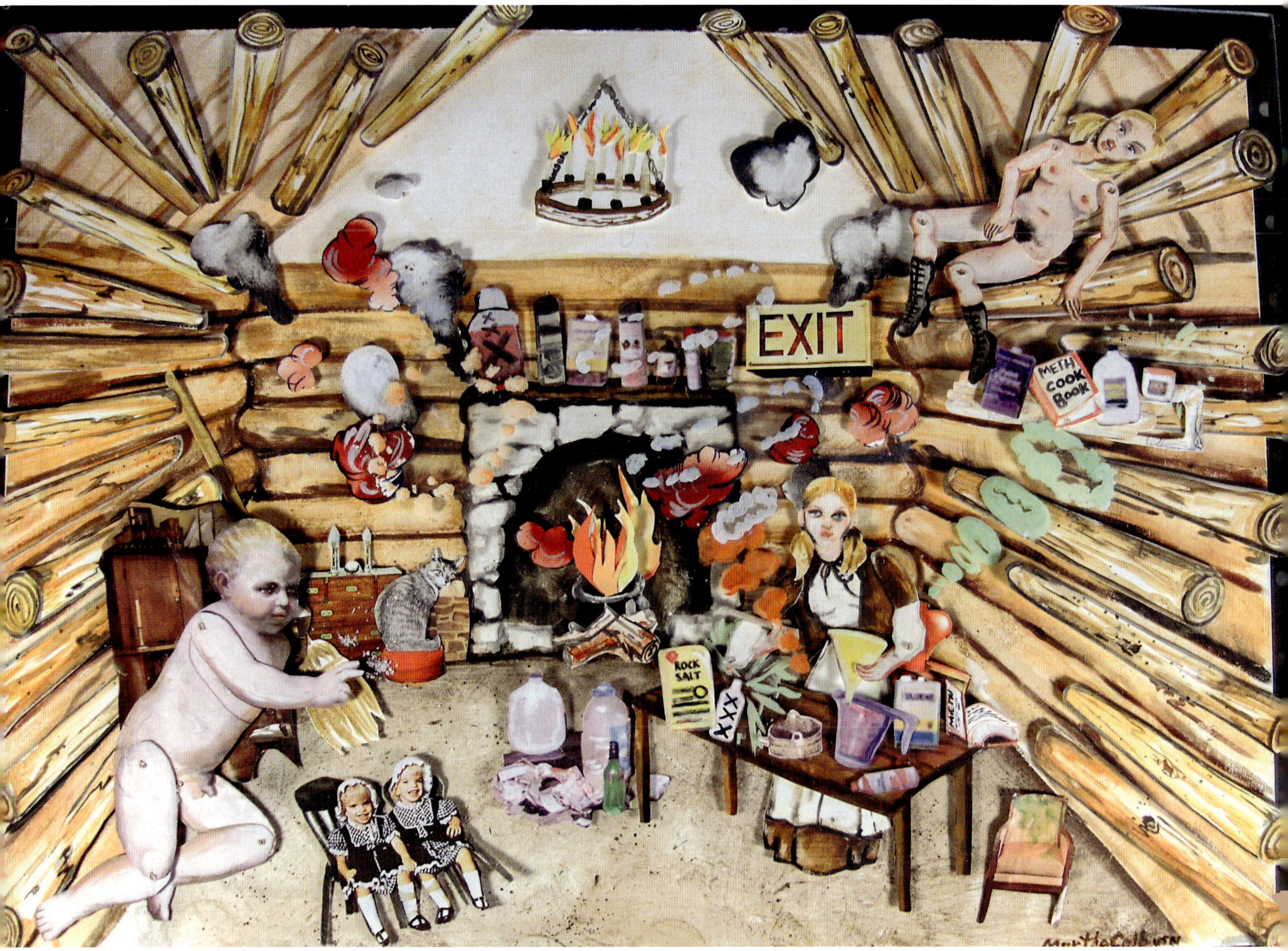

the dissolve

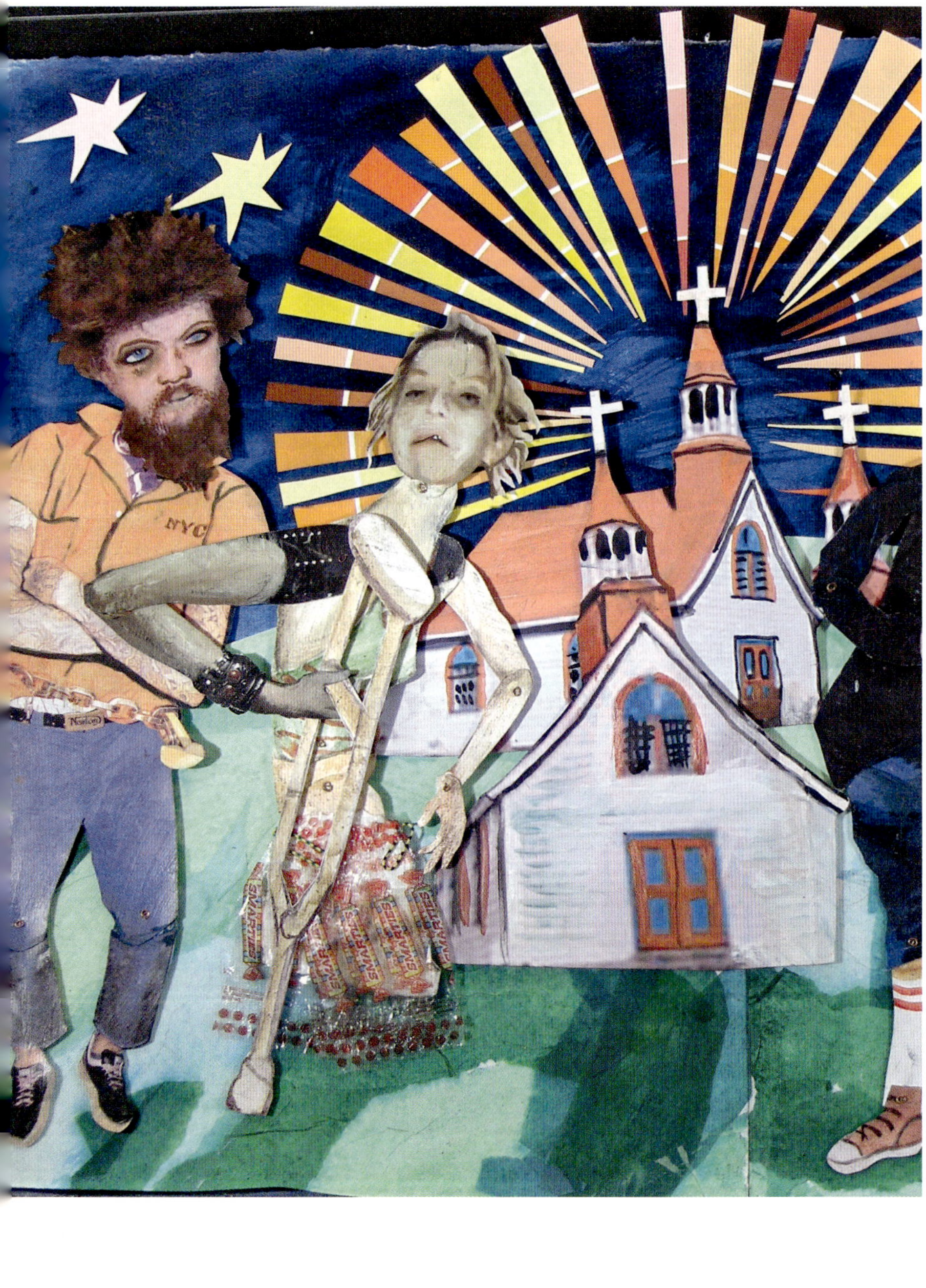

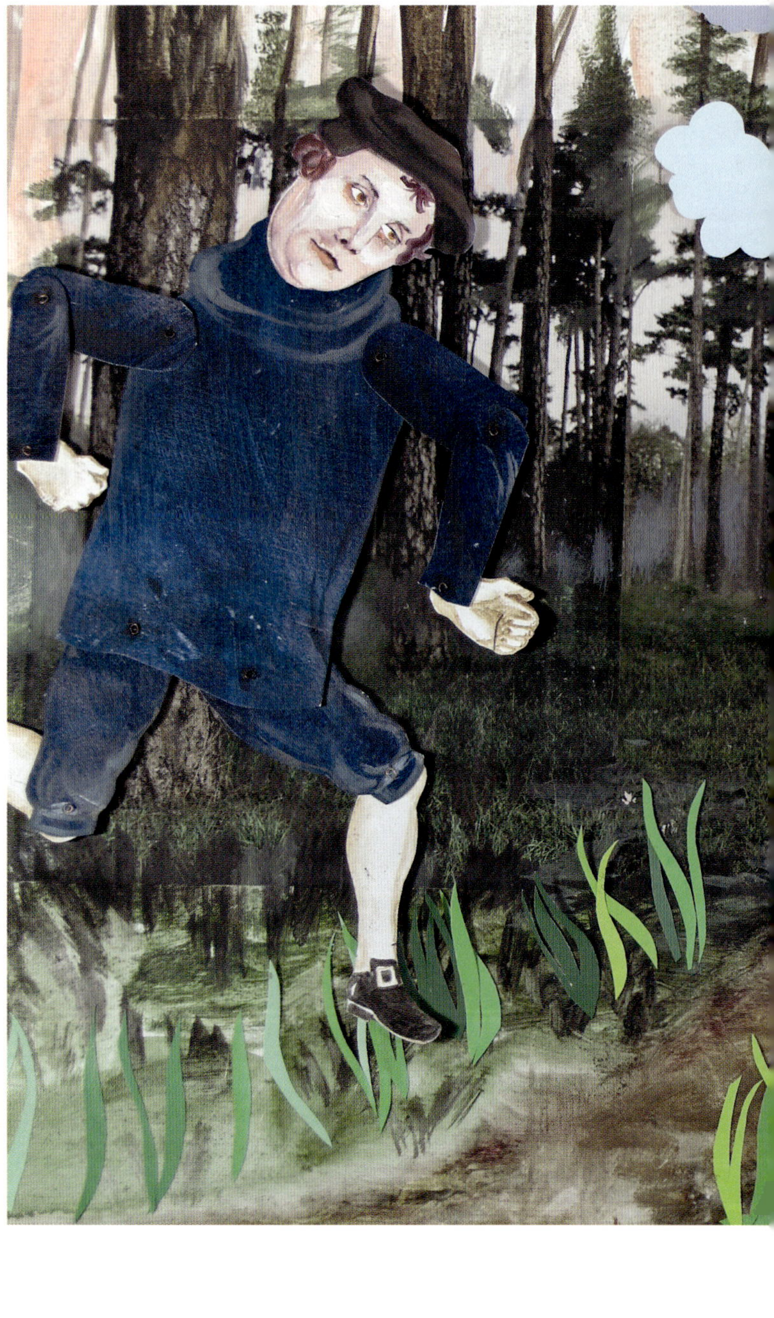

"...this bleak cultural and geographic landscape has finally broken people down, sending them in pursuit of some kind of escape; and so begins the drama between the persecutors and persecuted; the 'saved' and the saviors." — MC

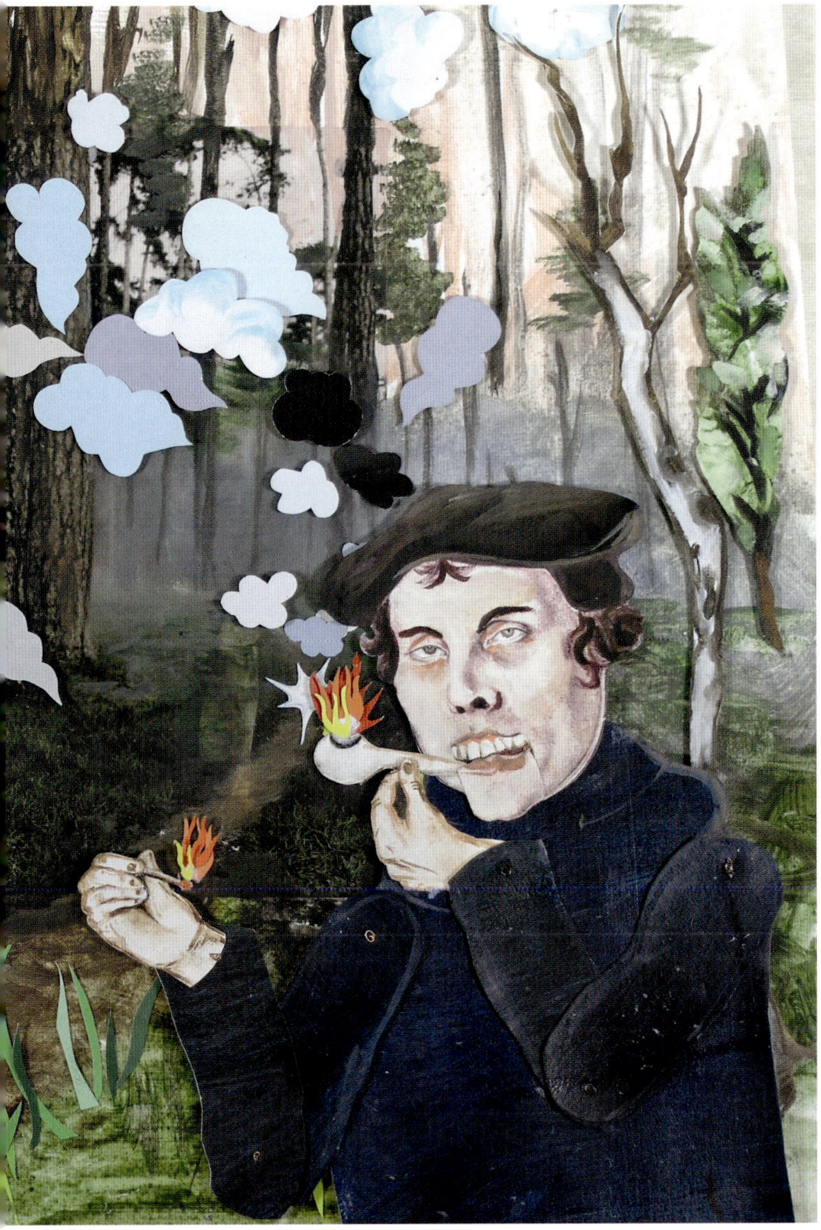

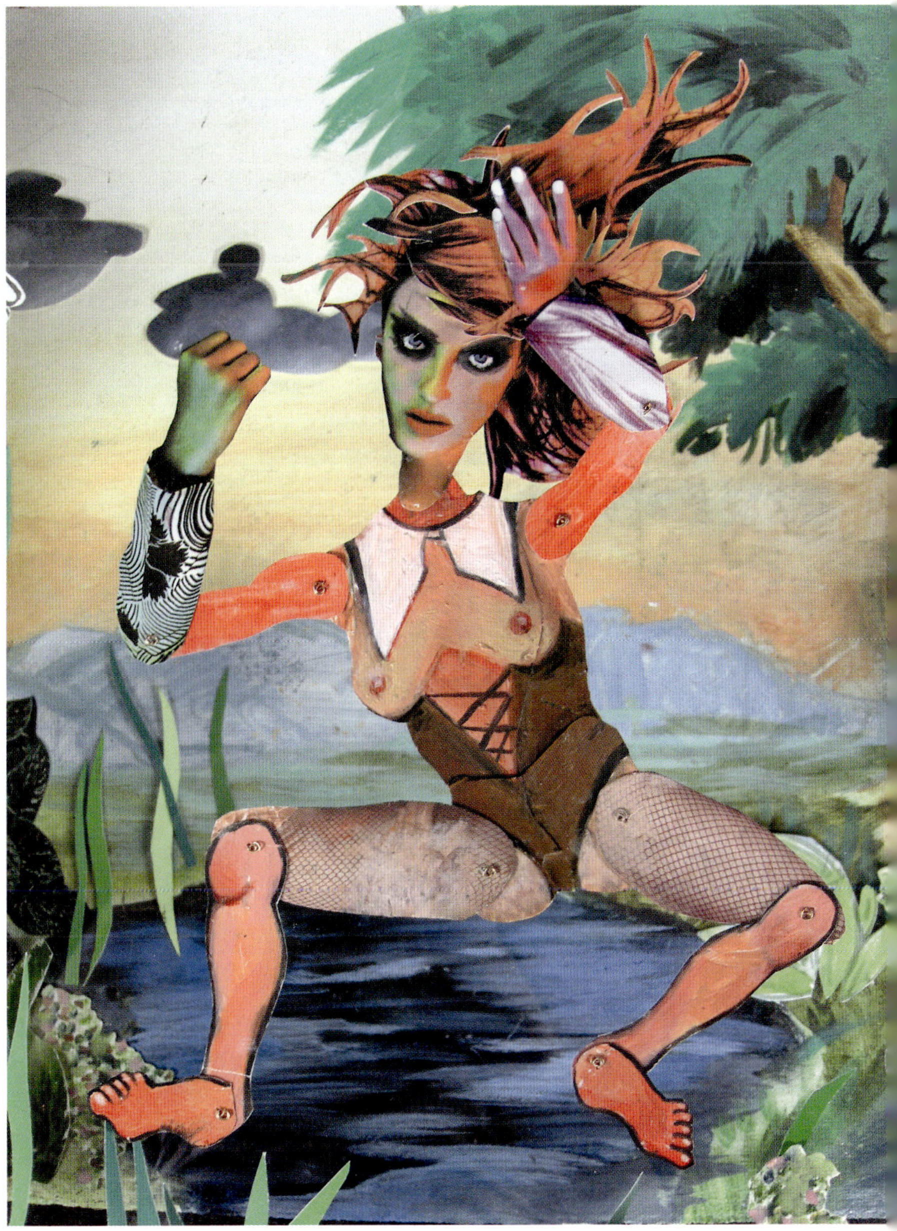

THOMAS **DEMAND**

BORN IN 1964, LIVES AND WORKS IN BERLIN

Rain, 2008

Thomas Demand's *Rain* is a 35mm film in which Demand has painstakingly re-created the effect of raindrops falling onto a hard surface. The precision with which these raindrops are rendered matches the handcrafted models he is known for in his photographs, and this work exhibits a similar interest in the simulation of the real that questions the parameters of representation. The raindrops dance across the screen, their movement creating an abstract painting in motion. The rhythmic patter offers a meditative soundtrack that reinforces the haunting quality of the film.

THOMAS DEMAND
Stills from *Rain*, 2008
35mm film loop

Images courtesy of the artist and Matthew Marks Gallery, New York

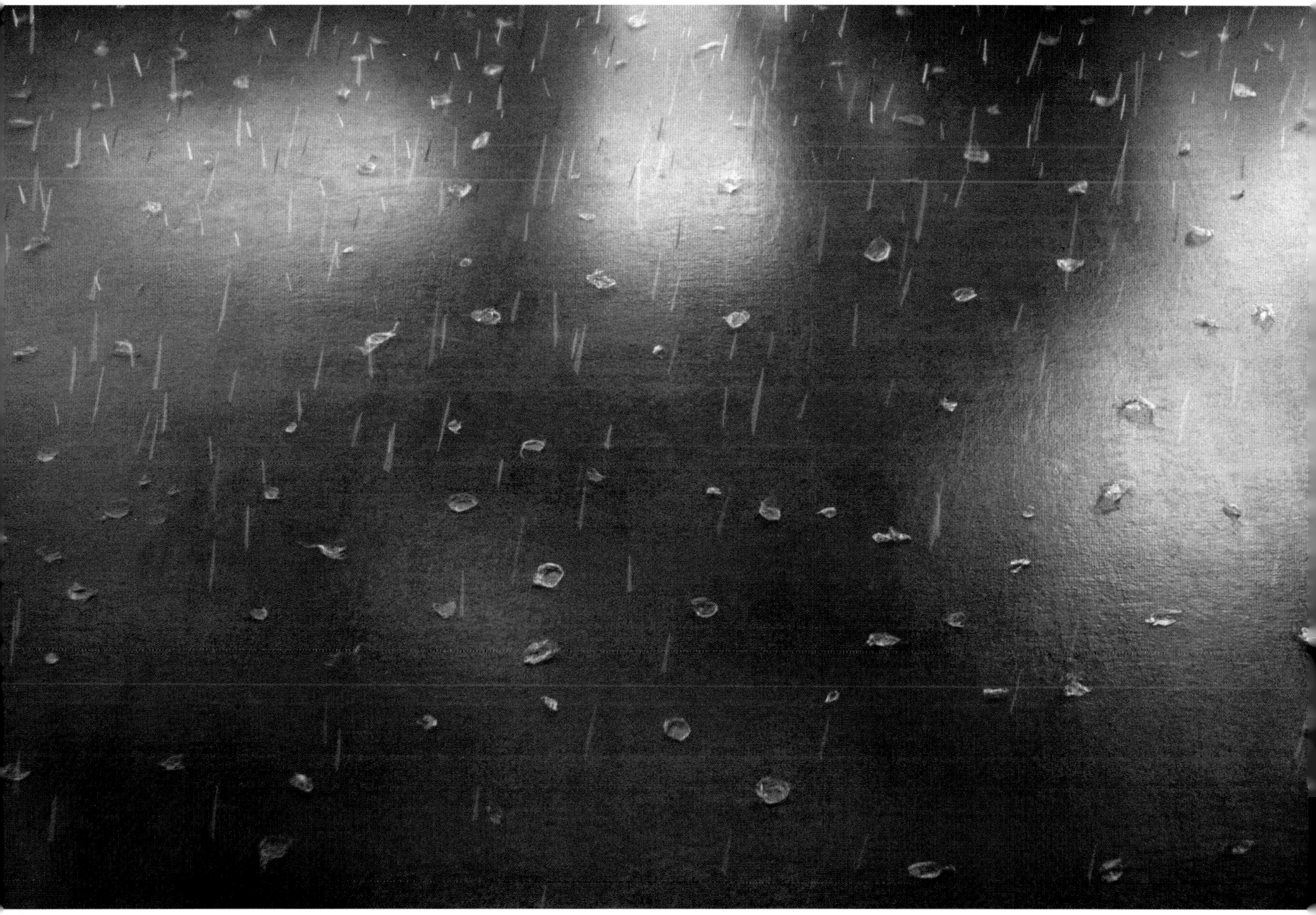

the dissolve

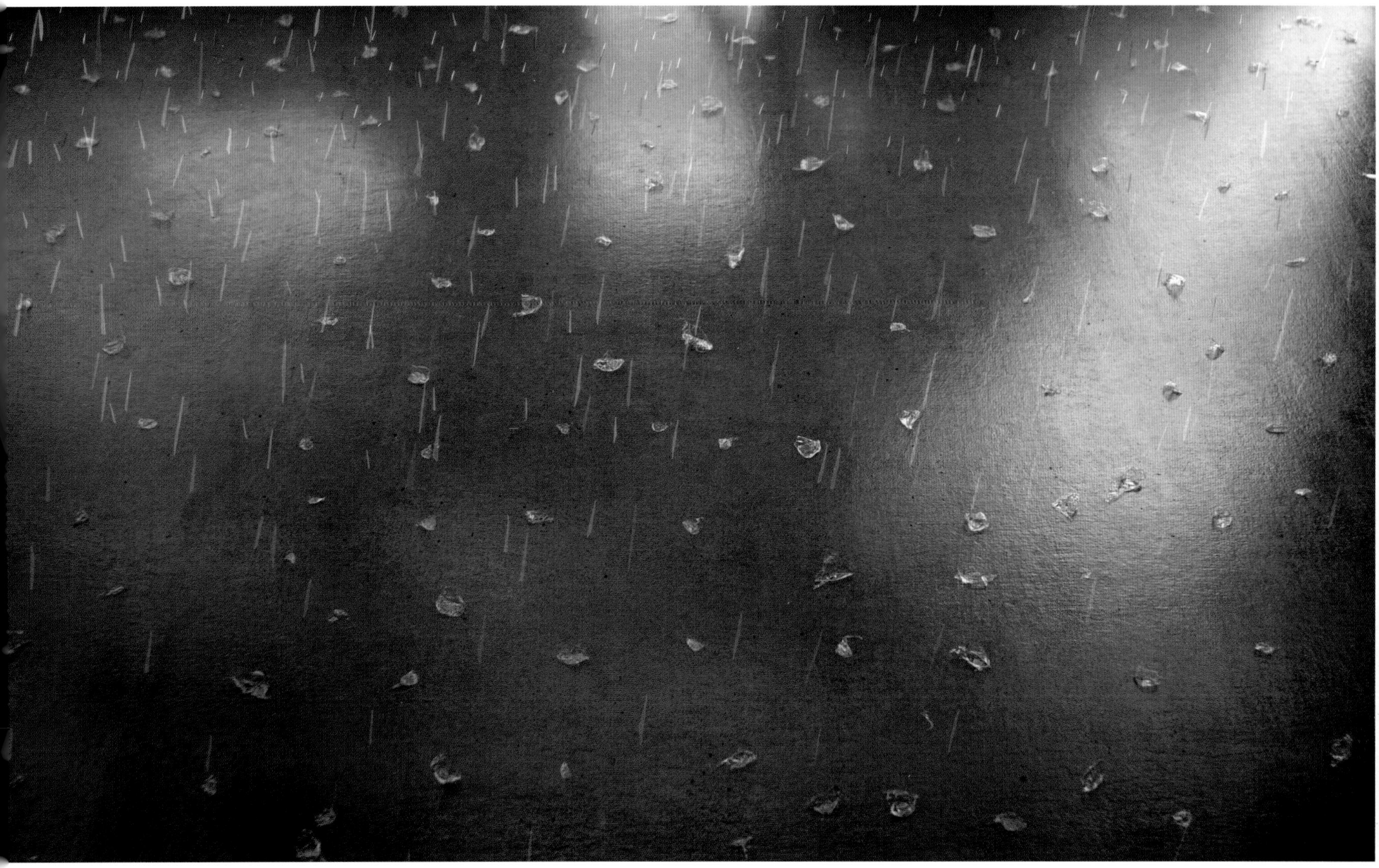

"Time, handmade!
Tautologies, looped!
Memory, reconstructed!
Images, mental!
Photography, stipulated!"
—TD

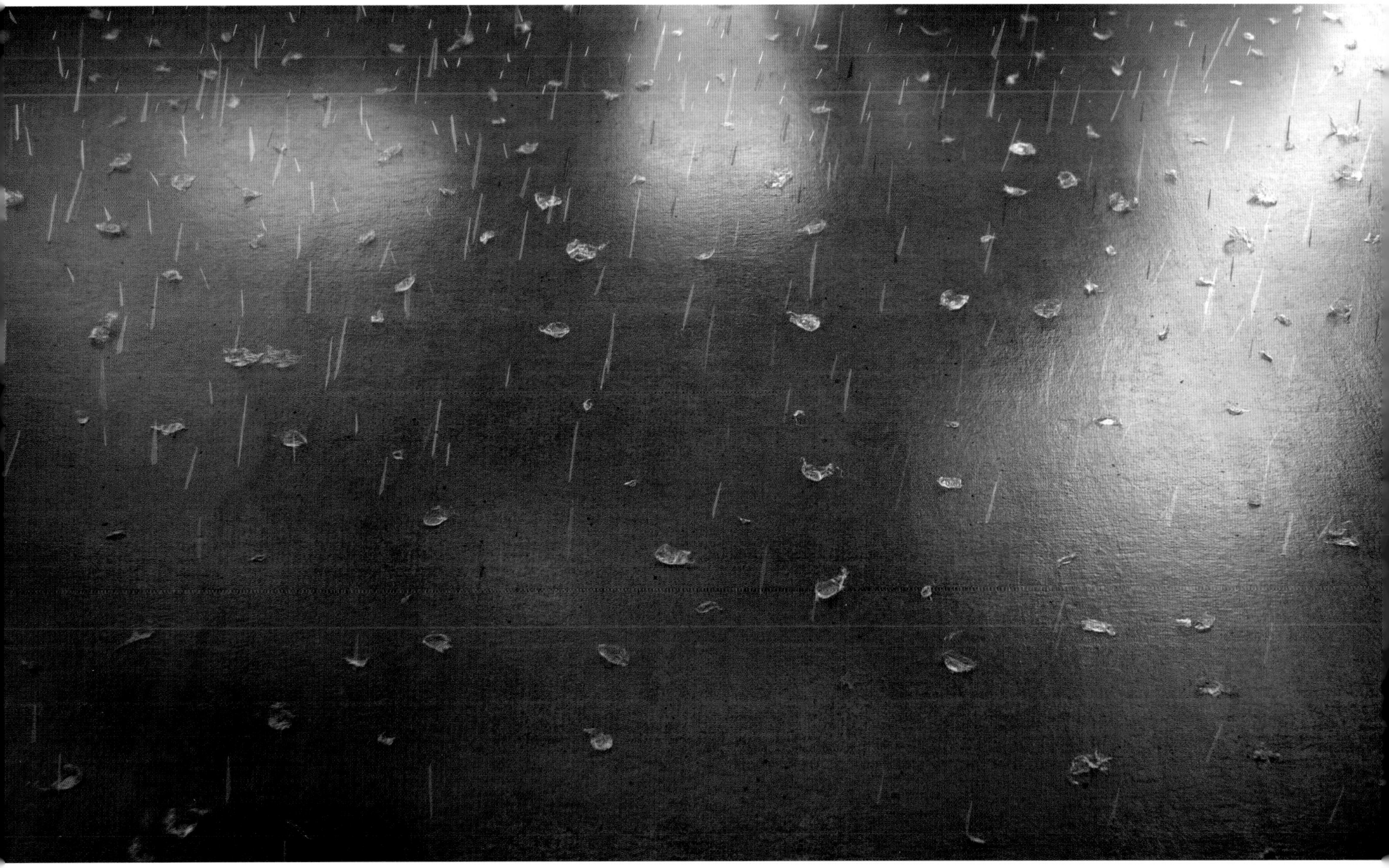

BRENT **GREEN**

BORN IN 1978, LIVES AND WORKS IN CRESSONA, PENNSYLVANIA

Paulina Hollers, 2006

Paulina Hollers reflects Brent Green's abiding interest in the strange characters and local tales of his childhood in Appalachia. The film tells the story of a woman whose son is hit by a bus and killed. She in turn kills herself to rescue his soul, and is taken on a harrowing journey through an idiosyncratic underworld. This stop-motion film combines hand-drawn animations, rickety handmade sets, and distinctive narrations. Scrawled inter-titles and atmospheric soundtracks recall the techniques of early film.

BRENT GREEN
Stills from *Paulina Hollers*, 2006
Video
Images courtesy of the artist and Andrew Edlin Gallery, New York

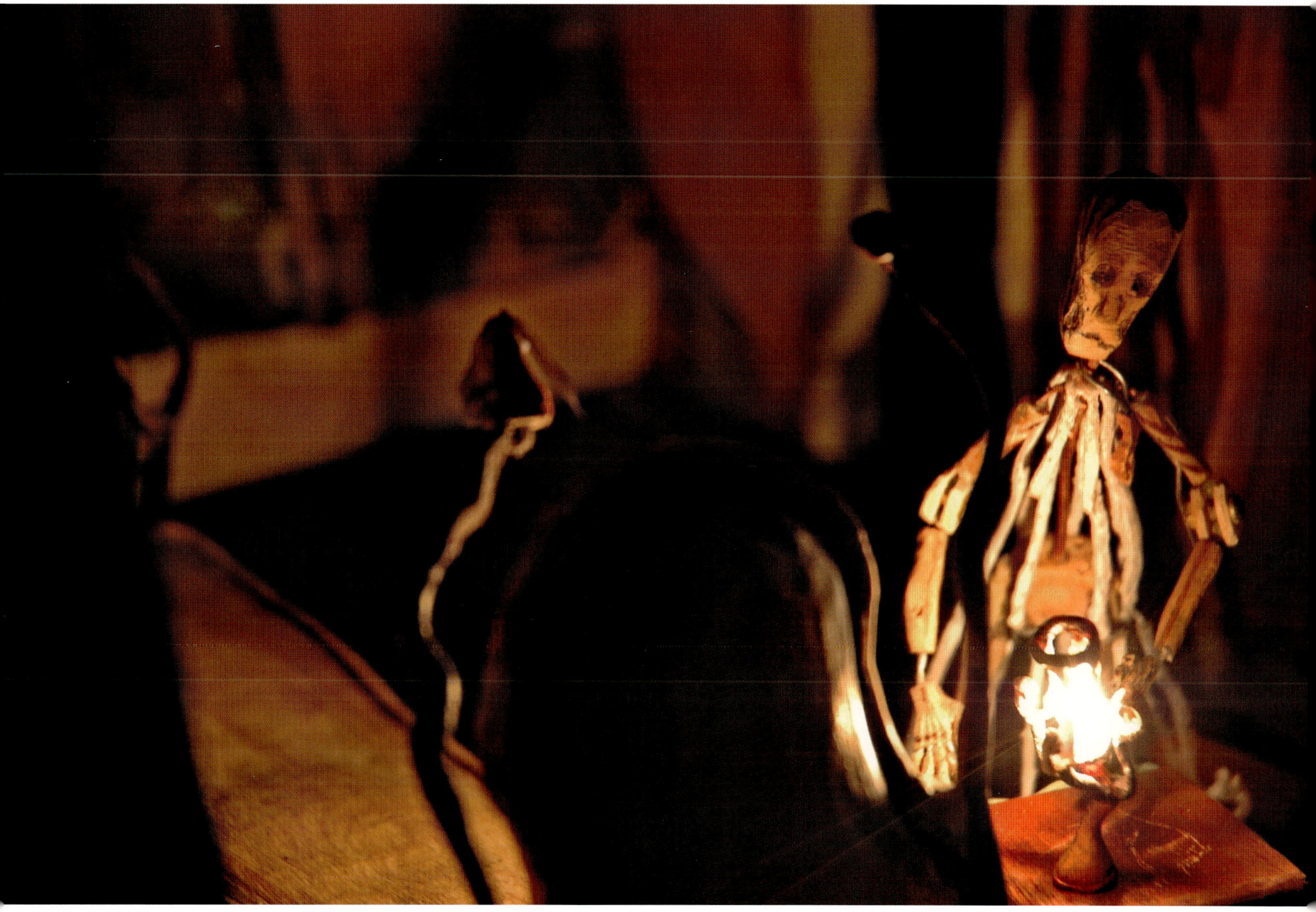

the dissolve

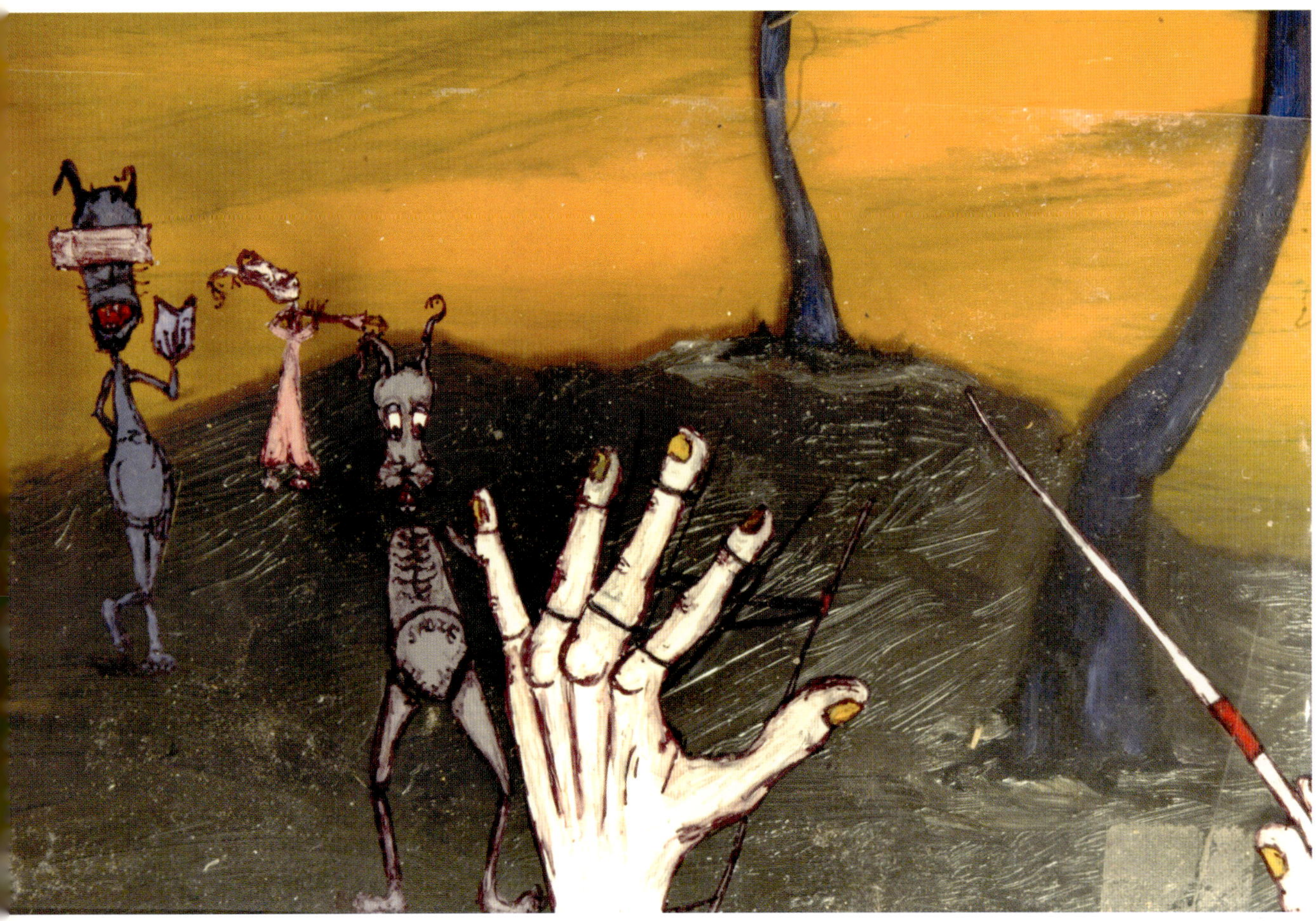

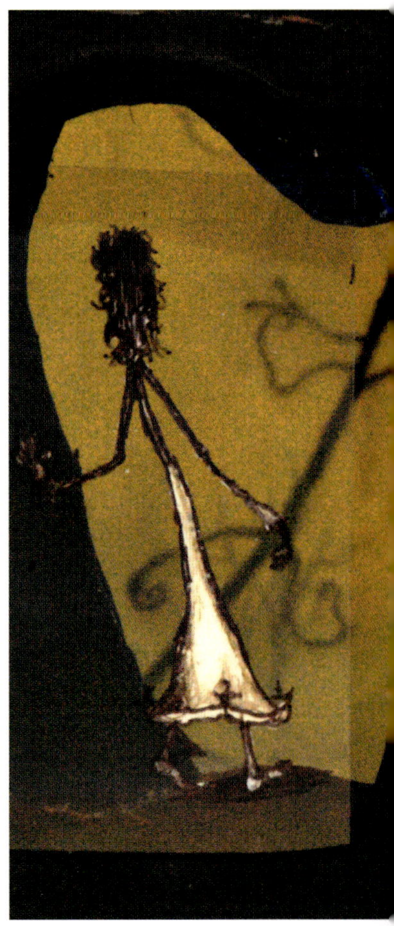

"The sun will shine on most everything." — BG

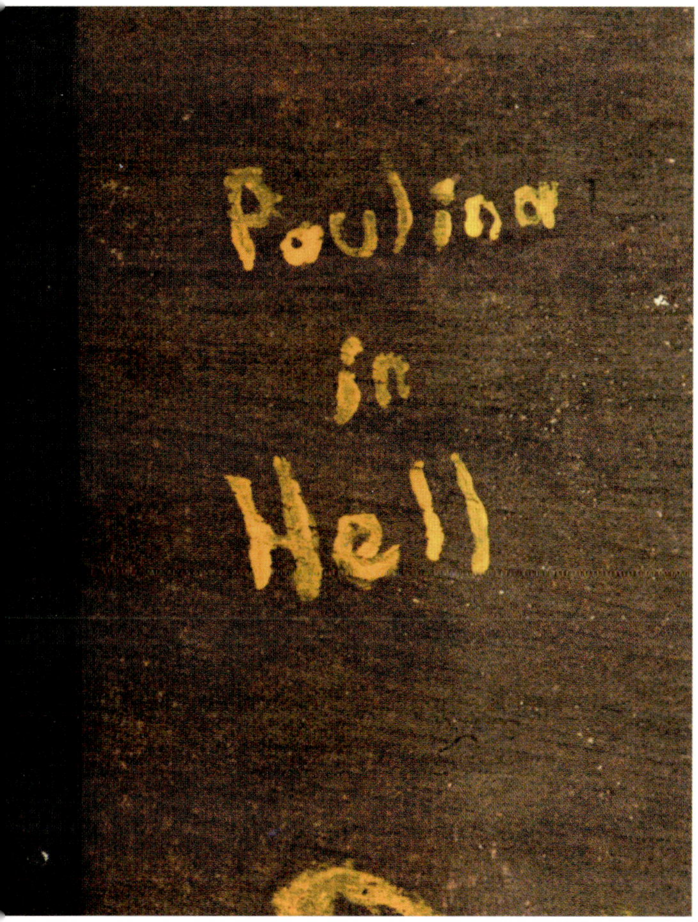

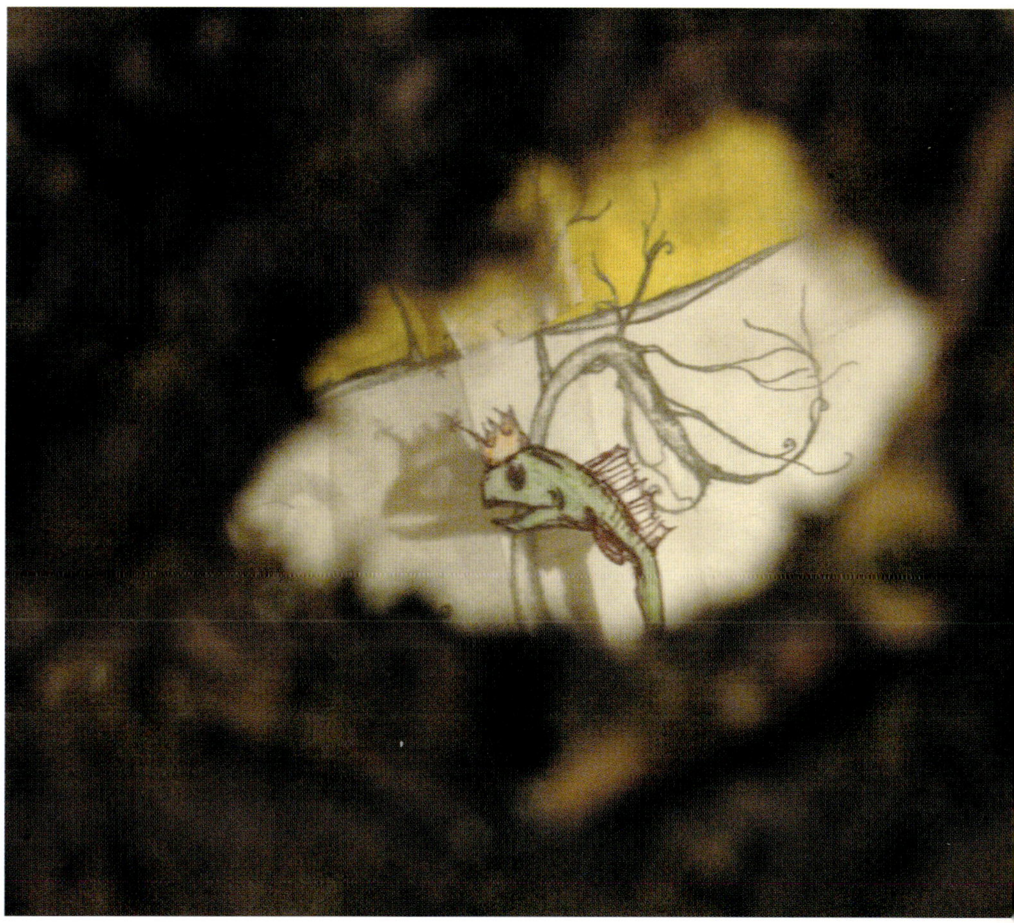

GEORGE **GRIFFIN**

BORN IN 1943, LIVES AND WORKS IN NEW YORK

Viewmaster, a digital mutoscope, 1976/2007

With *Viewmaster*, George Griffin has created a new digital context for his classic animation that riffed on Eadweard Muybridge's nineteenth-century motion studies. In Griffin's conceptually concise work, eight characters including a naked man, a naked woman, an anthropomorphic blob, and a stick-figure restaurant waiter are rendered in discrete drawings. The characters appear to continuously run in place and simultaneously chase after one another. The digital mutoscope ironically presents a computer animation in a nineteenth-century format.

GEORGE GRIFFIN
Stills from *Viewmaster, a digital mutoscope,* 1976/2007
35mm film original, digitally re-animated, MDF case, LCD monitor
Images courtesy of the artist

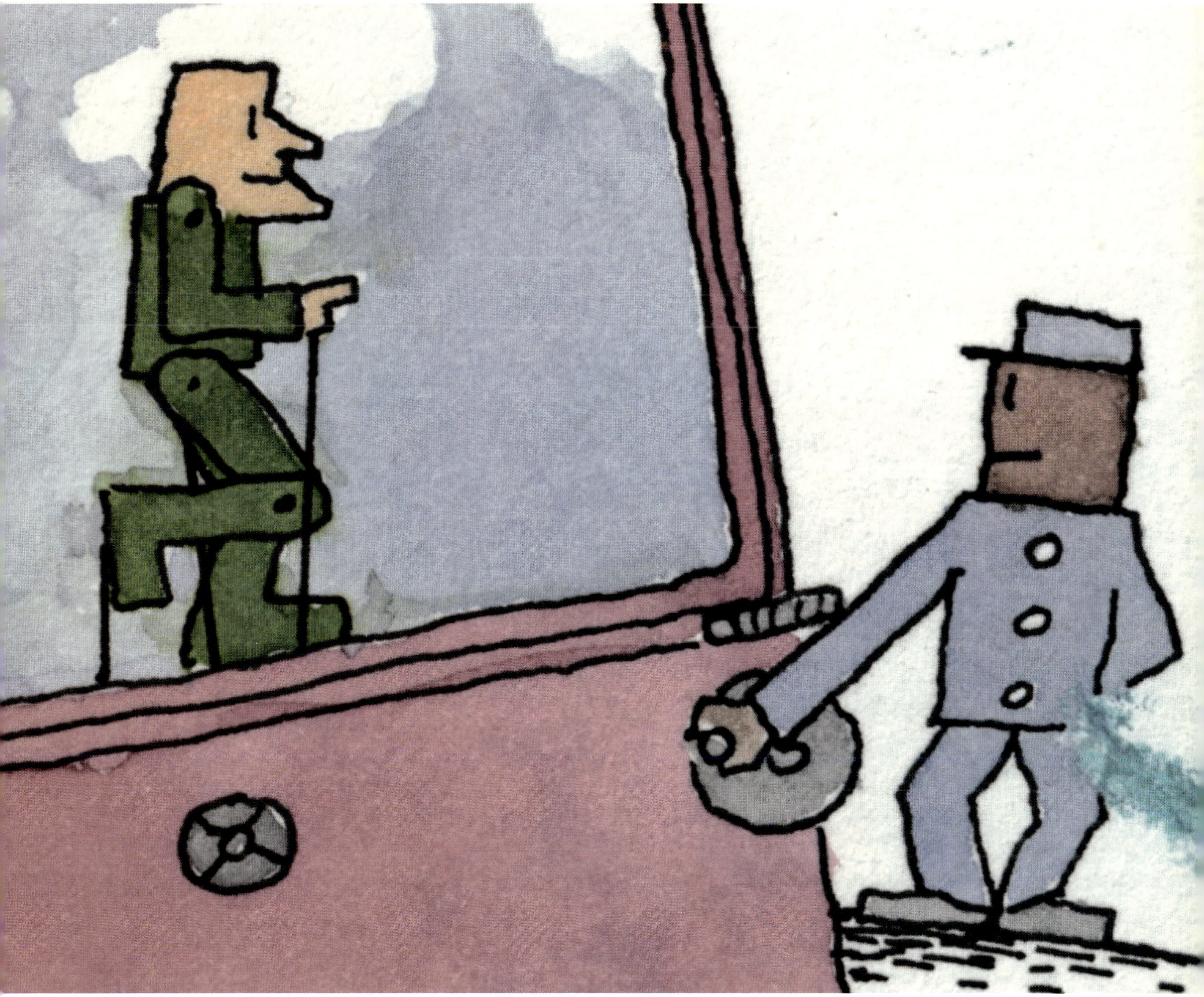

the dissolve

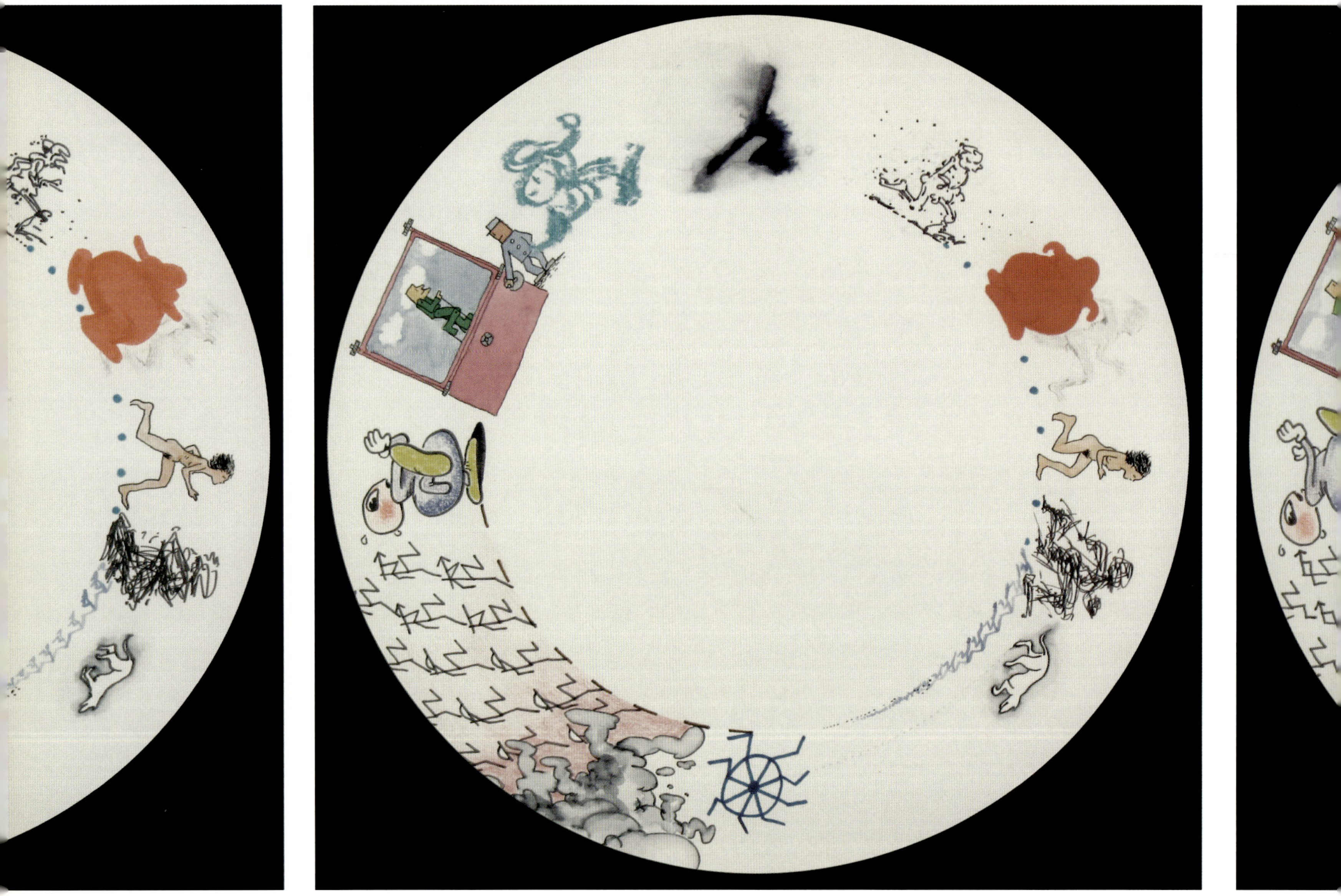

"Even though animation can now simulate a realistic performance, I am neither persuaded nor astonished; I am attracted to rowdy, discontinuous phases of perception and to performance that revels in its own synthetic construction." — GG

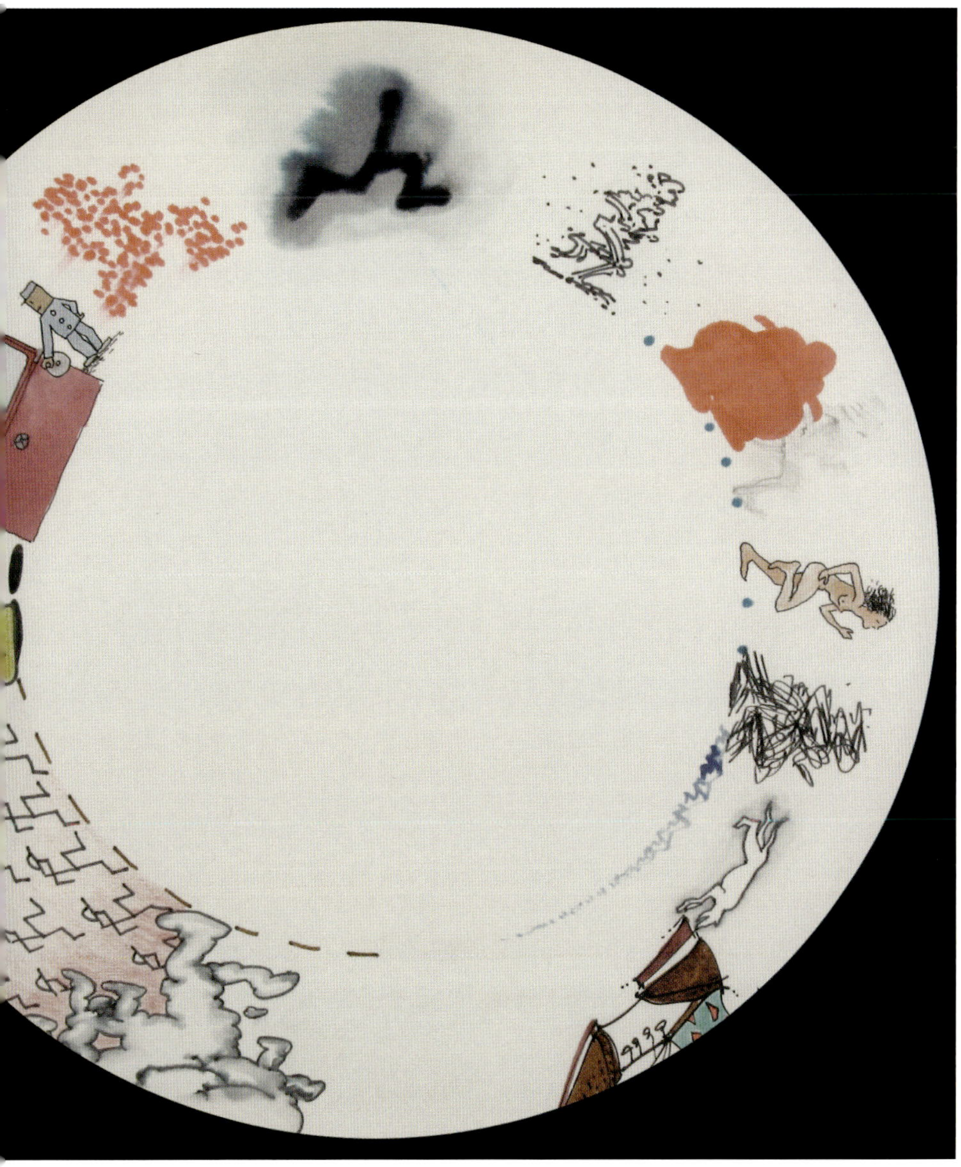

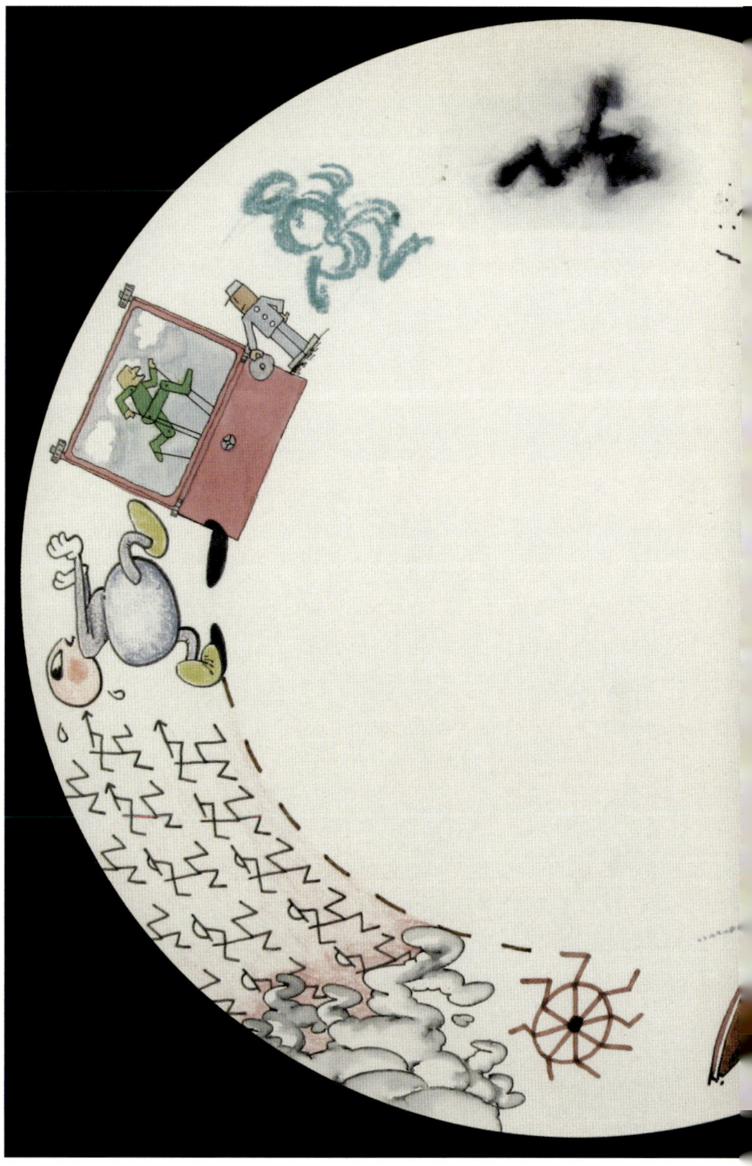

EZRA **JOHNSON**

BORN IN 1975, LIVES AND WORKS IN NEW YORK

What Visions Burn, 2006

Ezra Johnson's *What Visions Burn* relays the story of an art heist and its aftermath, in which Johnson intertwines content with style for a unique take on the robber-film genre. He paints and repaints his canvases to create each frame of his films, providing a rich visual texture and continuity. He uses the medium of painting to make a film about stolen paintings, and interjects newspaper headlines—made from newsprint collages—into the action. *What Visions Burn* is at once a meditation on art, film, and urban society.

EZRA JOHNSON
Stills from *What Visions Burn*, 2006
Video
Images courtesy the artist and Nicole Klagsbrun Gallery, New York

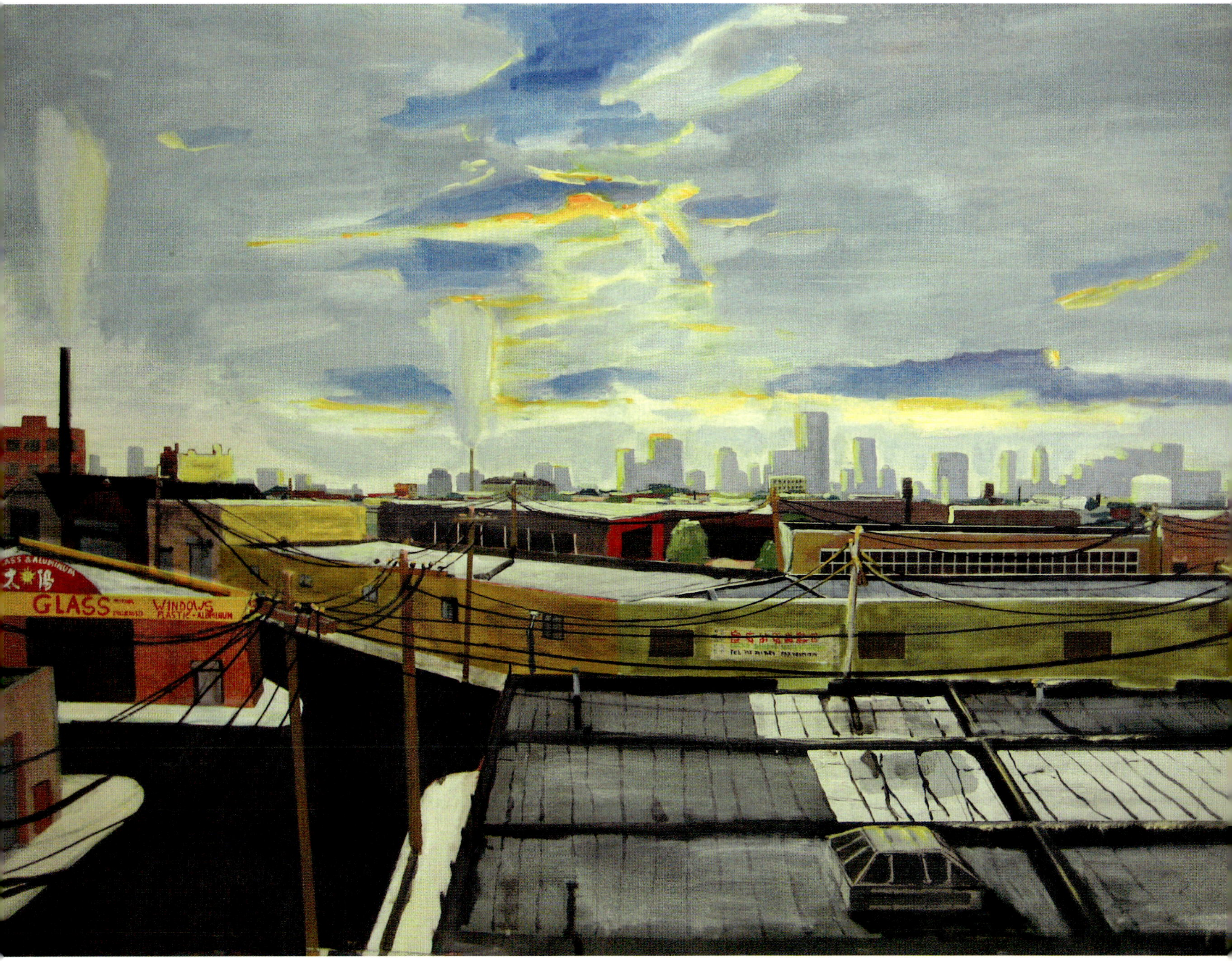

the dissolve

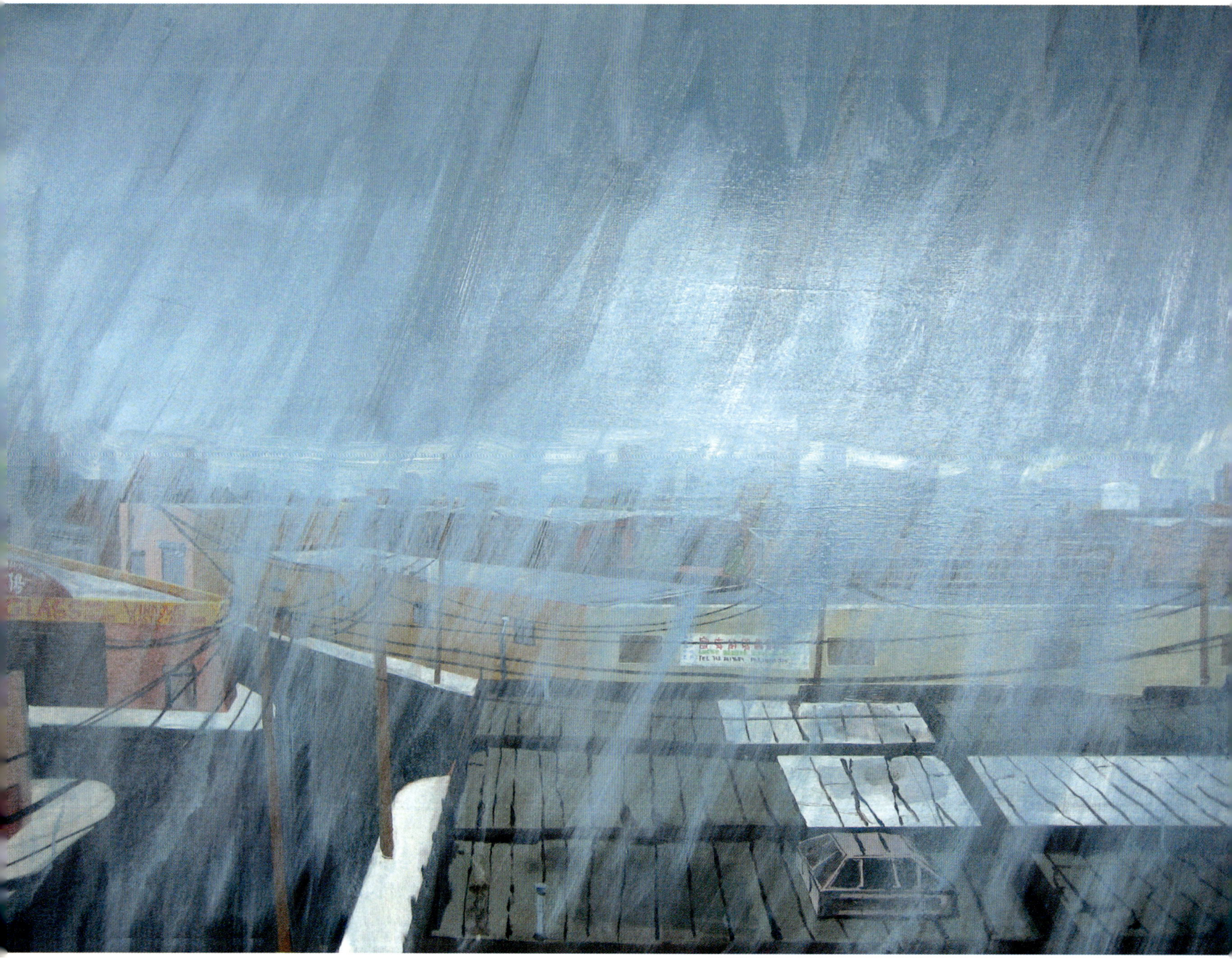

"I am a painter who makes animations that use movement to explore painting: materiality and color, space, light, and narrative. *What Visions Burn* is a movie about paintings and a painting about movies." — EJ

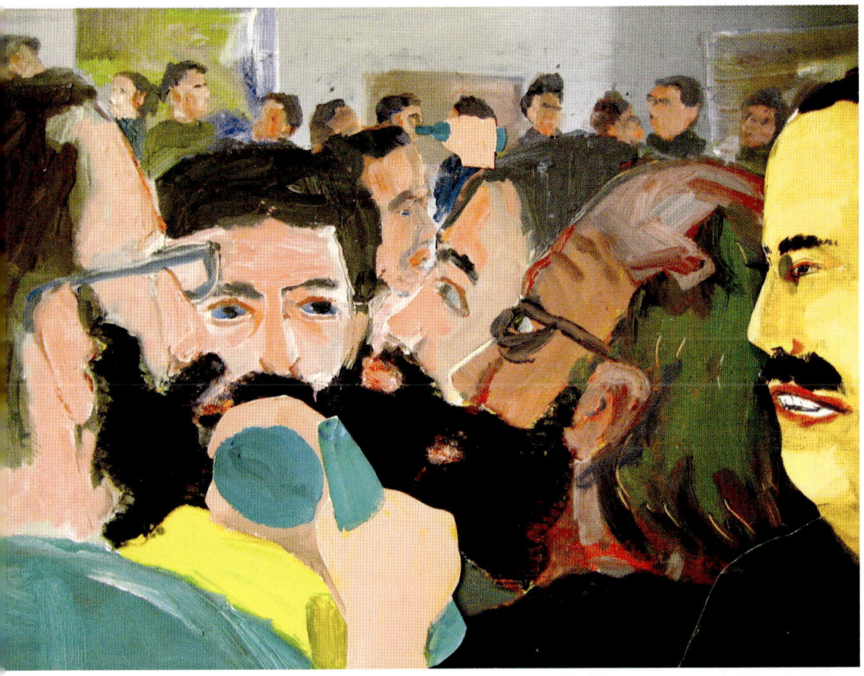

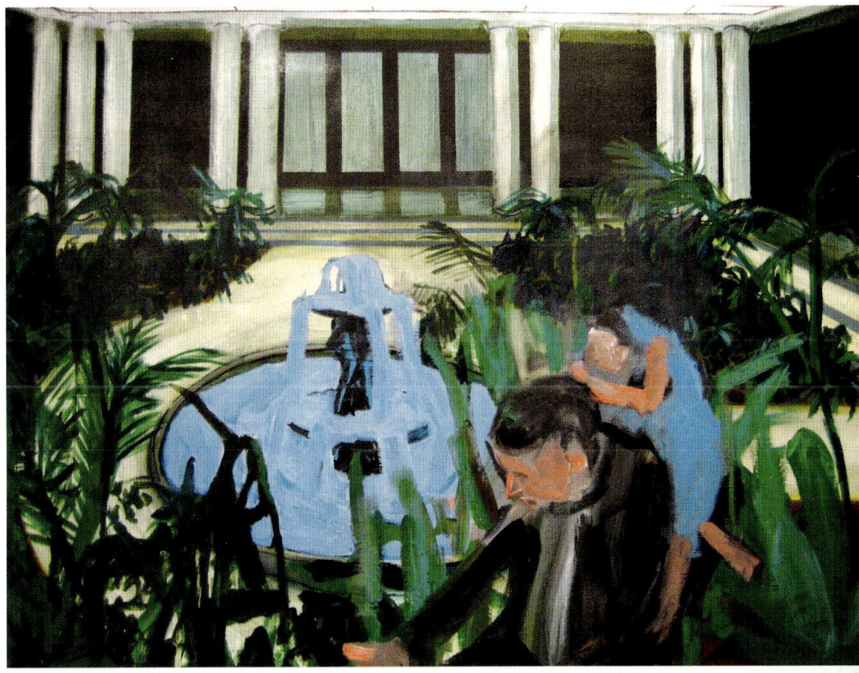

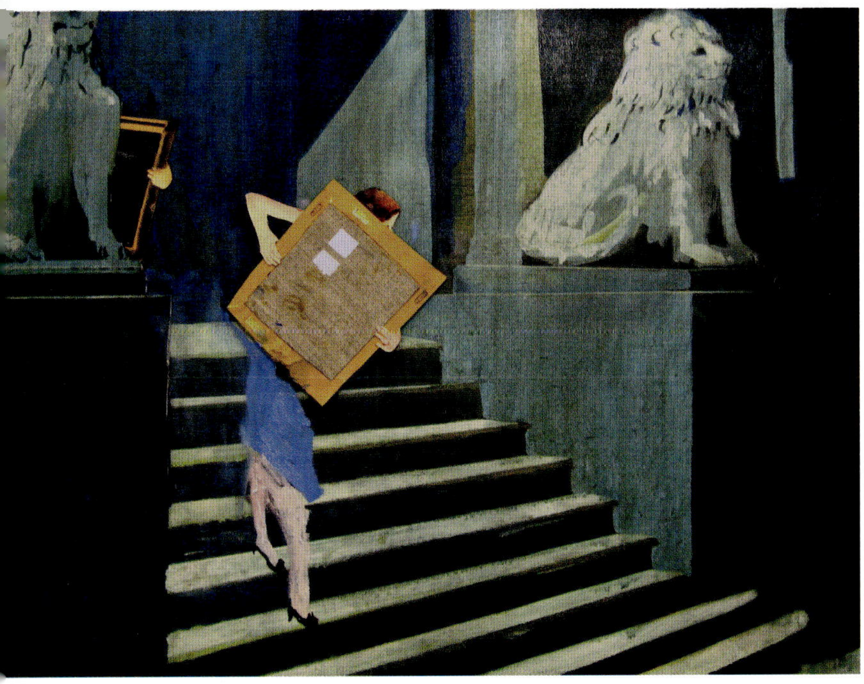

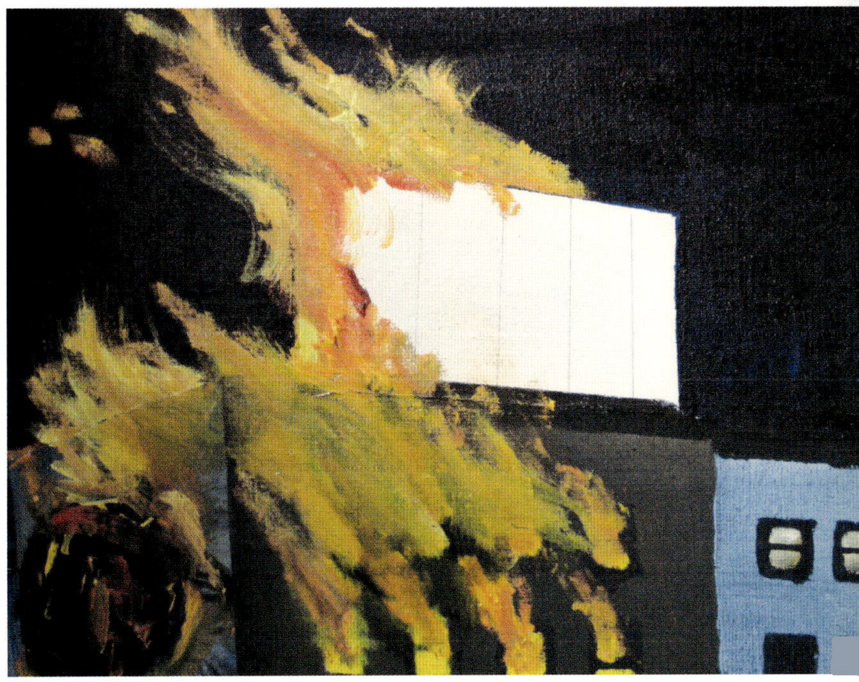

the dissolve

BILL T. **JONES** AND **OPENENDED GROUP**

BILL T. JONES, BORN IN 1952, LIVES AND WORKS IN NEW YORK

OPENENDED GROUP:
MARC DOWNIE, BORN IN 1977, LIVES AND WORKS IN CHICAGO
SHELLEY ESHKAR, BORN IN 1970, LIVES AND WORKS IN NEW YORK
PAUL KAISER, BORN IN 1956, LIVES AND WORKS IN NEW YORK

After Ghostcatching, 2010

After Ghostcatching is a stereoscopic version of a work created from a collaboration between Bill T. Jones and OpenEnded Group. Jones's distinctive movements are transformed into a three-dimensional moving drawing through the use of motion-capture technology. Abstract lines are created by the fading traces of Jones's body while the sound of Jones's rhythmic humming and breathing punctuate his gestures. This tenth anniversary reworking of the original edition takes advantage of the evolution of 3-D and projection technology to create an enhanced version of *Ghostcatching* in which art, dance, and technology are seamlessly integrated.

BILL T. JONES AND OPENENDED GROUP
Stills from *Ghostcatching*, 1999
Images courtesy of Bill T. Jones, Shelley Eshkar, and Paul Kaiser

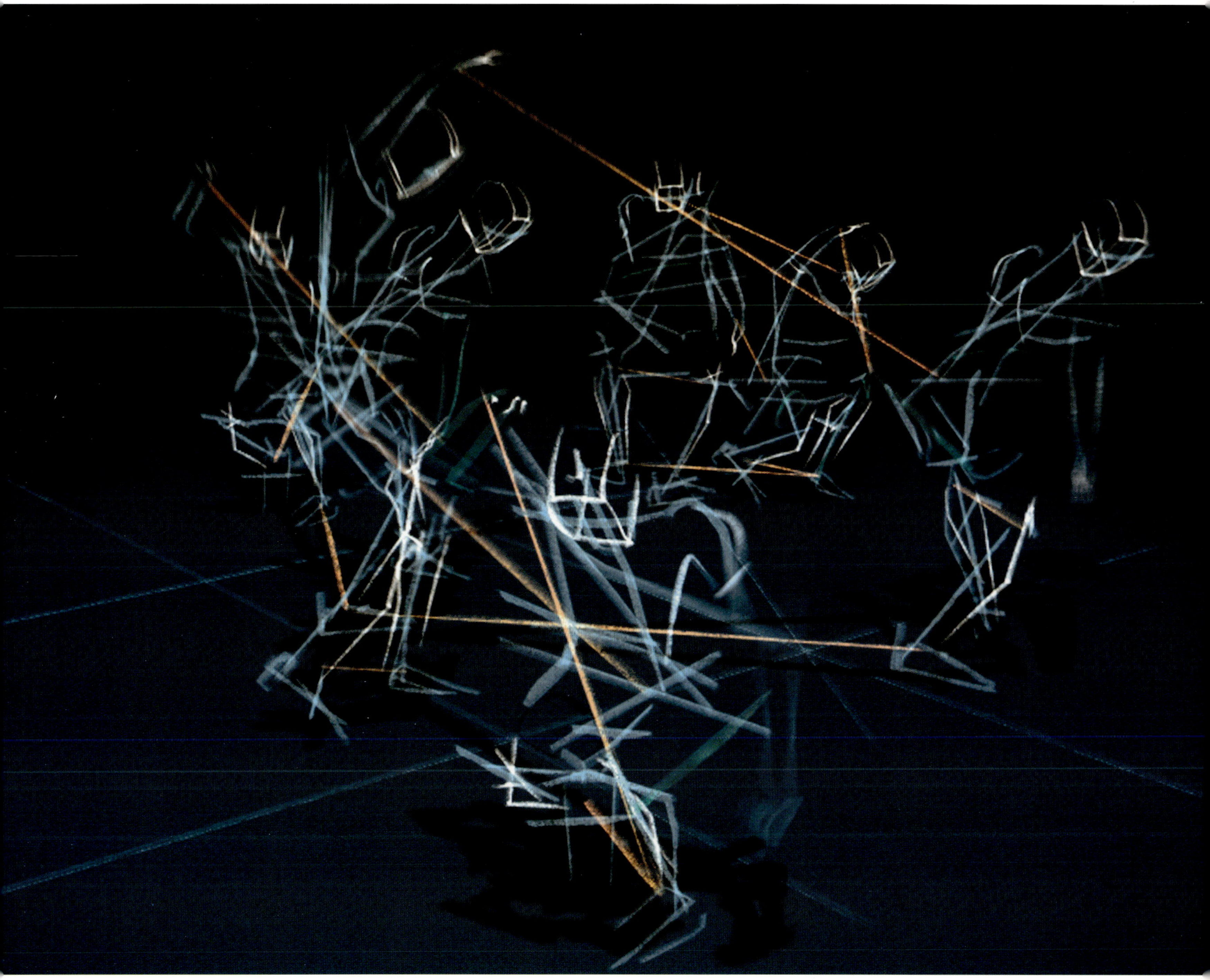

the dissolve

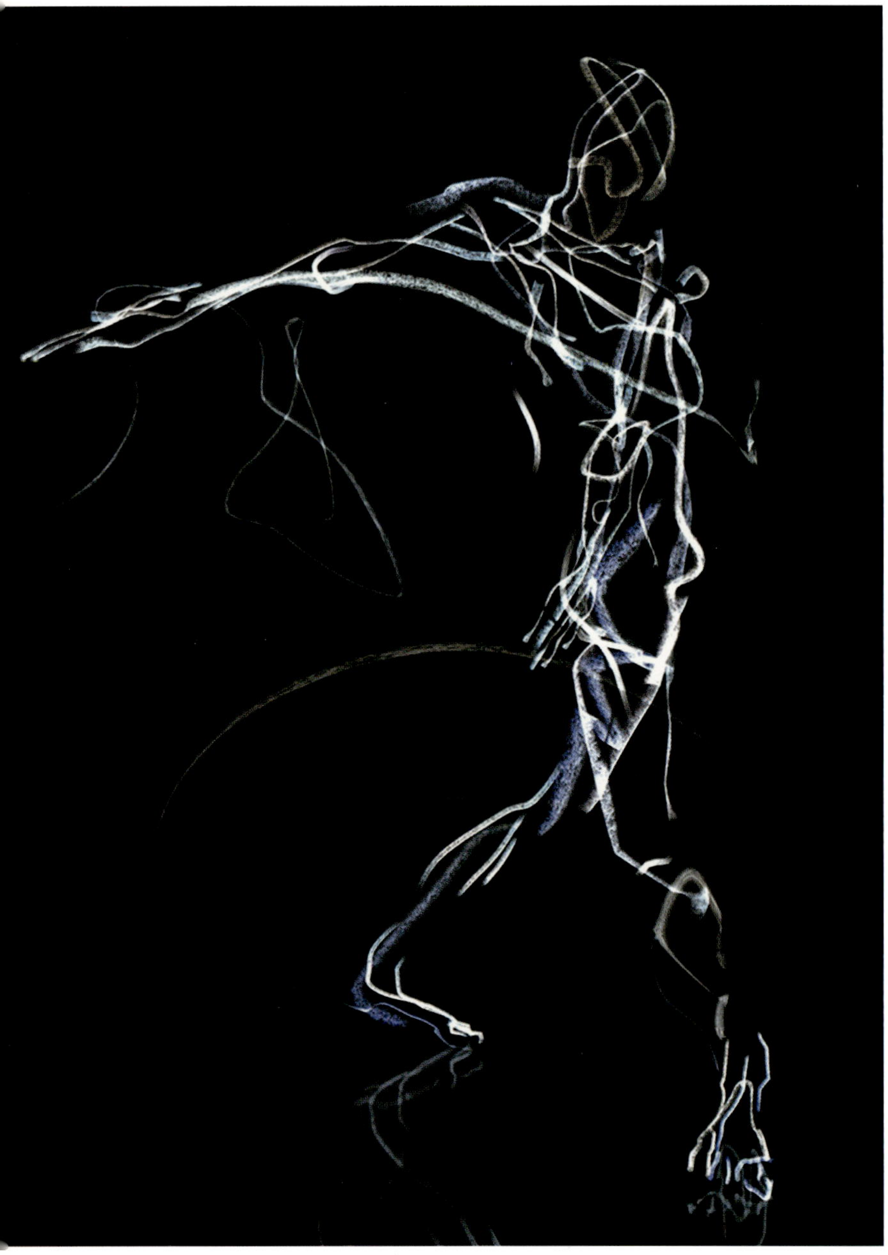

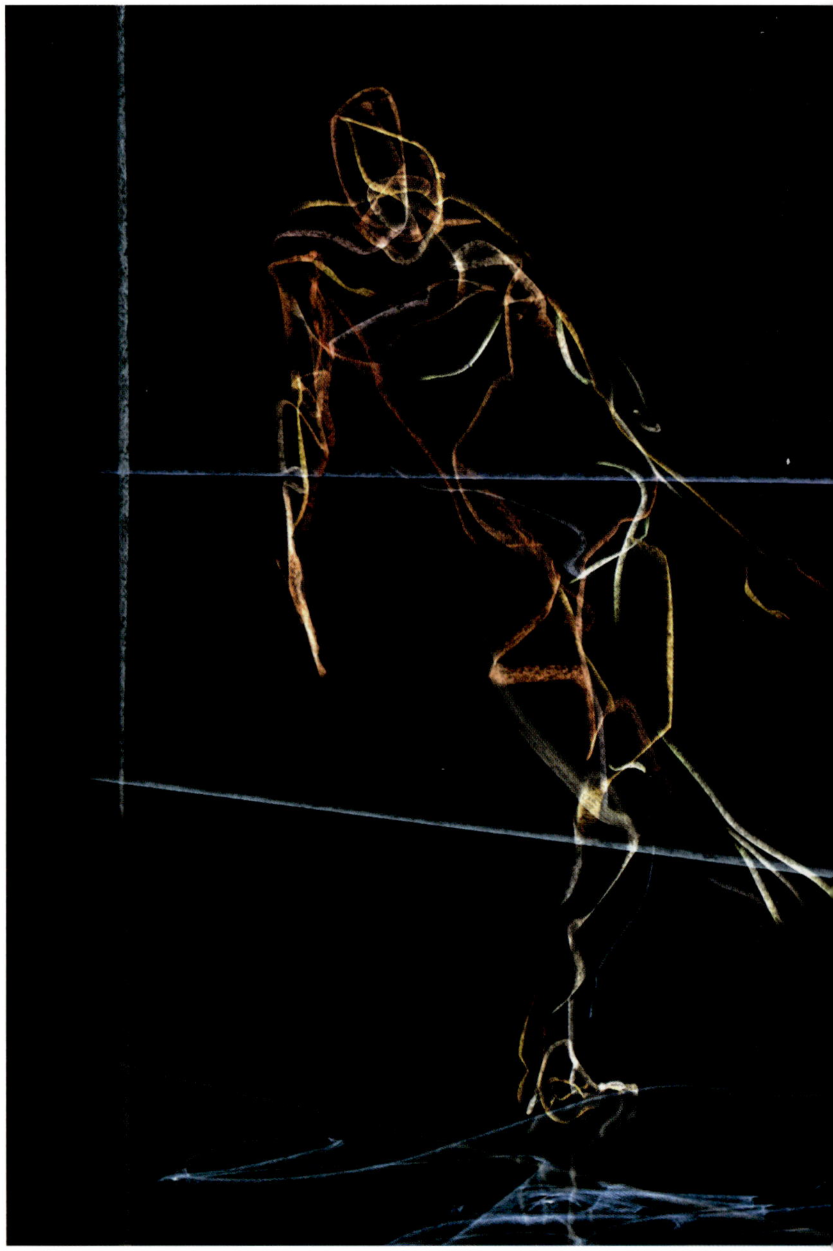

"I think back to the mystery and excitement I felt participating in this landmark collaboration that set out to use digital technology to, in some way, free my movement from my person, my personality, and time and space—the natural arena for my art form. Now, three years after deciding to stop performing, and approximately ten years after the original *Ghostcatching* was created, it is gratifying to see how technology has continued to evolve and that this artifact of my performing remains fresh, offering what every dancer relishes: a glimpse of immortality!" — BTJ

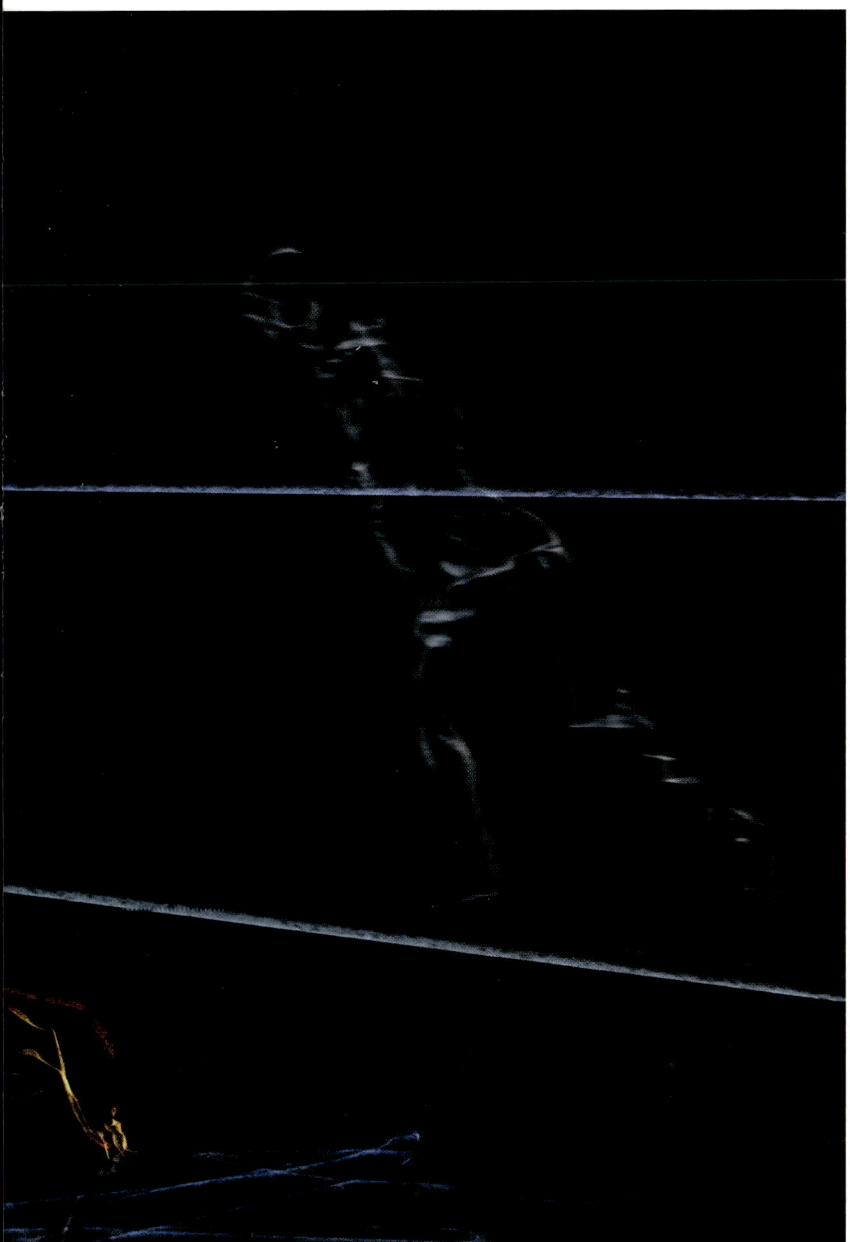

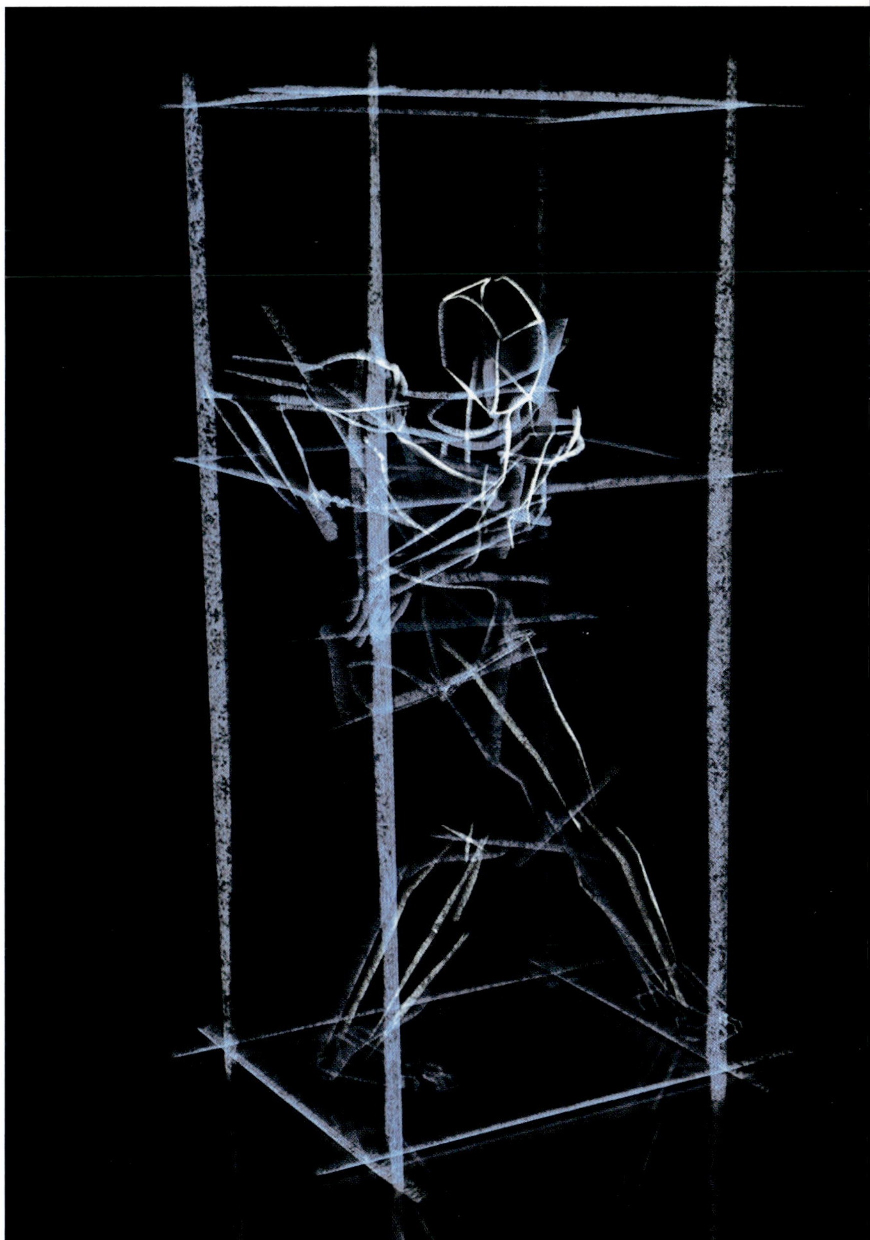

the dissolve

WILLIAM **KENTRIDGE**

BORN IN 1955, LIVES AND WORKS IN JOHANNESBURG

History of the Main Complaint, 1996

History of the Main Complaint is the sixth work in William Kentridge's landmark *Drawings for Projection* series of innovative stop-motion films made from meticulously rendered and erased charcoal drawings. This animation is constructed from a body of approximately twenty-one drawings. Created shortly after the establishment of the Truth and Reconciliation Commission in 1995, the piece investigates the complicated legacy of South Africa's Apartheid system by tracing a journey through the conflicted unconscious of its white protagonist, Soho Eckstein.

WILLIAM KENTRIDGE
Stills from *History of the Main Complaint*, 1996
35mm film transferred to DVD
Images courtesy of the artist and Marian Goodman Gallery, New York

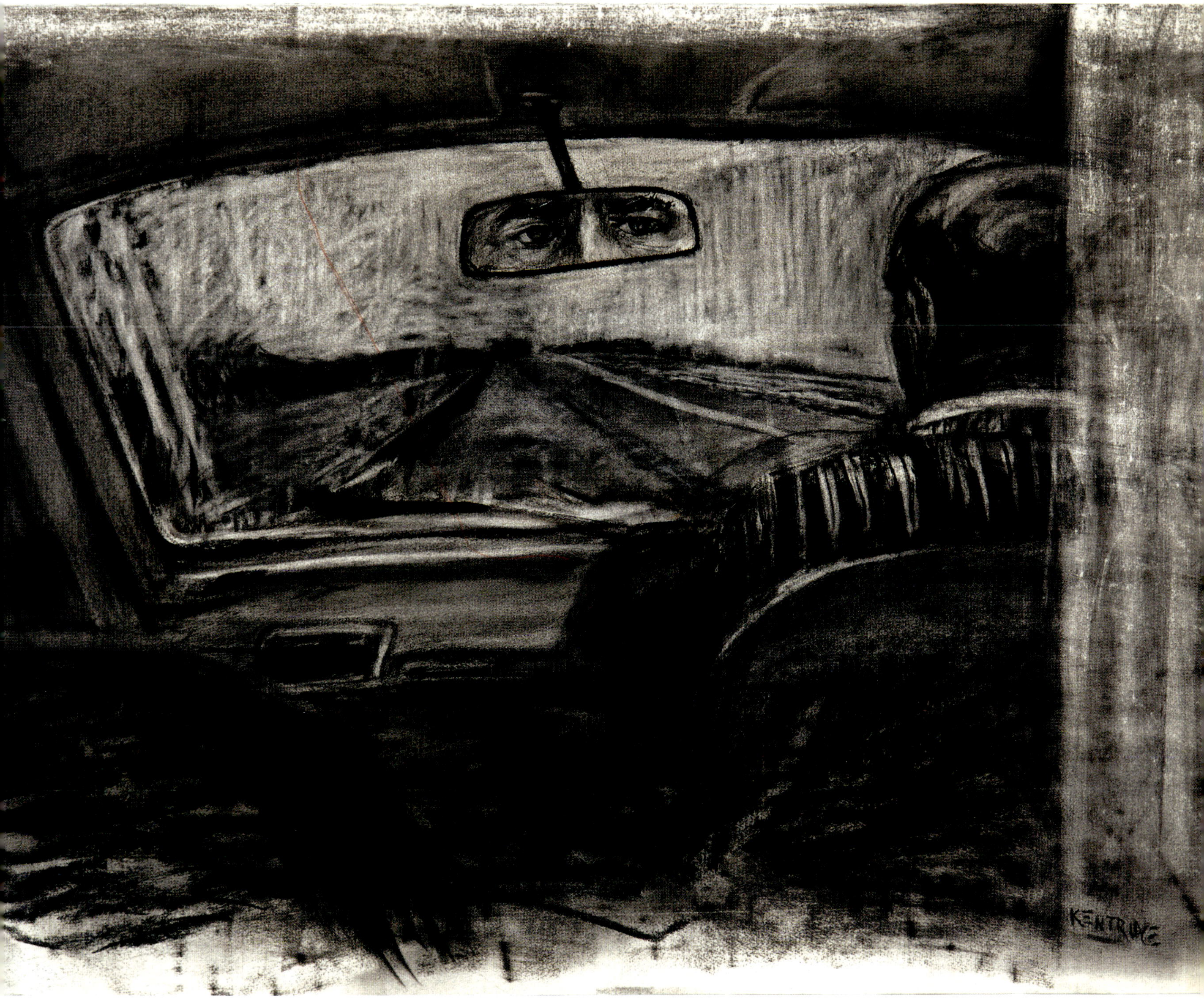

the dissolve

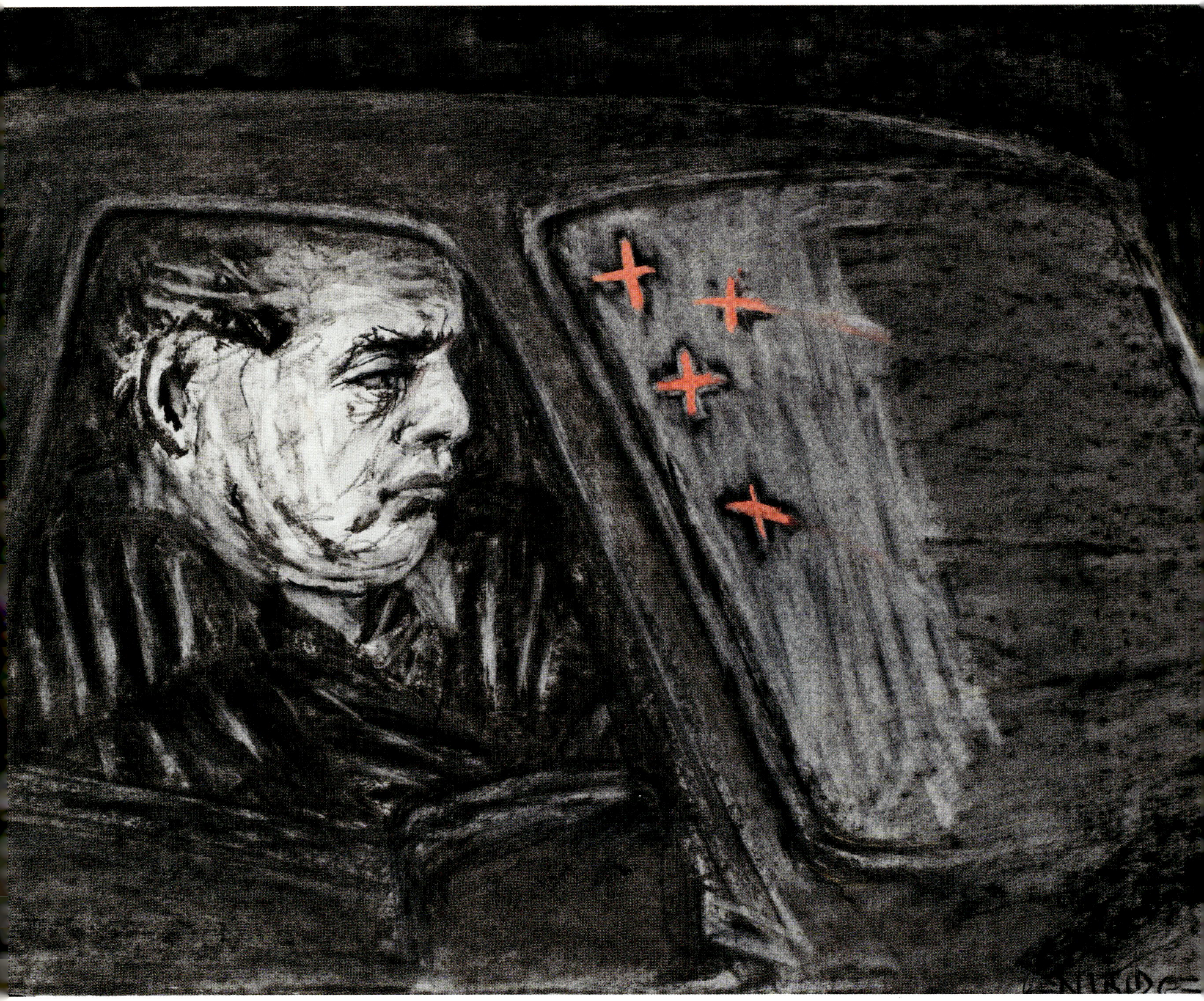

"Well, everything is drawing. Sometimes the drawings are primarily charcoal on paper, but (occasionally) the drawings are simply two-dimensional drawings—straightforward charcoal drawing on paper. Sometimes I film those drawings in progress, stage-by-stage as the drawing is completed…the movement is adjusted, and shifted, and becomes the basis for pieces that are finished as films. Two dimensions moving through time." —WK

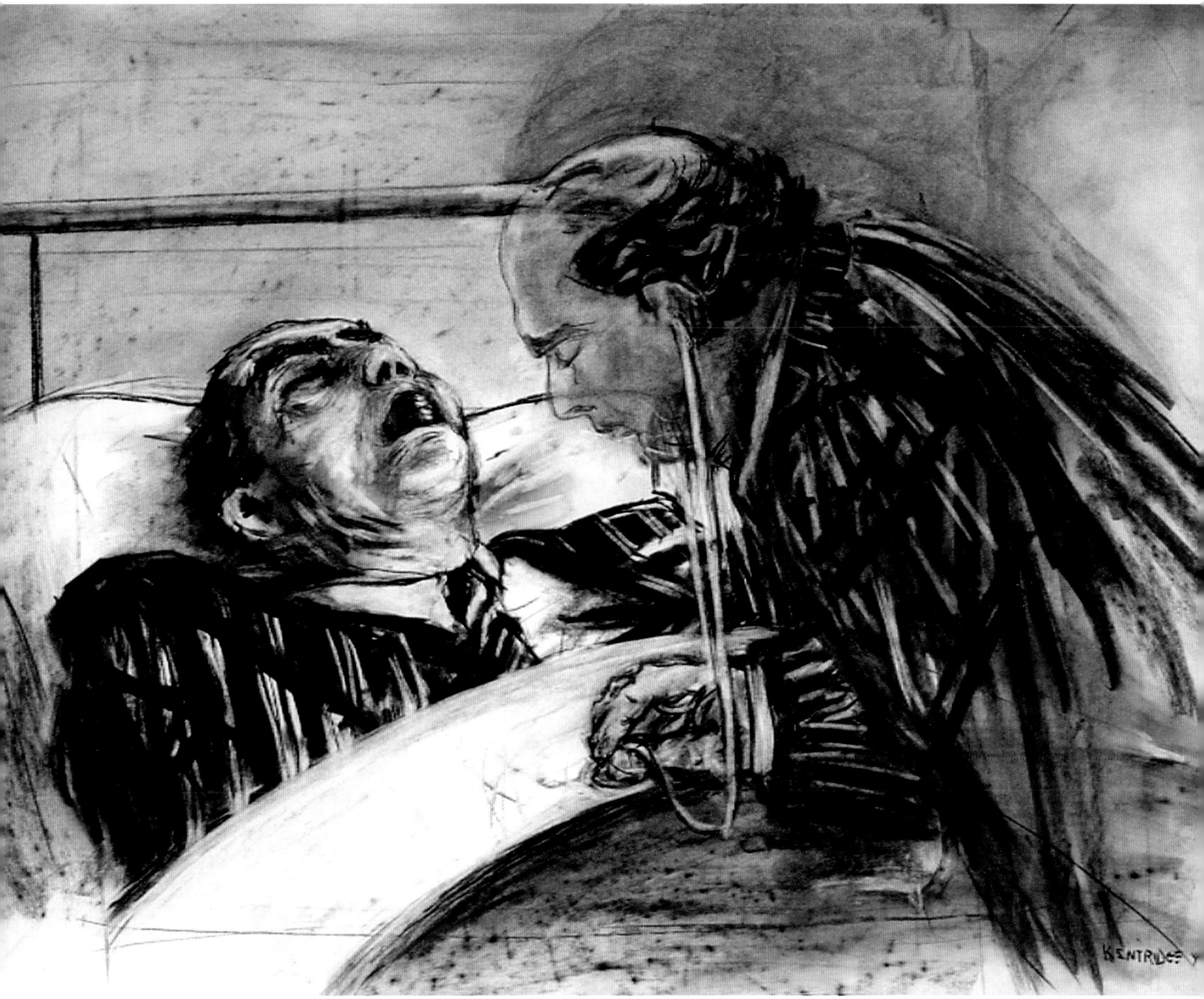

AVISH **KHEBREHZADEH**

BORN IN 1969, LIVES AND WORKS IN WASHINGTON, D.C. AND ROME

Theater III and *Edgar*, 2010

Avish Khebrehzadeh's painting and video form one integrated work. *Theater III* is the ground for the projected animated narrative *Edgar*. In *Edgar*, three loosely linked vignettes unfold. A pregnant woman is carried past a village into the desert where the three men who have been carrying her, leave her. She then disappears down a hole with the man who has been digging it. Khebrehzadeh's works evoke fairy tales and dreamscapes, often inspired by her actual dreams and memories.

AVISH KHEBREHZADEH
Stills from *Edgar*, 2010
Video
Images courtesy of the artist

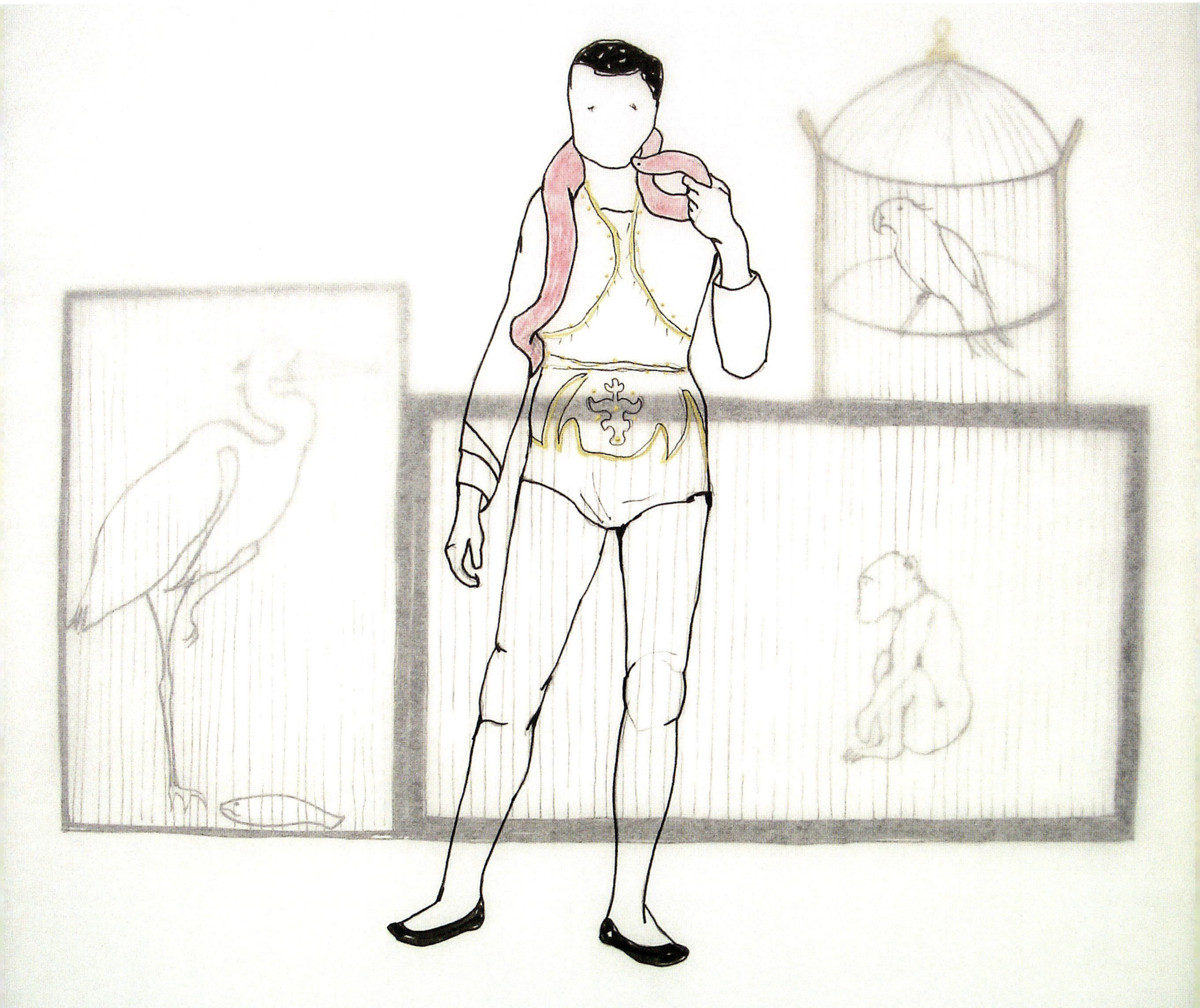

the dissolve

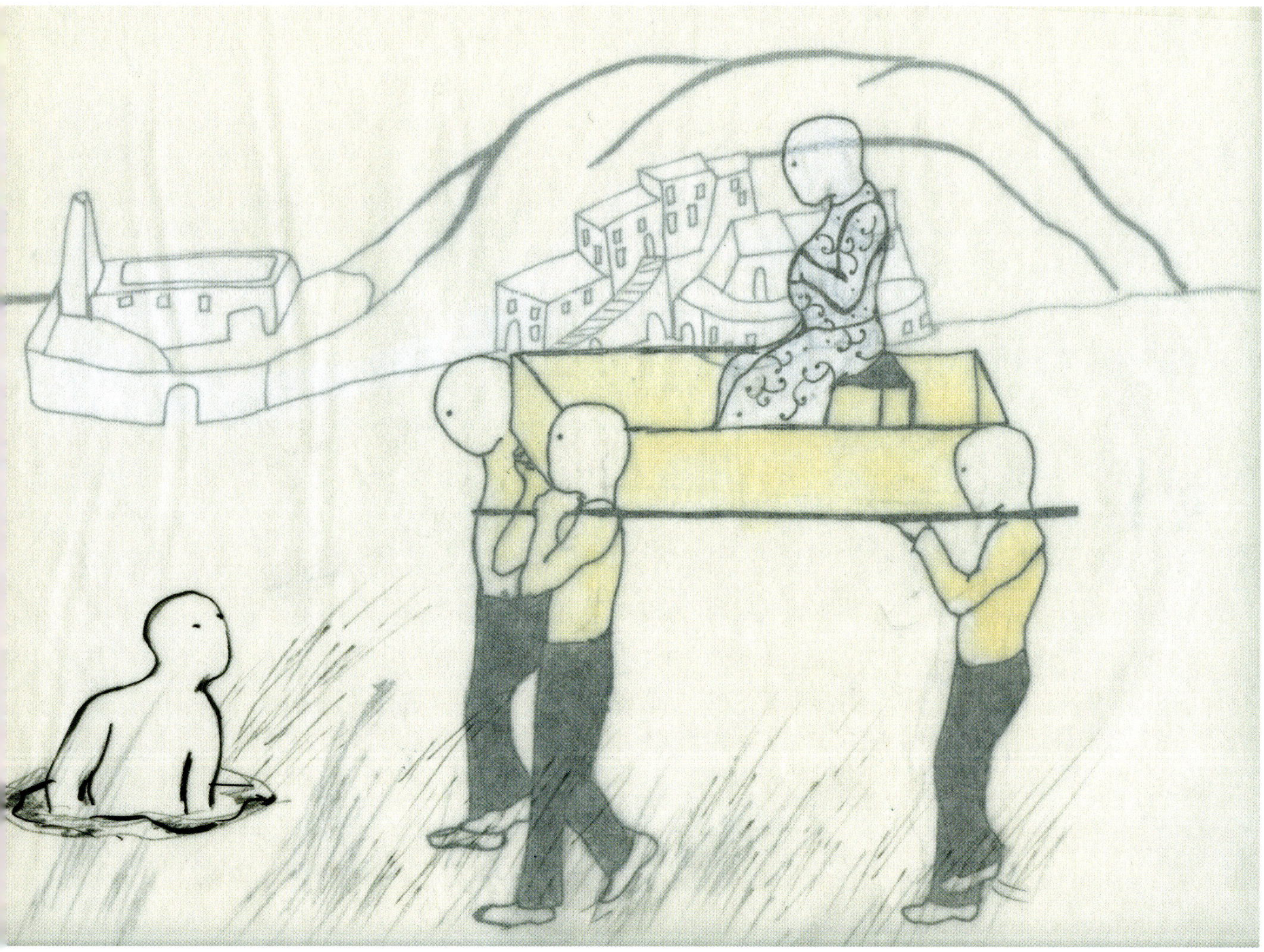

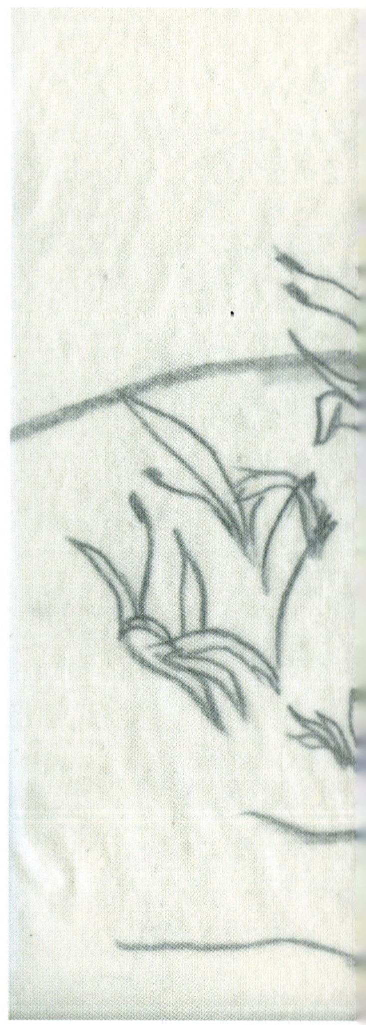

"There is no future or past—only a colorful, silent, and infinitesimal 'now.' Depict the silence and speak the colors sheltered in fragments of time." — AK

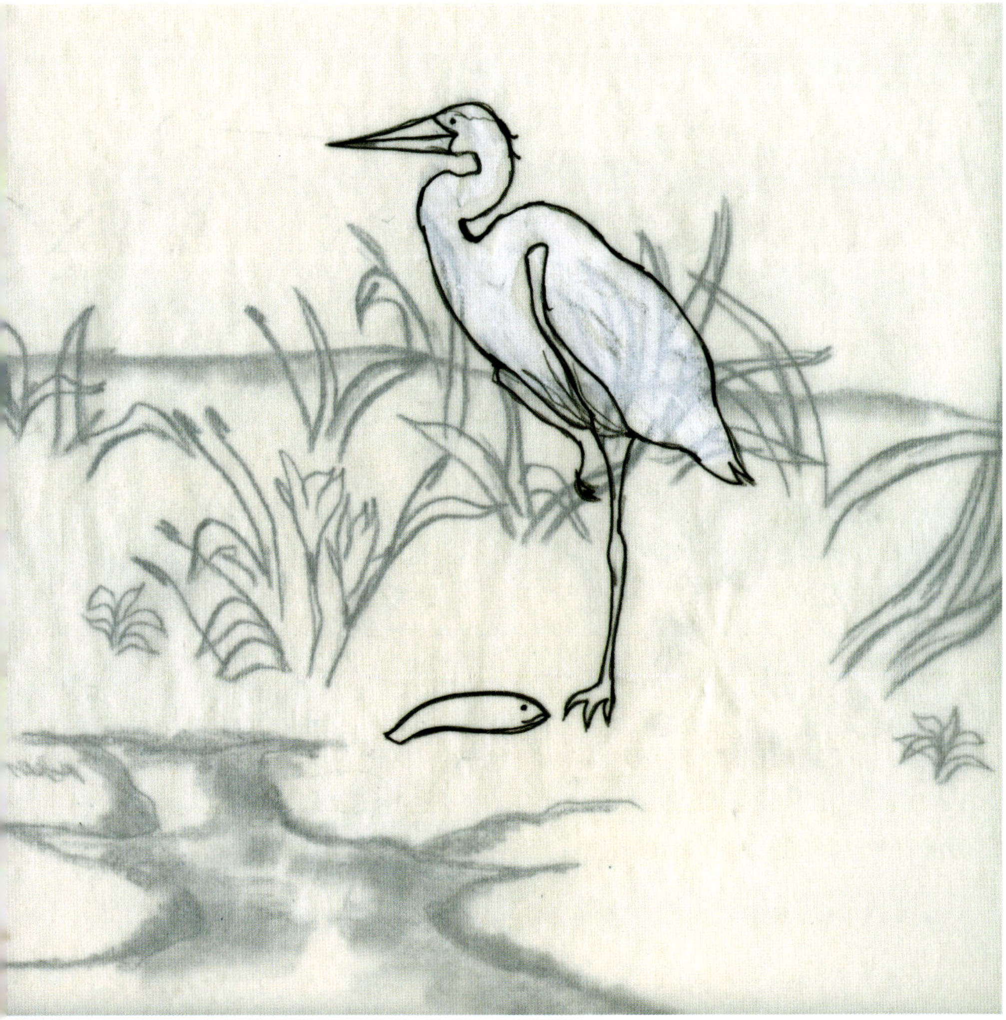

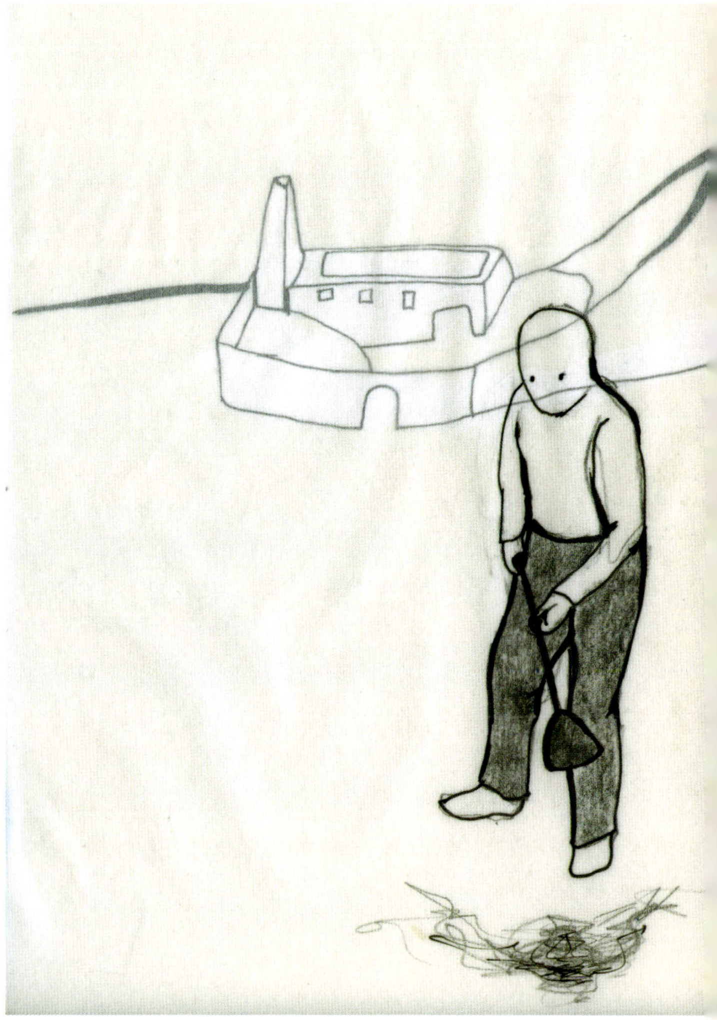

LALEH **KHORRAMIAN**

BORN IN 1974, LIVES AND WORKS IN NEW YORK

Water Panics in the Sea, 2010

Laleh Khorramian's *Water Panics in the Sea* is the fourth in a series of films by the artist that is based on the five elements: earth, air, fire, water, and ether. The hallucinatory voyage of landscapes and occurrences explores of the artificial as real and the real versus the imagined. Khorramian combines stop-motion animation and the magnifications of her monotypes with collages and live-action film. The soundtrack, created through a similar process of layering, sampling, and selecting, underscores the theatrical, epic, and absurd quality of the film.

LALEH KHORRAMIAN
Stills from *Water Panics in the Sea*, 2010
Digital animation
Images courtesy of the artist and Salon 94, New York

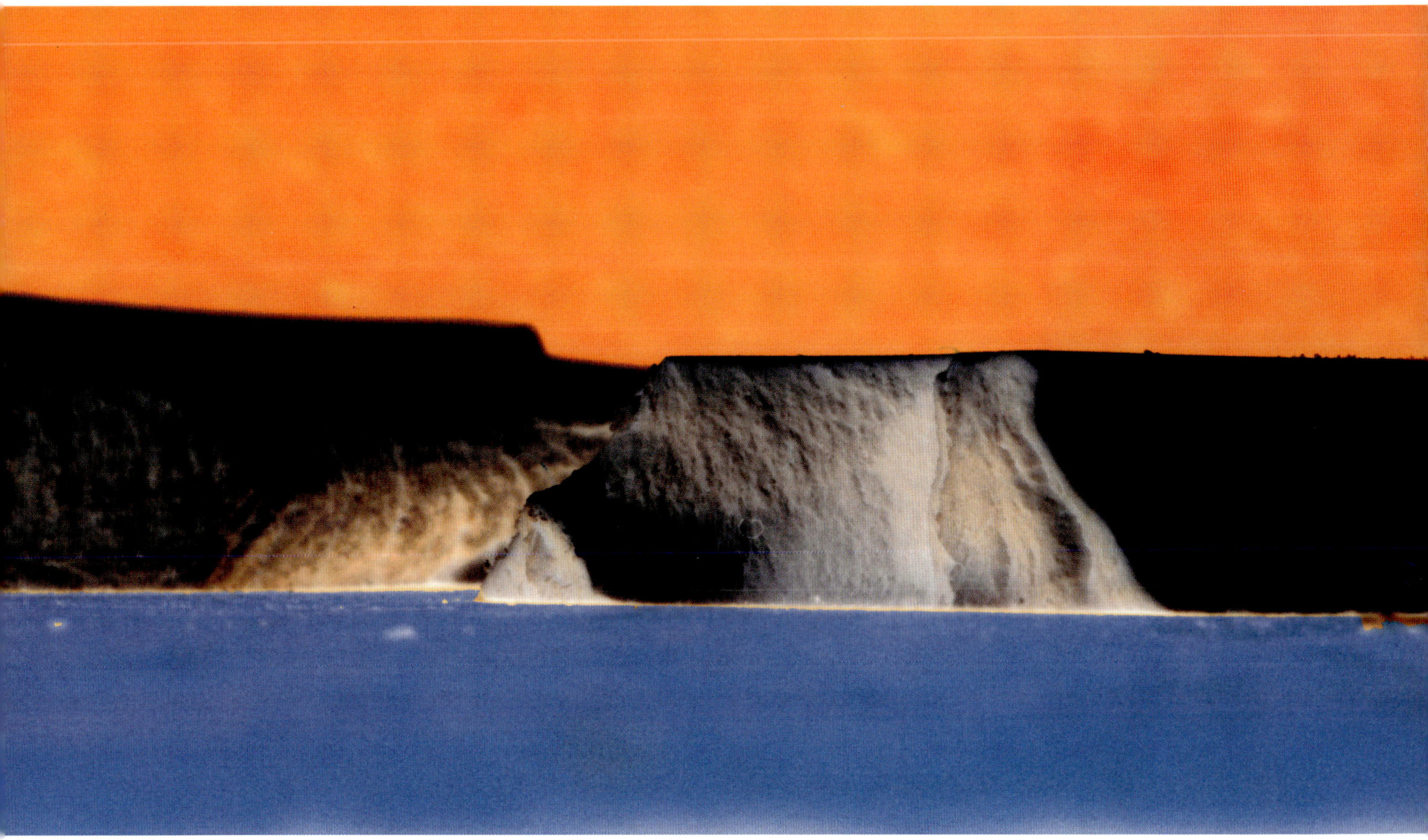

the dissolve

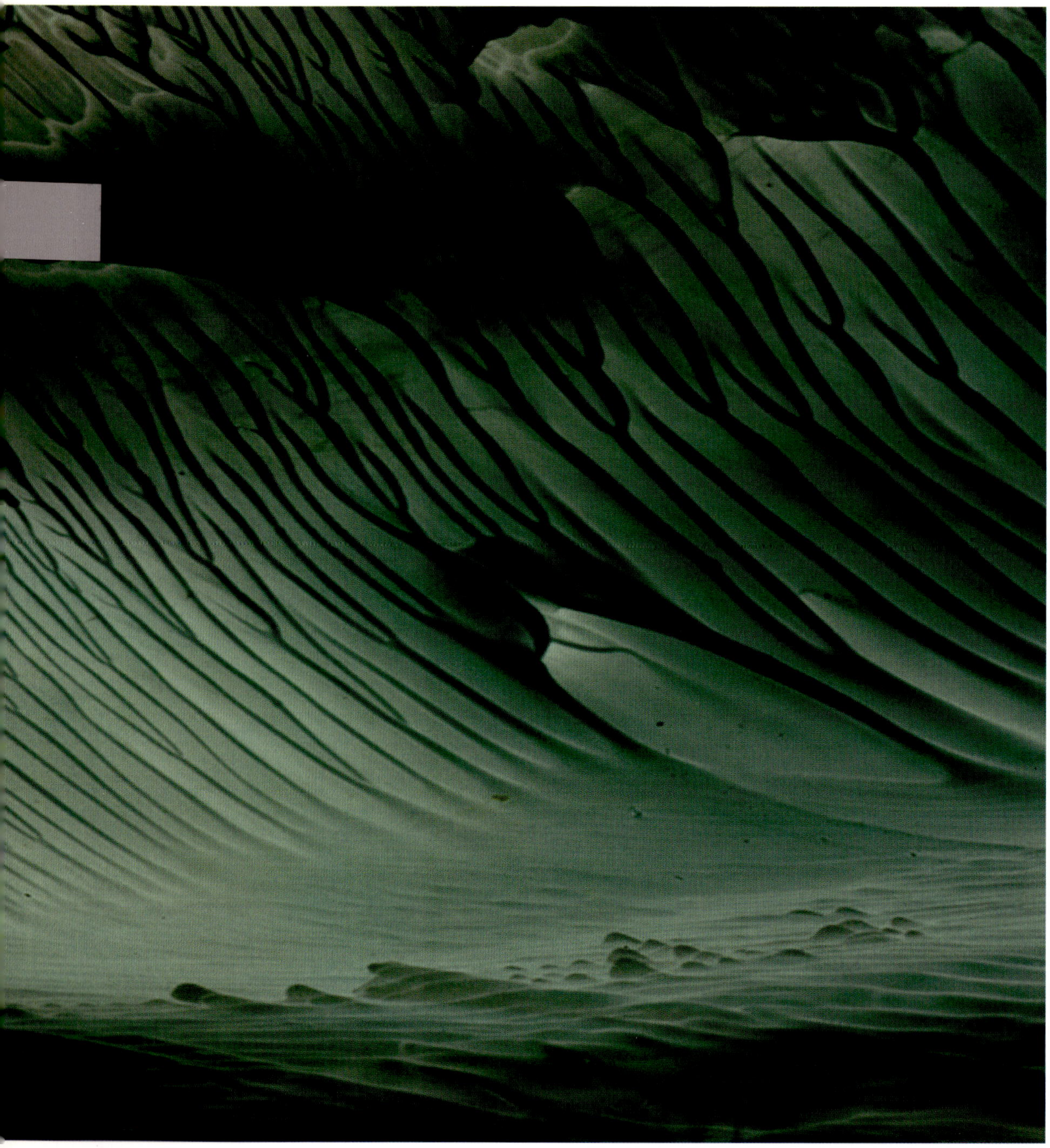

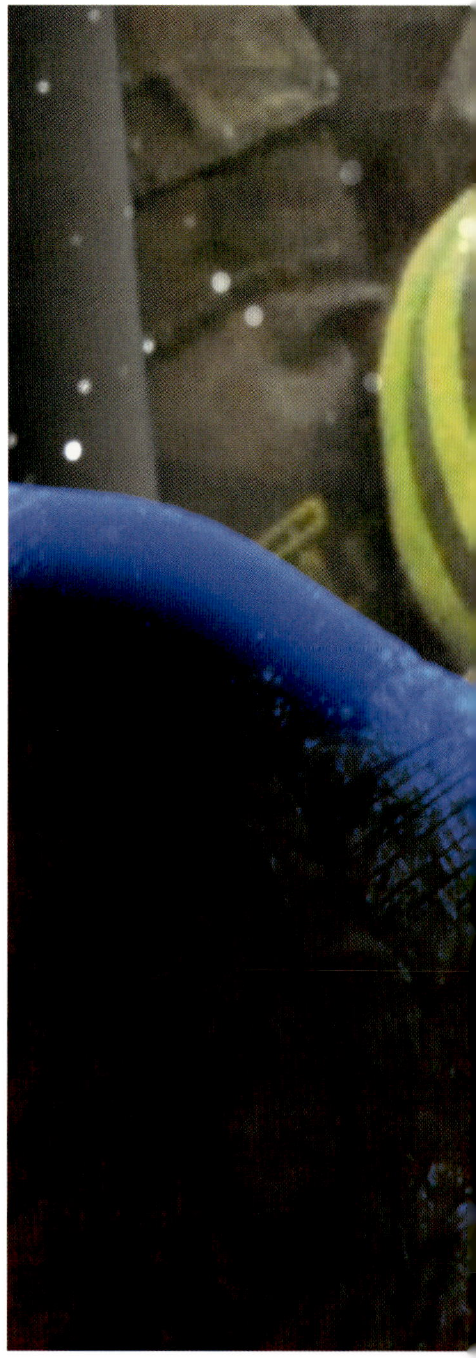

"I like to experiment with the process of chance as a starting point, then investigate its details and outcomes. Bizarrely personal and absurd, these explorations communicate the uncanny as a constructed parallel universe. From there, I attempt to open up an unpredictable space, a space where fiction can capture aspects of life not normally visible to us." — LK

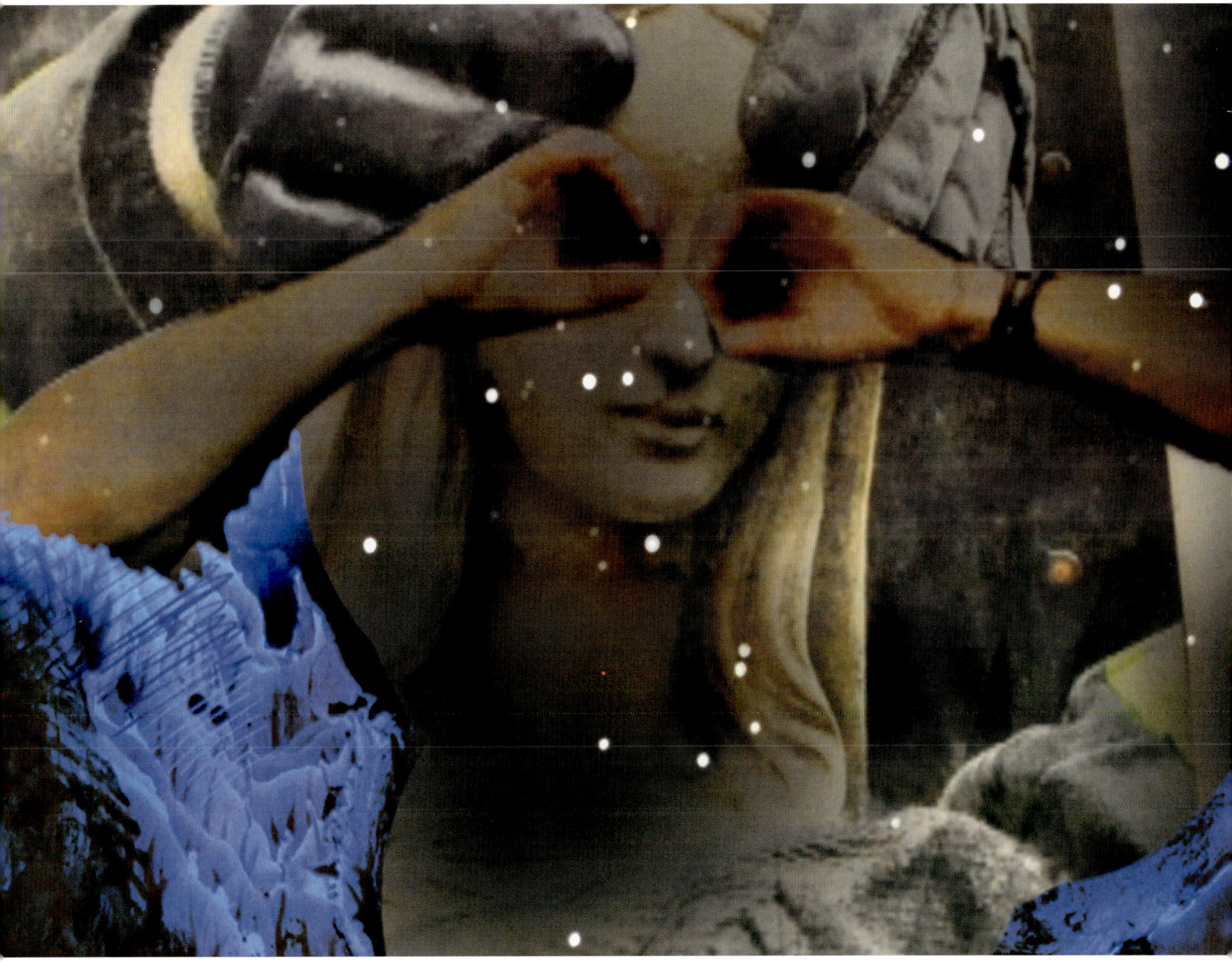

MARIA **LASSNIG**

BORN IN 1919, LIVES AND WORKS IN VIENNA

Maria Lassnig Kantate, 1992

Maria Lassnig's film *Maria Lassnig Kantate* integrates live action, animation, and found photography to present a humorous, semi-autobiographical narrative that outlines the contours of her life—from her Austrian childhood to her development as an artist in Europe and the United States. Lassnig sings the German narration in a faux folk style and changes costume to punctuate the story. The highly personal and expressive film represents what she terms "body-awareness," positing the body as a conduit to explore the interior worlds of human psychology and emotion.

MARIA LASSNIG
Stills from *Maria Lassnig Kantate*, 1992
35mm film transferred to DVD
Images courtesy of sixpackfilm, Wien, Austria

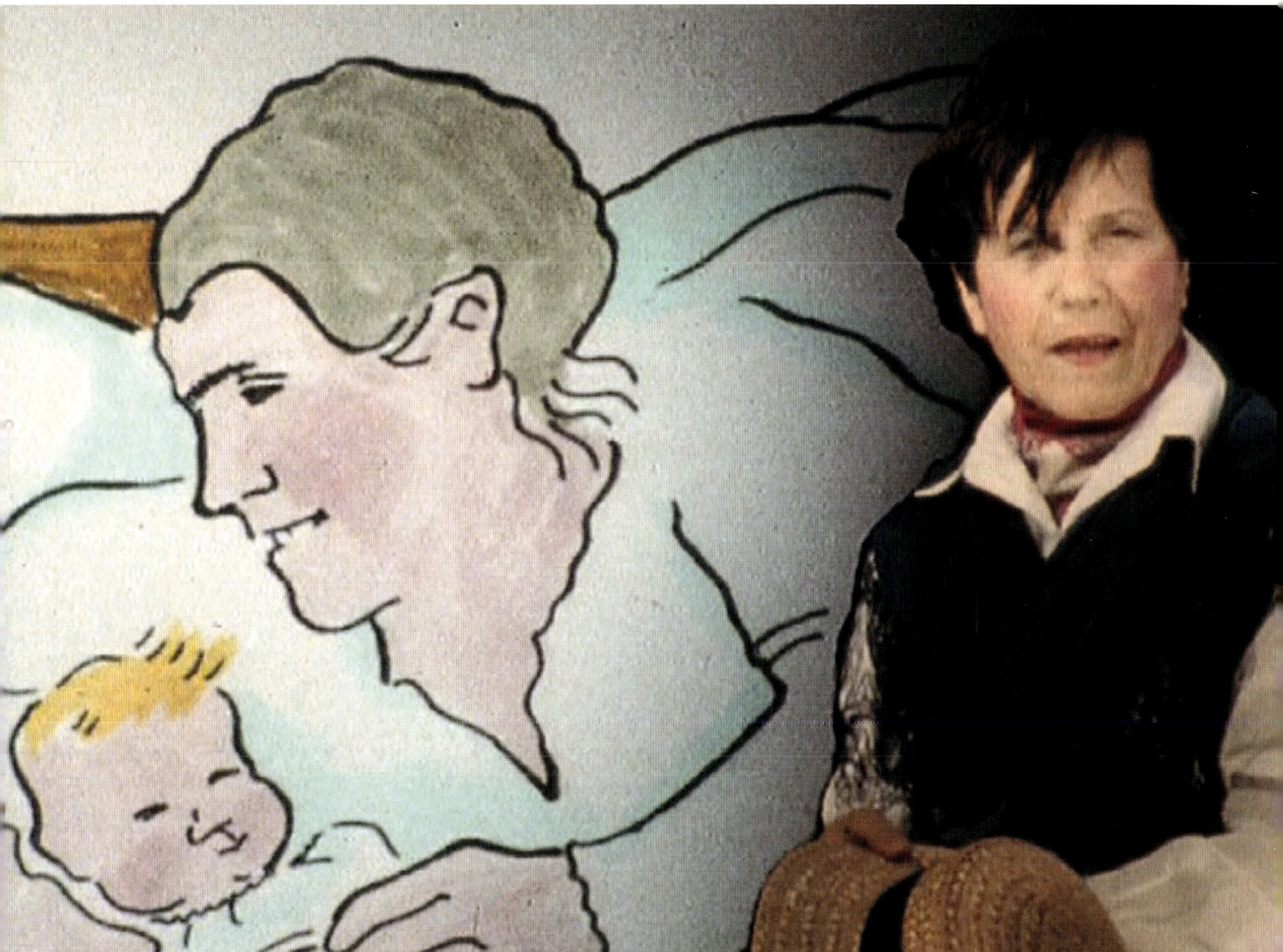

the dissolve

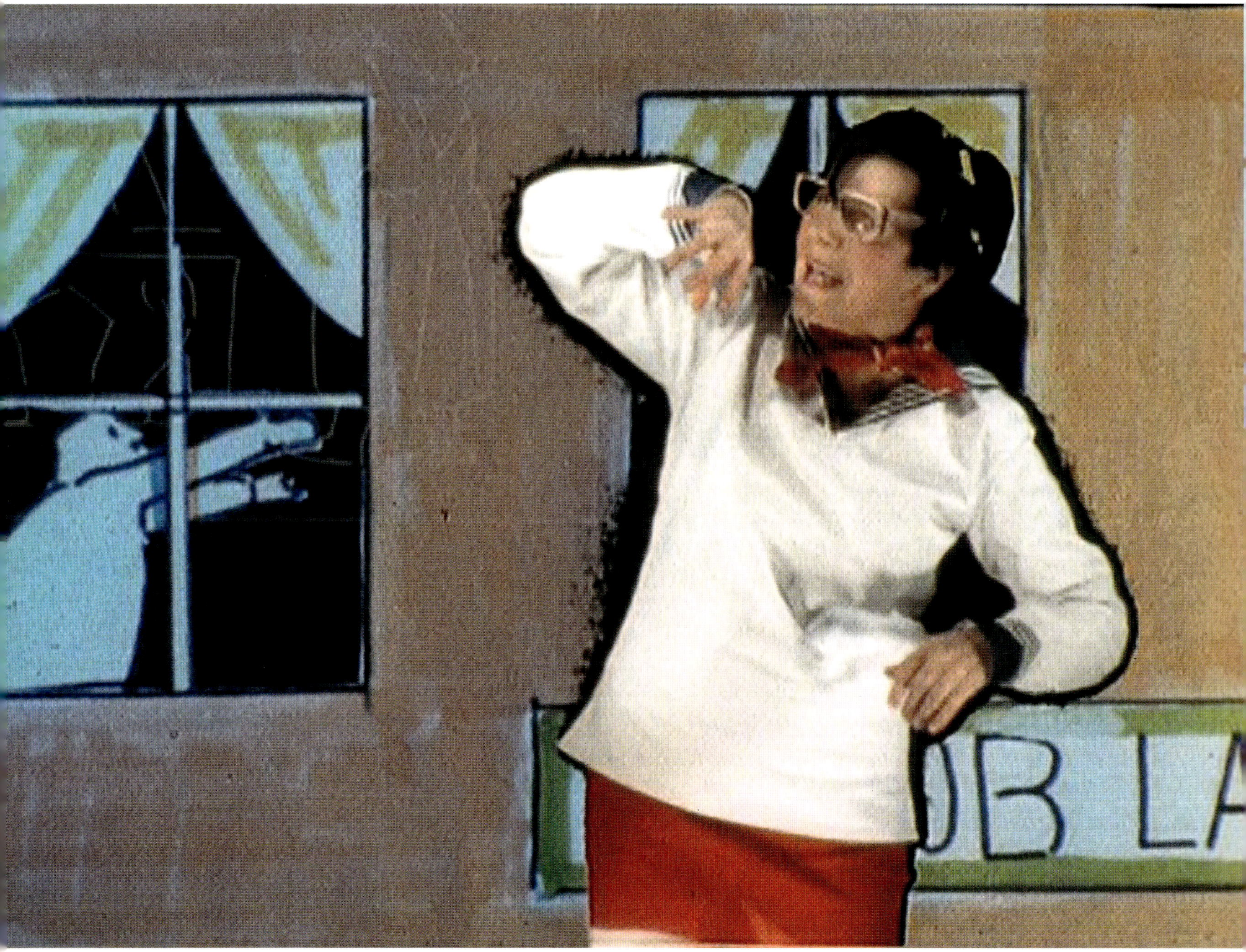

"My heart is beating so hard it makes the world outside tremble." — ML

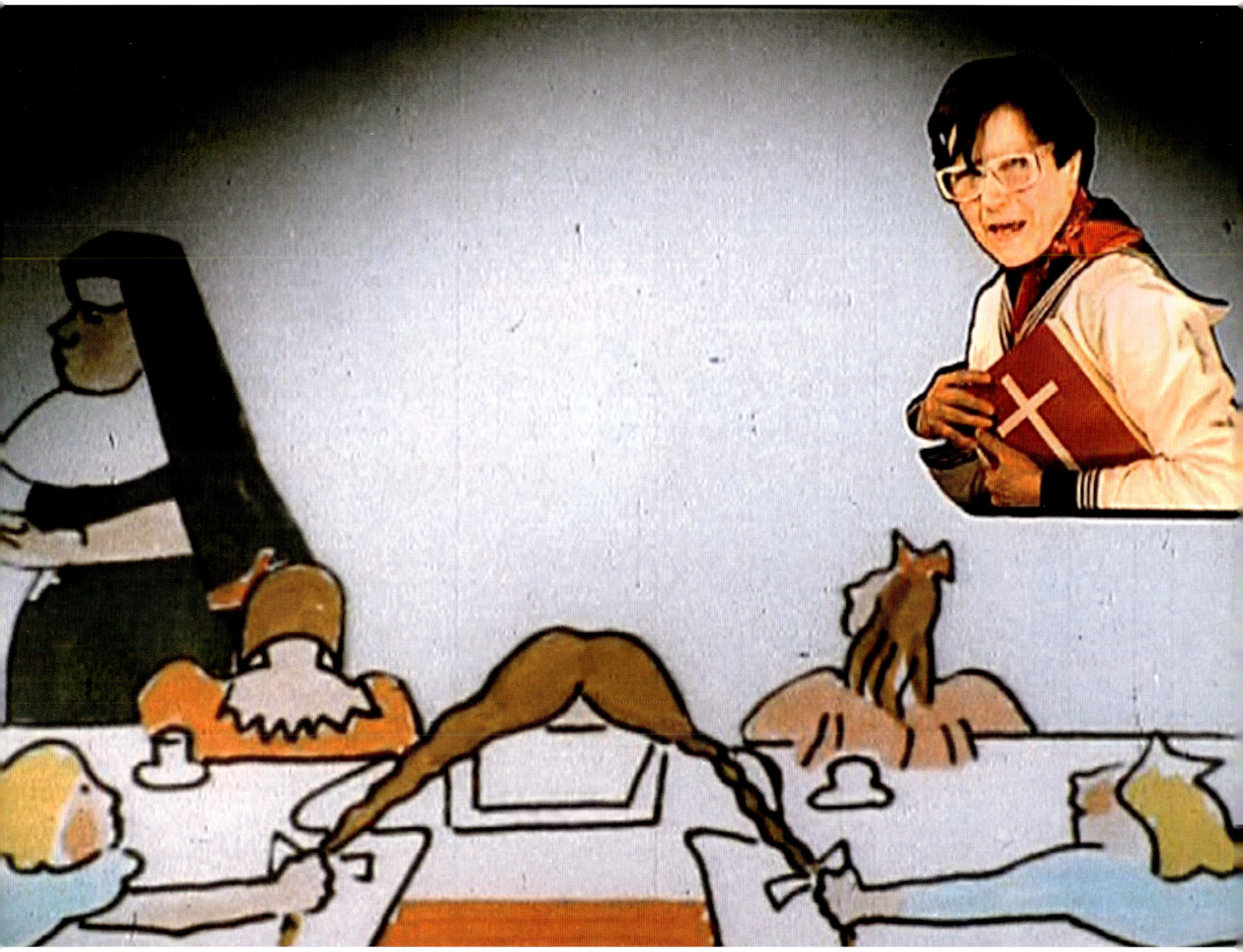

JENNIFER AND KEVIN **McCOY**

BORN IN 1968/1967, LIVE AND WORK IN NEW YORK

Traffic #1: Our Second Date, 2004

Traffic #1: Our Second Date emphasizes the ways in which cultural phenomena become integrated into and shaped by personal histories. This work re-imagines the traffic-jam scene from the 1967 Jean-Luc Godard film *Week End*, which the couple saw together in Paris. A meticulously constructed miniature diorama occupies a rotating tabletop. As it turns, cameras project the changing scenes from Godard's movie onto the gallery wall, and the piece as a whole merges the sculptural with the cinematic.

JENNIFER AND KEVIN McCOY
Details from *Traffic #1: Our Second Date*, 2004
Tabletop installation with plastic figures, plastic and metal model vehicles, LCD monitor, electronics, lights, video cameras, and video projection
Images courtesy of the artists

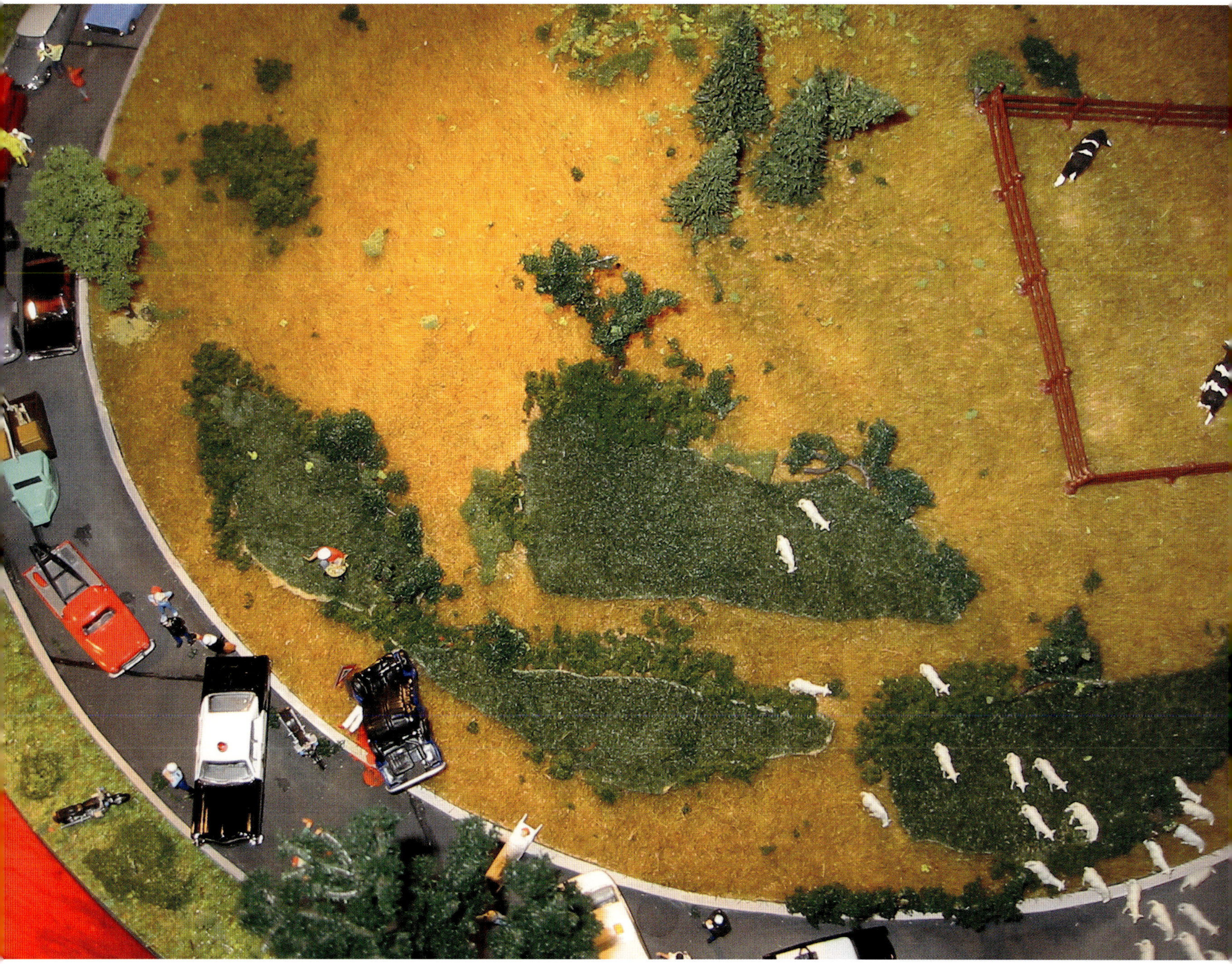

the dissolve

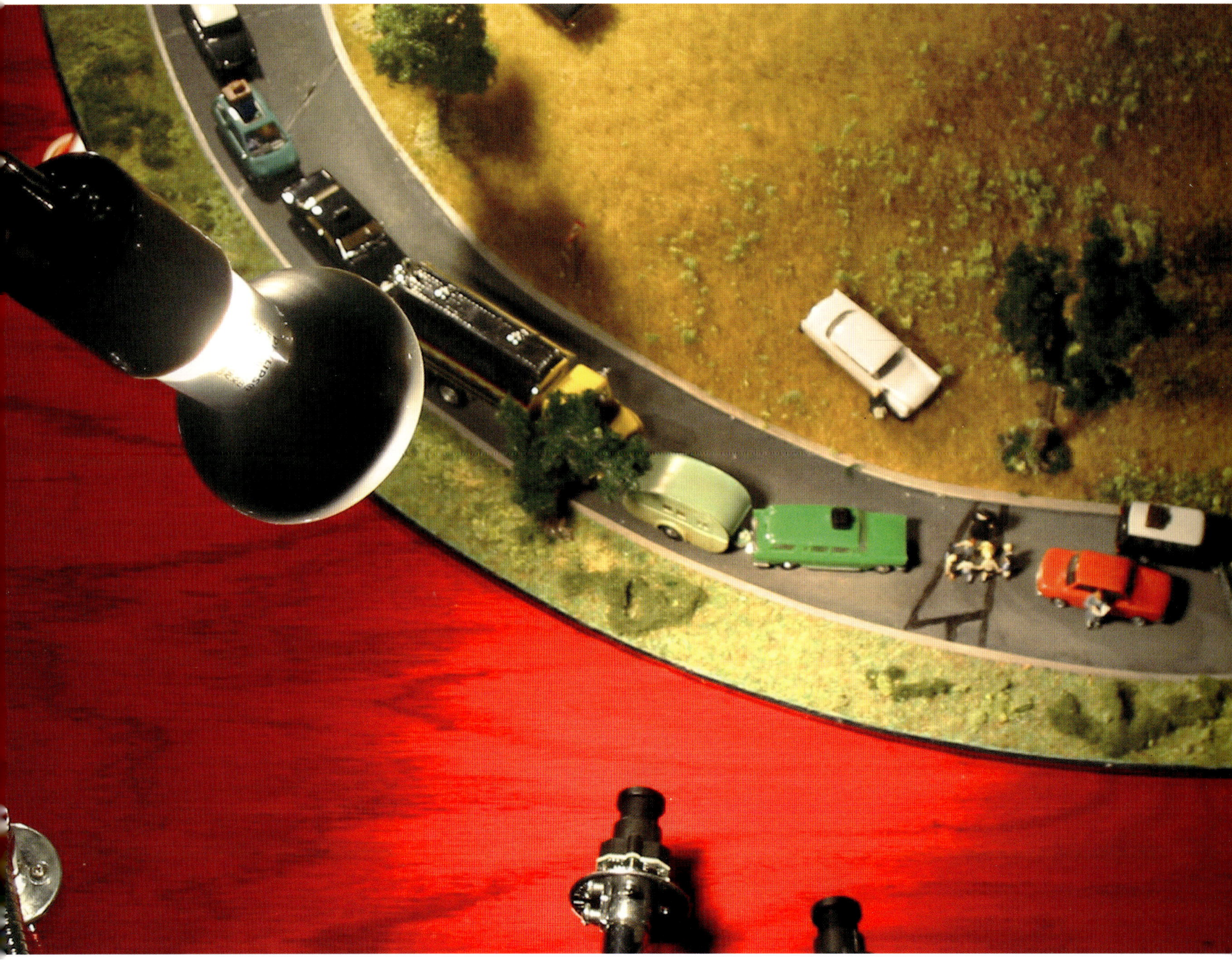

"Isn't the essential shot in cinema the reaction shot? In it, the face mirrors the position of the active viewer and meaning hovers—floating free." — J and KMcC

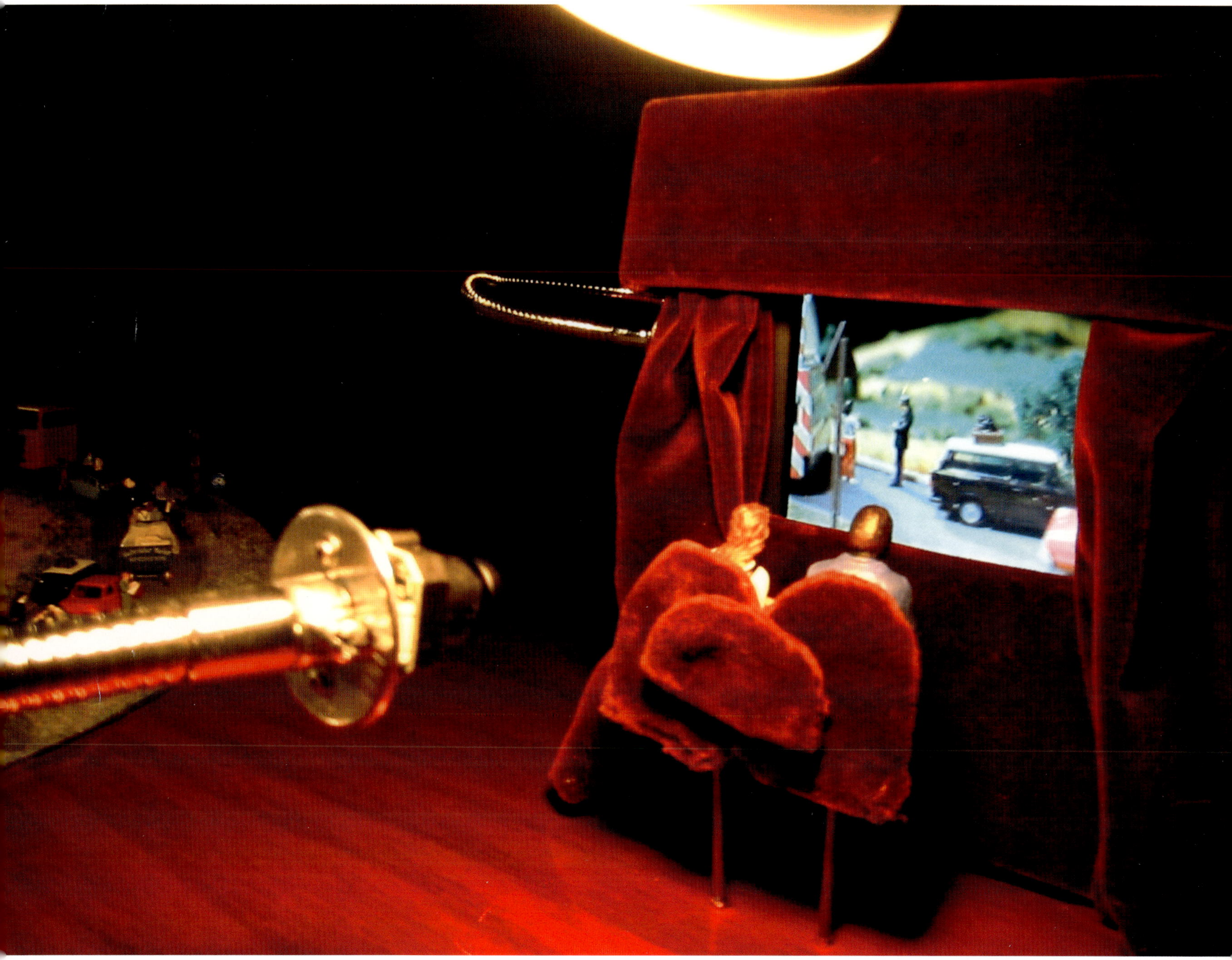

JOSHUA **MOSLEY**

BORN IN 1974, LIVES AND WORKS IN PHILADELPHIA

A Vue, 2004

Joshua Mosley's *A Vue* employs a combination of hand-drawn, computer-generated, and stop-motion techniques to investigate philosophical topics that emerge from everyday situations. Its narrative focuses on a park ranger and his interaction with a woman who works for a fiber-optics company. The term "a vue" is used in rock climbing to describe an ascent without prior knowledge of the route. As such, it serves as a powerful metaphor for the unpredictable life paths of the characters within Mosley's film.

JOSHUA MOSLEY
Stills from *A Vue*, 2004
Mixed-media animation transferred to DVD
Images courtesy of the artist and Donald Young Gallery, Chicago, IL

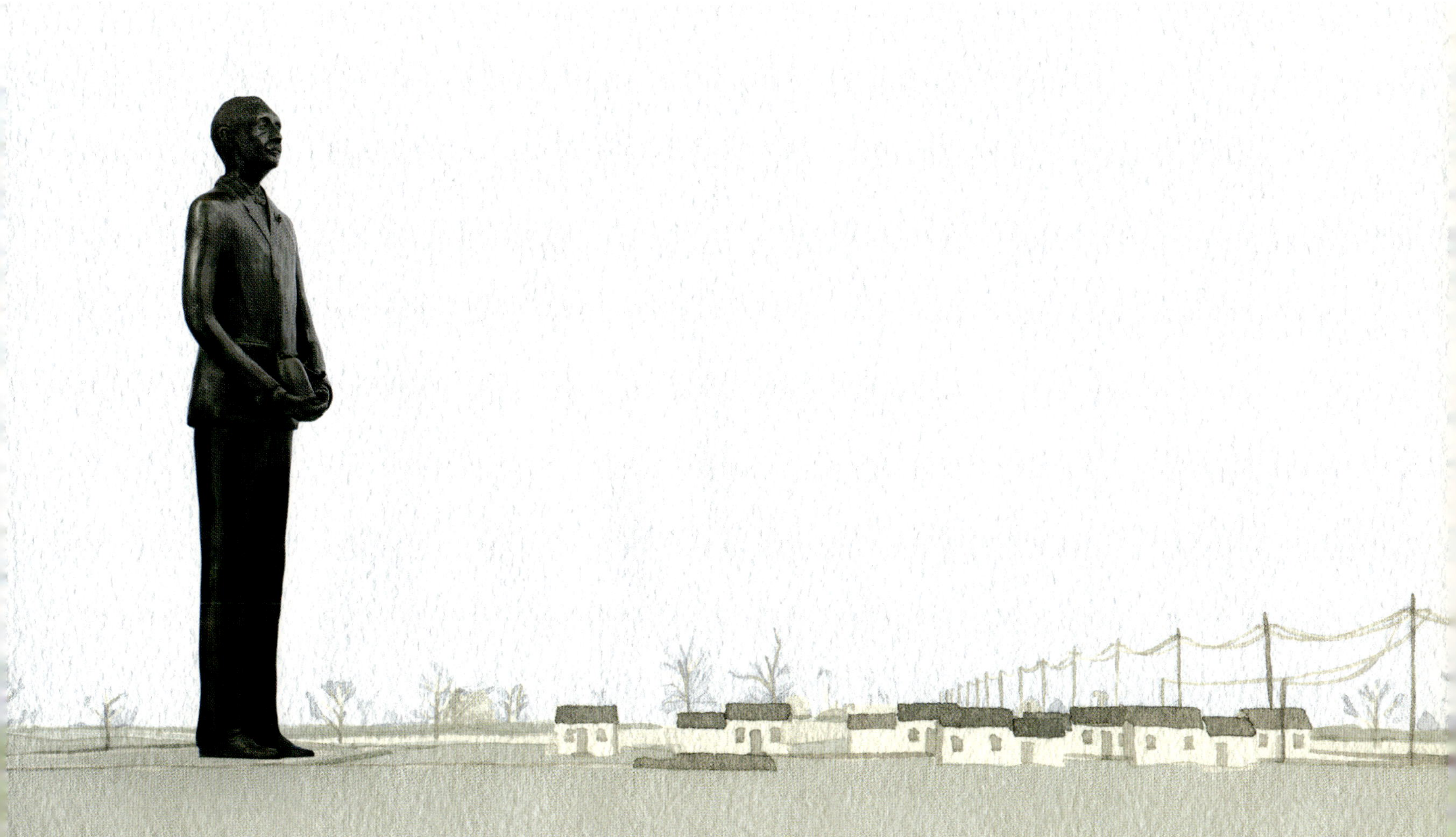

the dissolve

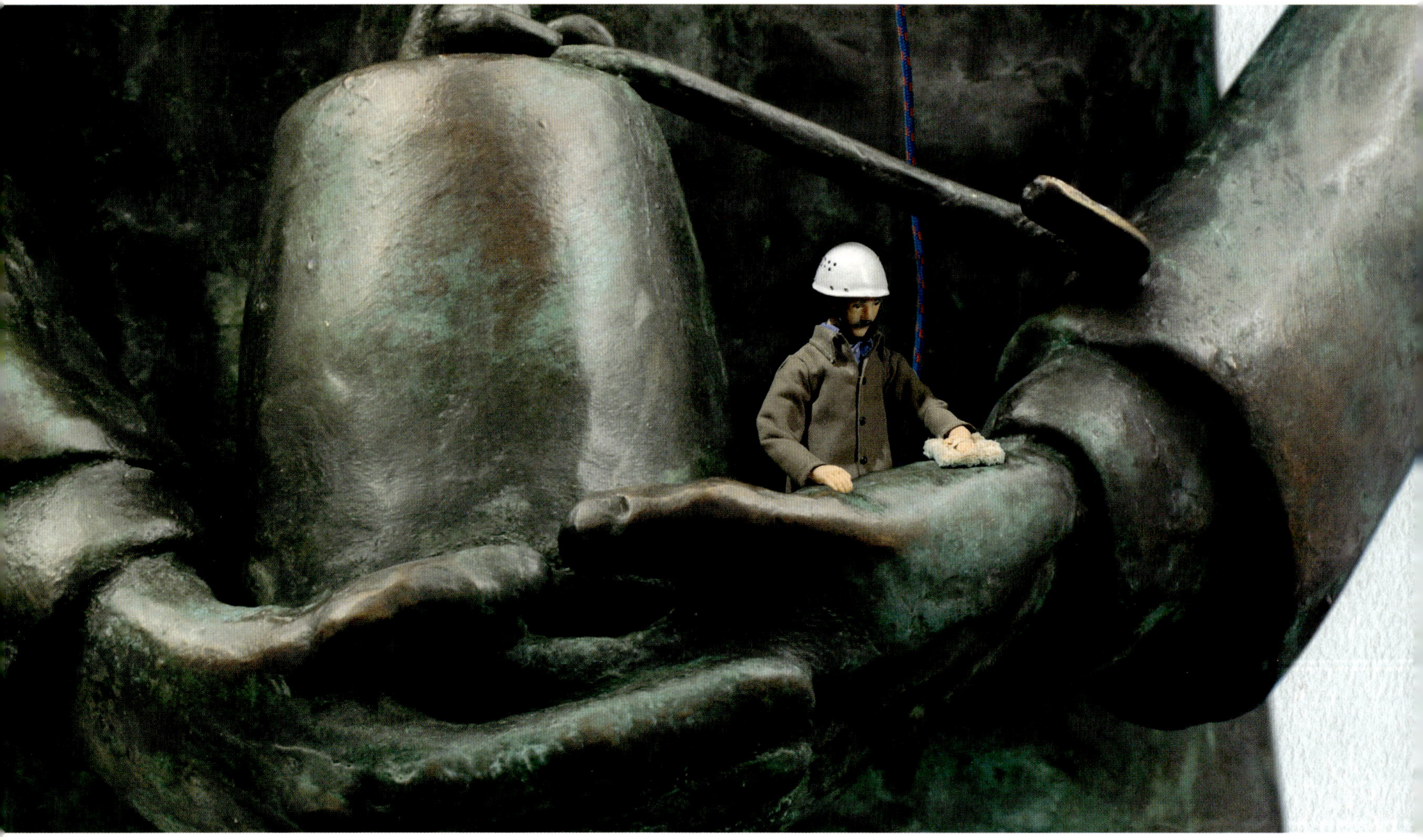

"Not everything that we see can be understood.
I've been thinking about not-fully-understanding as an experience. And I've been making these animations to think about how we live with partial awareness." — JM

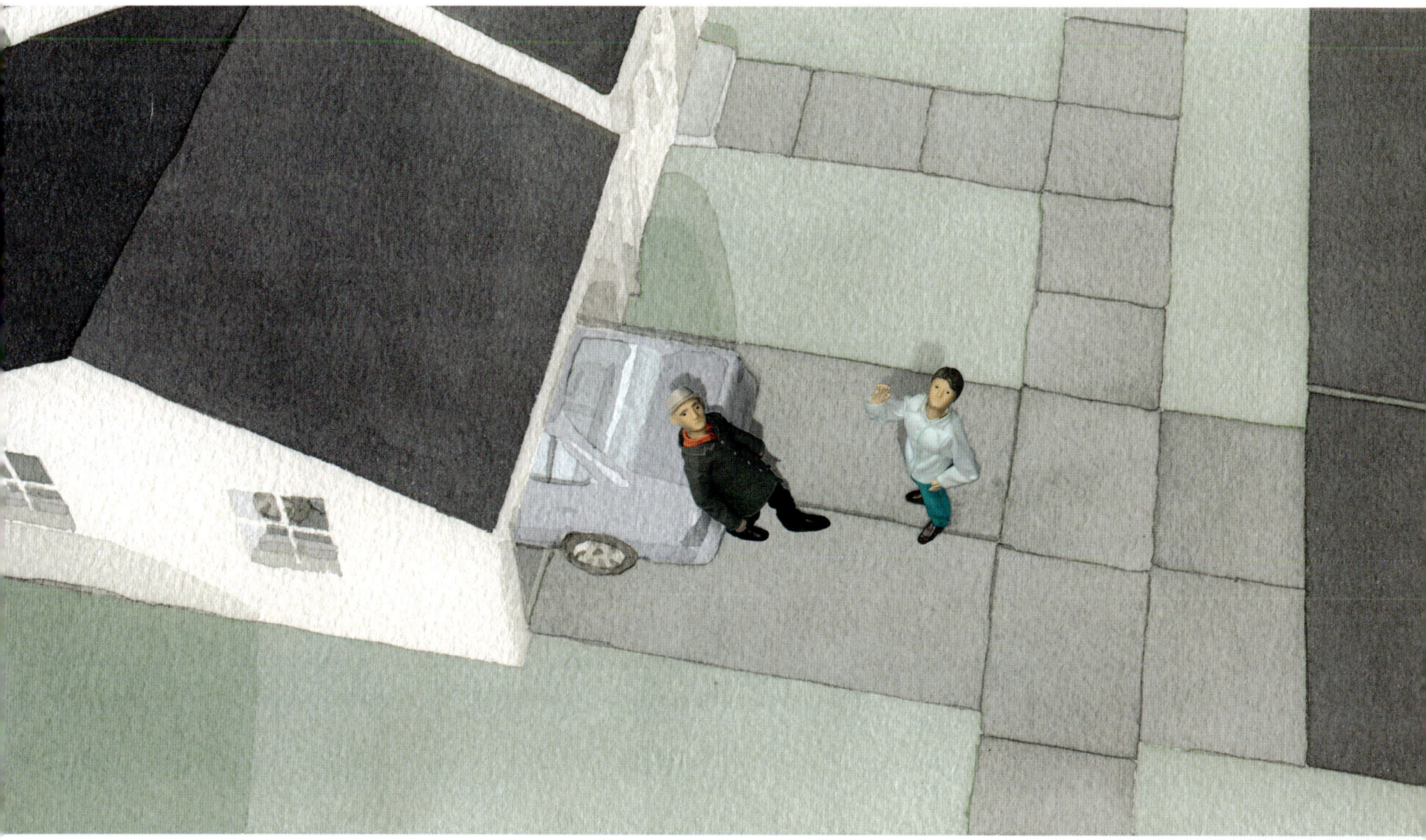

the dissolve

OSCAR **MUÑOZ**

BORN IN 1951, LIVES AND WORKS IN CALI, COLOMBIA

Re/trato, 2003

In Oscar Muñoz's *Re/trato,* a hand uses a brush to paint a face on a concrete sidewalk with water. Before the image is finished, the beginning of the portrait has evaporated. The painting continues, and the portrait is in a constant state of reconstruction. Muñoz's ephemeral material creates a work that meditates on the impermanent nature of images and the transient nature of life.

OSCAR MUÑOZ
Stills from *Re/trato*, 2003
Video
Images courtesy of the artist and Sicardi Gallery, Houston, TX

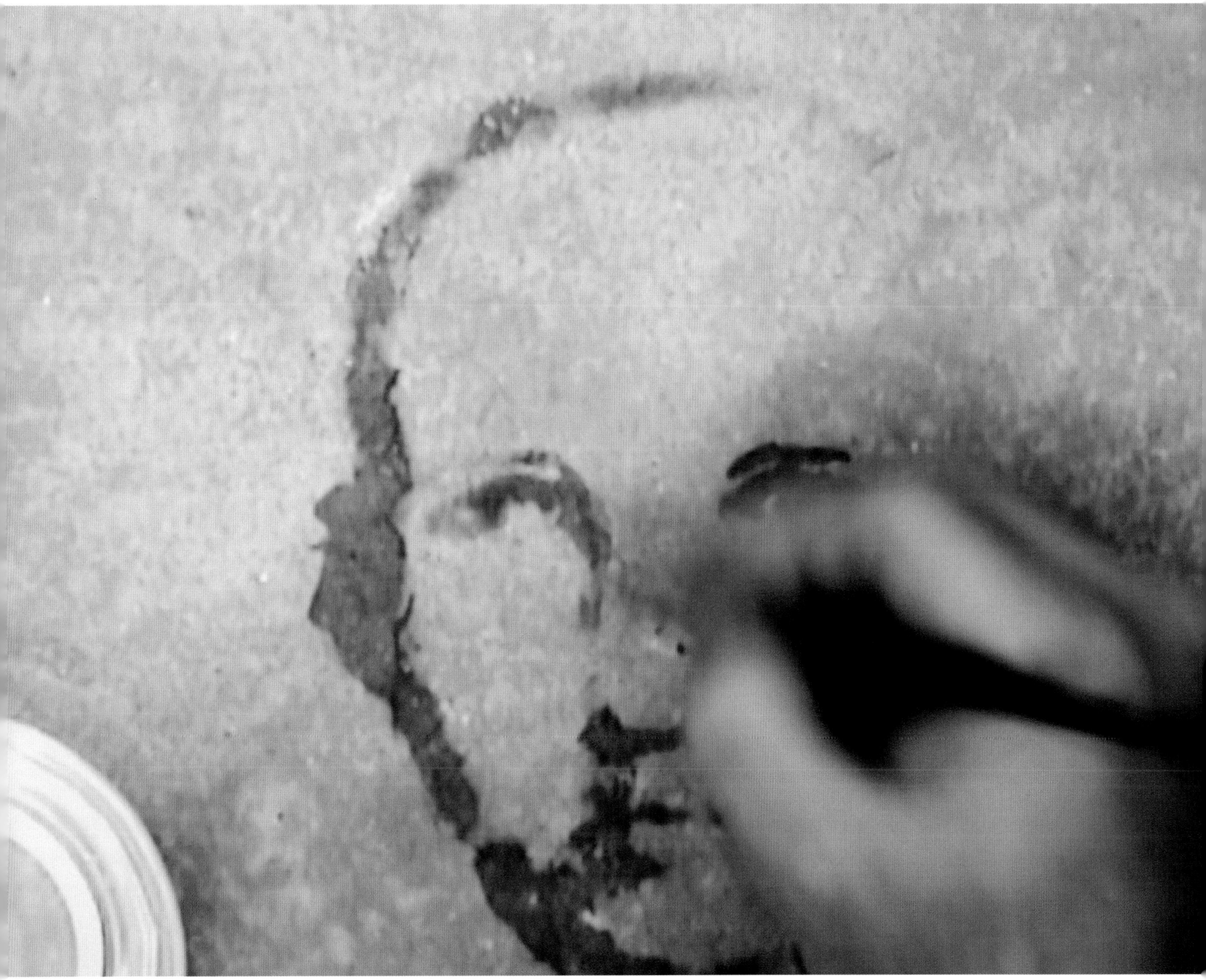

the dissolve

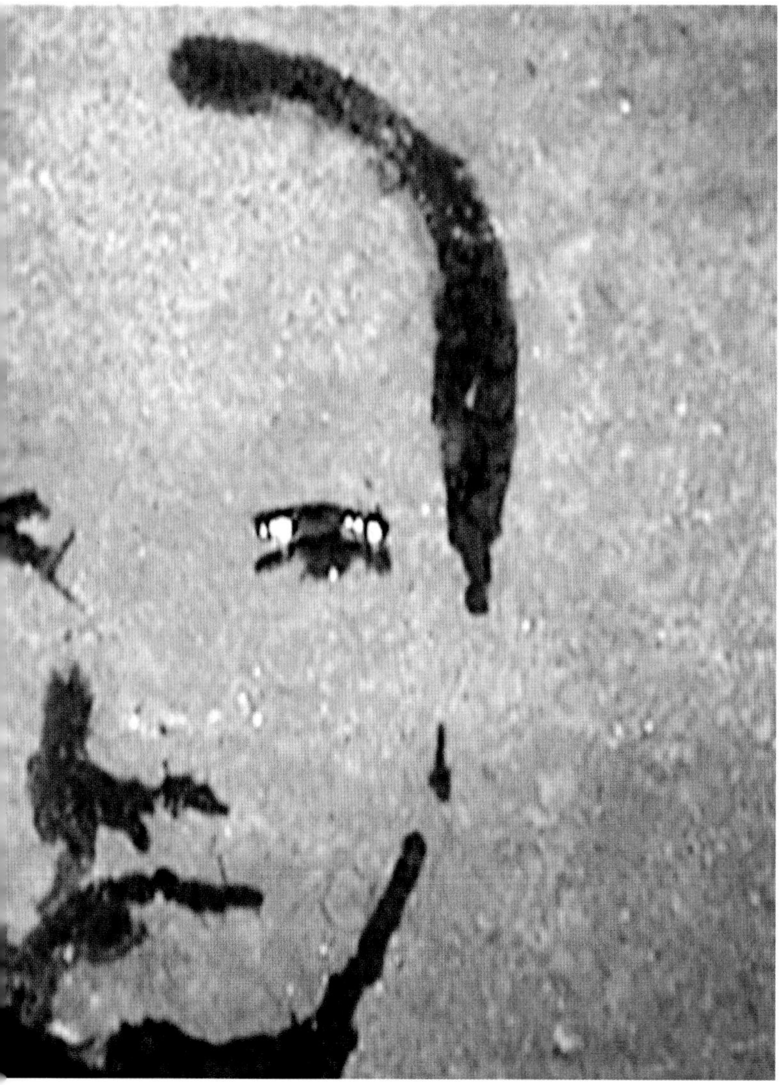

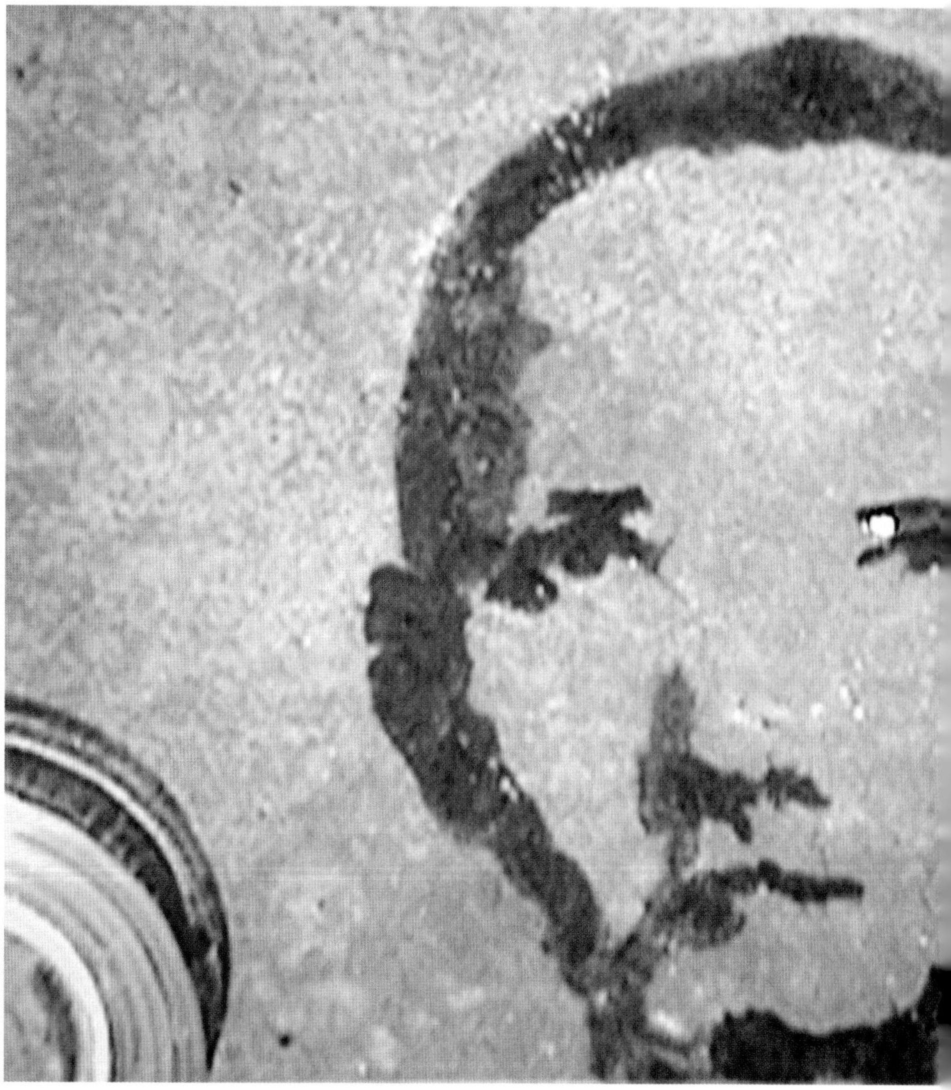

"My work focuses in particular on the genre of the portrait, always using the photographic act and its chemical essentiality as a reference and a metaphor. I want to evoke the timeless theme of the impossibility of retaining events of the past, and attempt, on the other hand, to create memory using similar mechanics of impermanence, which are ungraspable." — OM

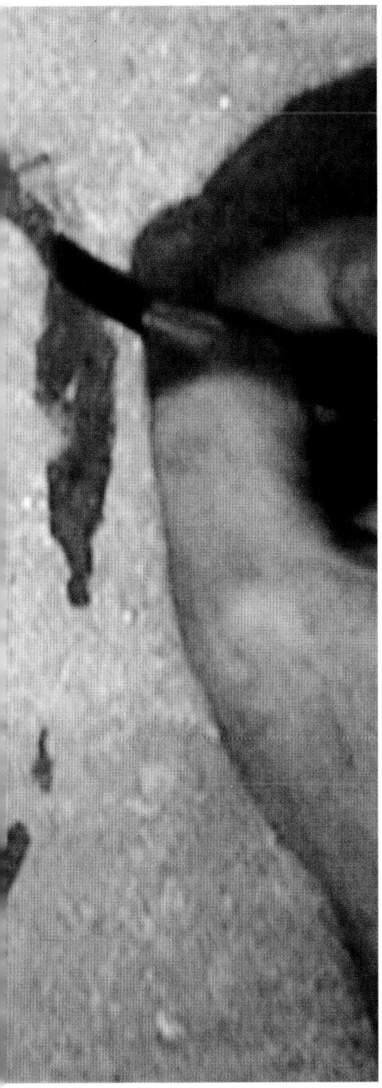

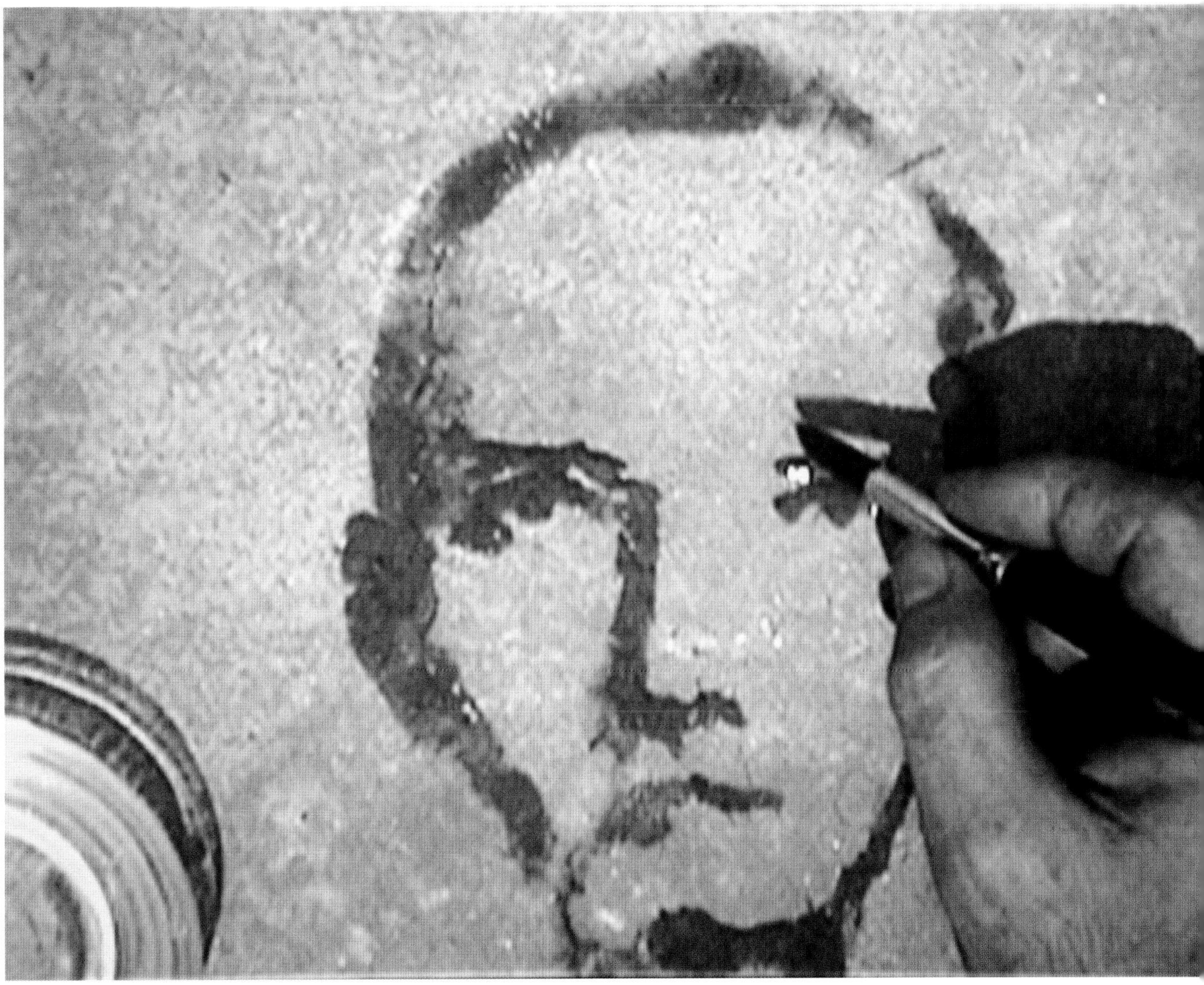

JACCO **OLIVIER**

BORN IN 1972, LIVES AND WORKS IN AMSTERDAM

Almost, 2009

Jacco Olivier's *Almost* provides the feeling of entering an action already in progress and departing before it is resolved. The opening image of a clothesline gives way to a dense and richly colored landscape. A running figure serves as a device to guide the viewer's eye through the lush composition. Olivier uses a composite technique that combines painting and photography to create visual texture. The enigmatic and subtle nature of the action draws attention to the film's formal qualities, which include pronounced brushstrokes in velvety hues of green, red, orange, and gold.

JACCO OLIVIER
Stills from *Almost*, 2009
Video
Images courtesy of the artist and Marianne Boesky Gallery, New York

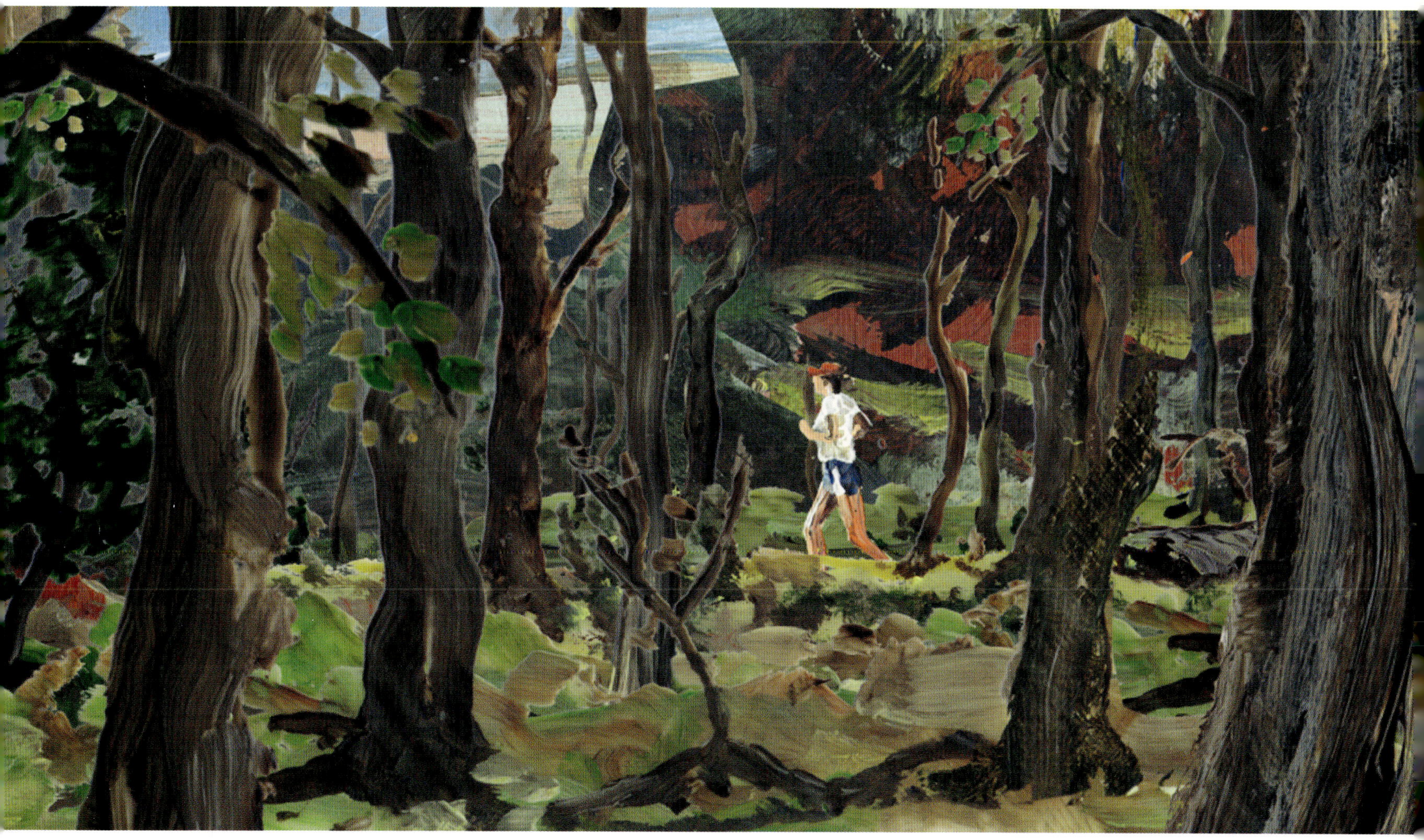

the dissolve

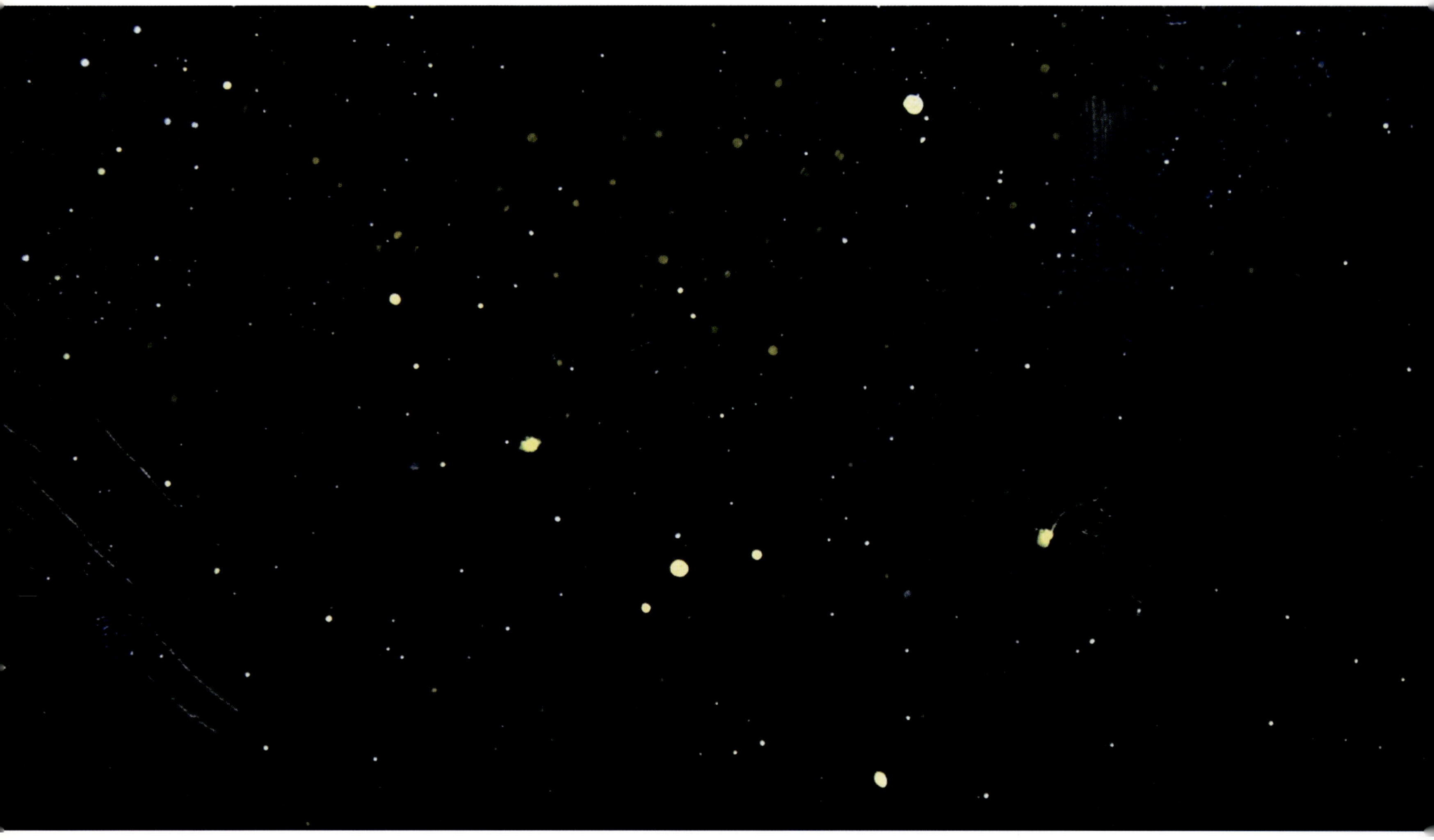

"In my 'moving paintings,' I connect all the bits and pieces that hold the universe together." — JO

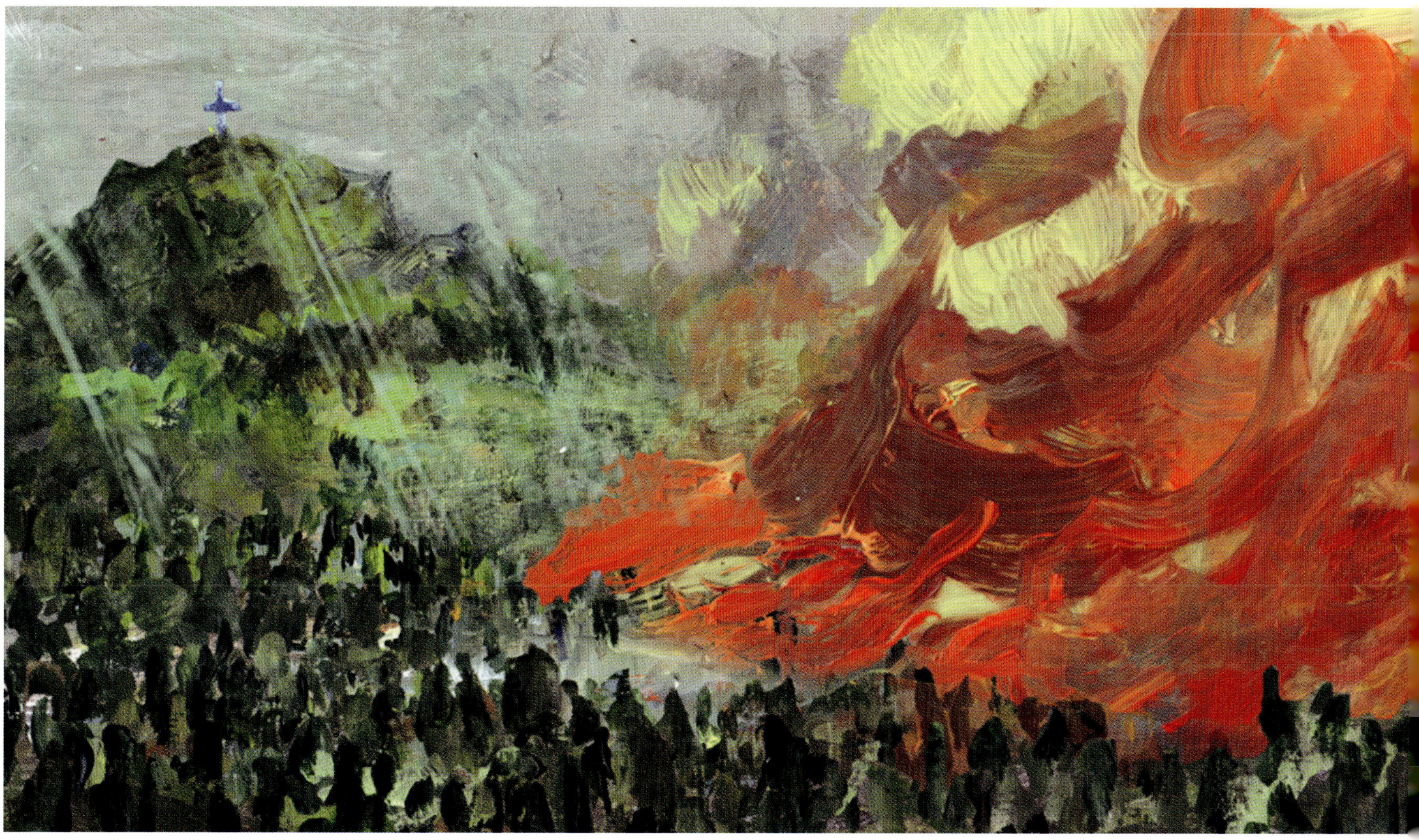

the dissolve

RAYMOND **PETTIBON**

BORN IN 1957, LIVES AND WORKS IN SOUTHERN CALIFORNIA

Sunday Night and Saturday Morning, 2005

With *Sunday Night and Saturday Morning,* Raymond Pettibon activates his body of figurative drawings—influenced in style and content by American popular culture: literature, film noir, pulp fiction, and punk rock—through Flash animation. This piece consists of several vignettes linked by the recurring imagery of trains and a beating heart. As in his drawings, the narration in this film is created from a patchwork of textual sources that triggers a disjunctive relationship to the imagery.

RAYMOND PETTIBON
Drawings for *Sunday Night and Saturday Morning*, 2005
Video
Images courtesy of Regen Projects, Los Angeles, CA

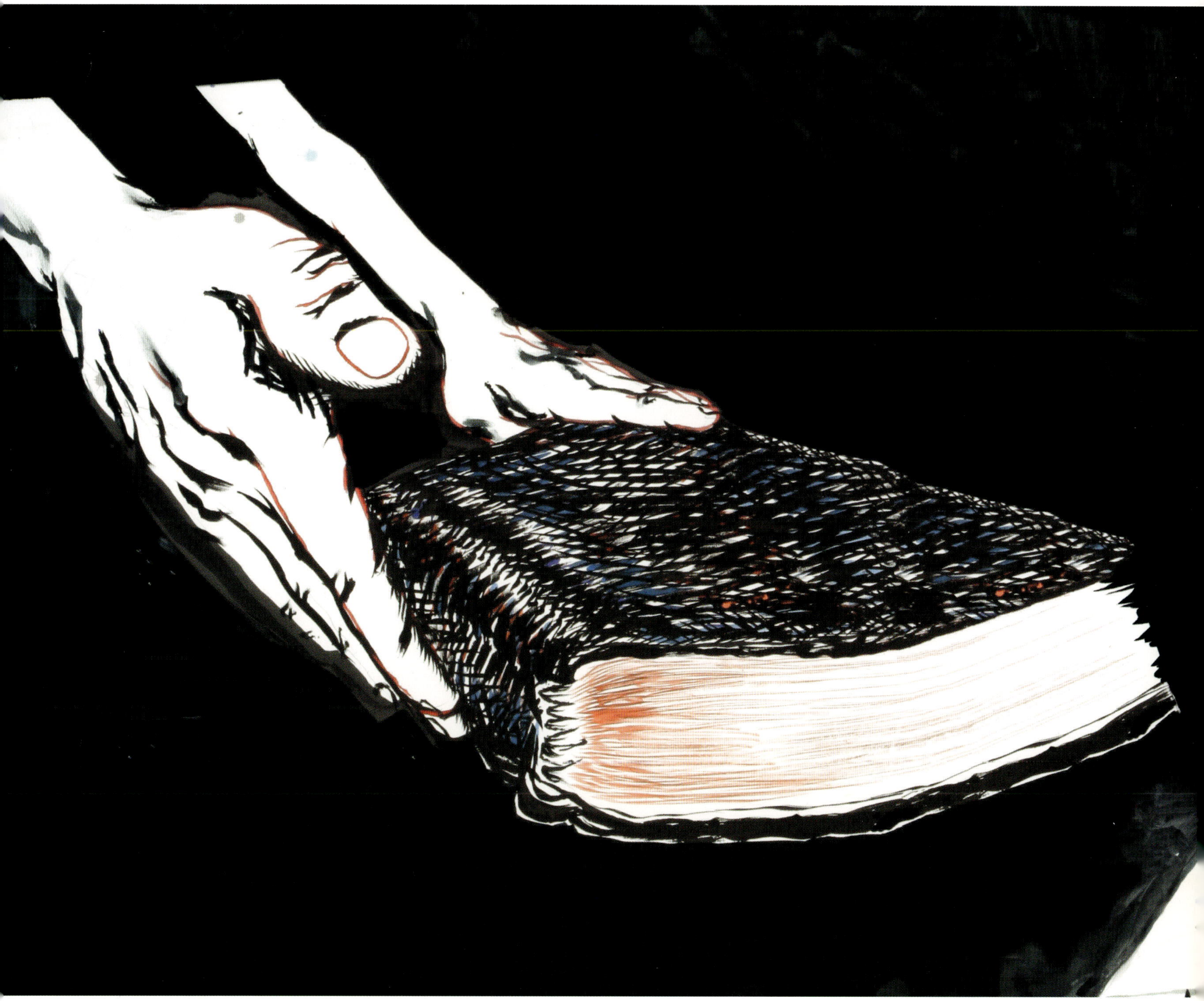

the dissolve

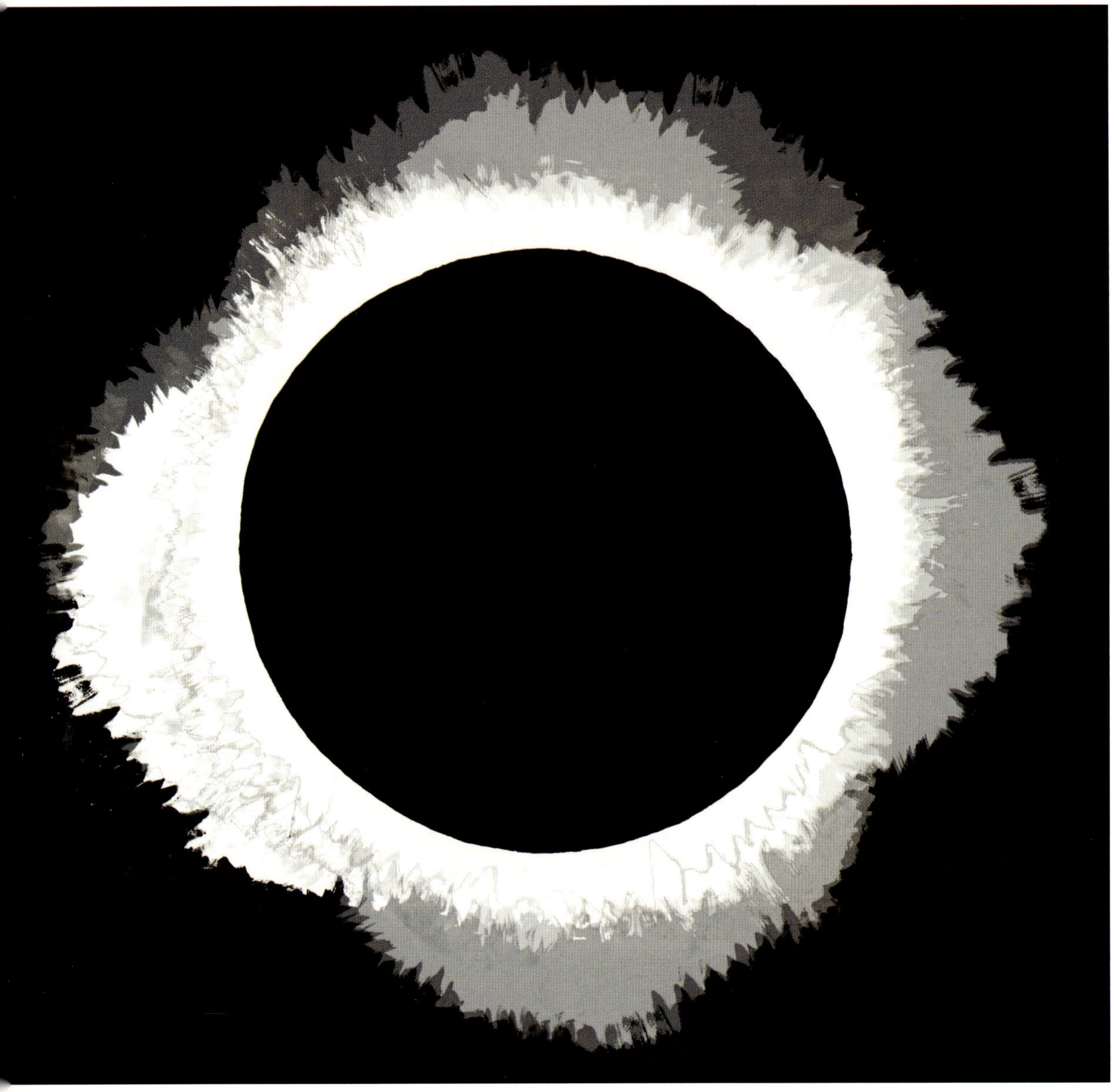

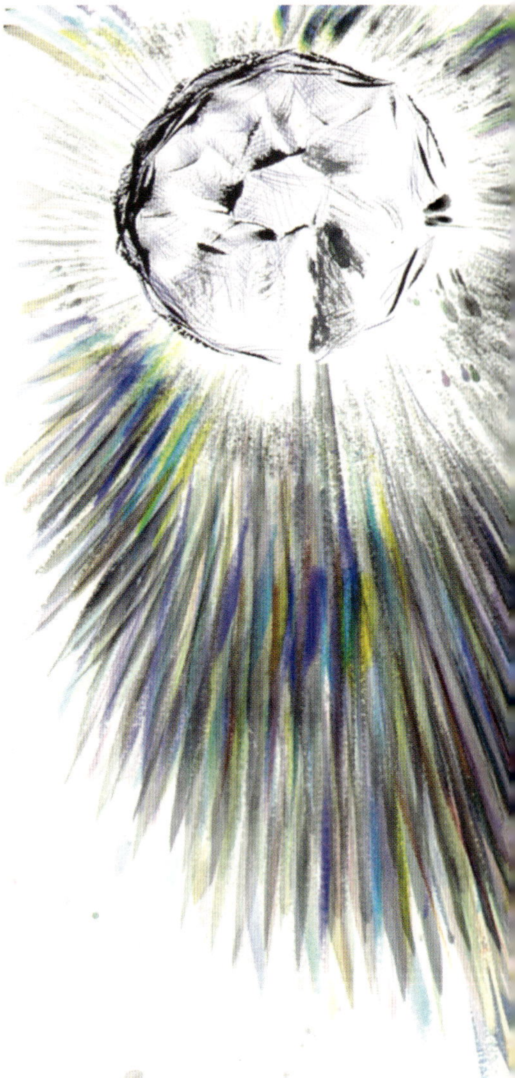

"Most of my interests come more from writing, but it doesn't take away from my artwork… It's something I work on and spend a lot of time with. After all these years, it's still kind of awkward, and I'm still learning, and I'm always struggling. In a way, with each drawing, it's almost like starting over and looking to find my place and re-learn." — RP

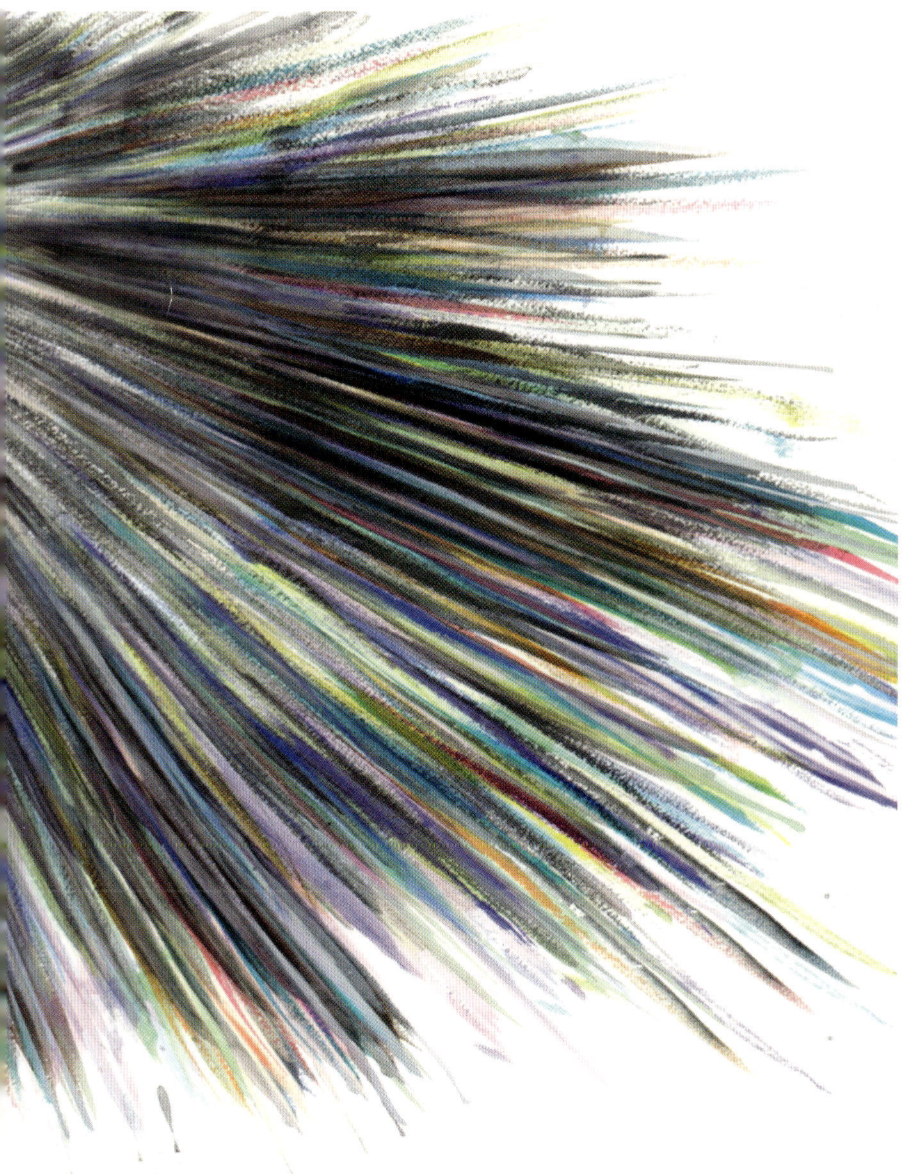

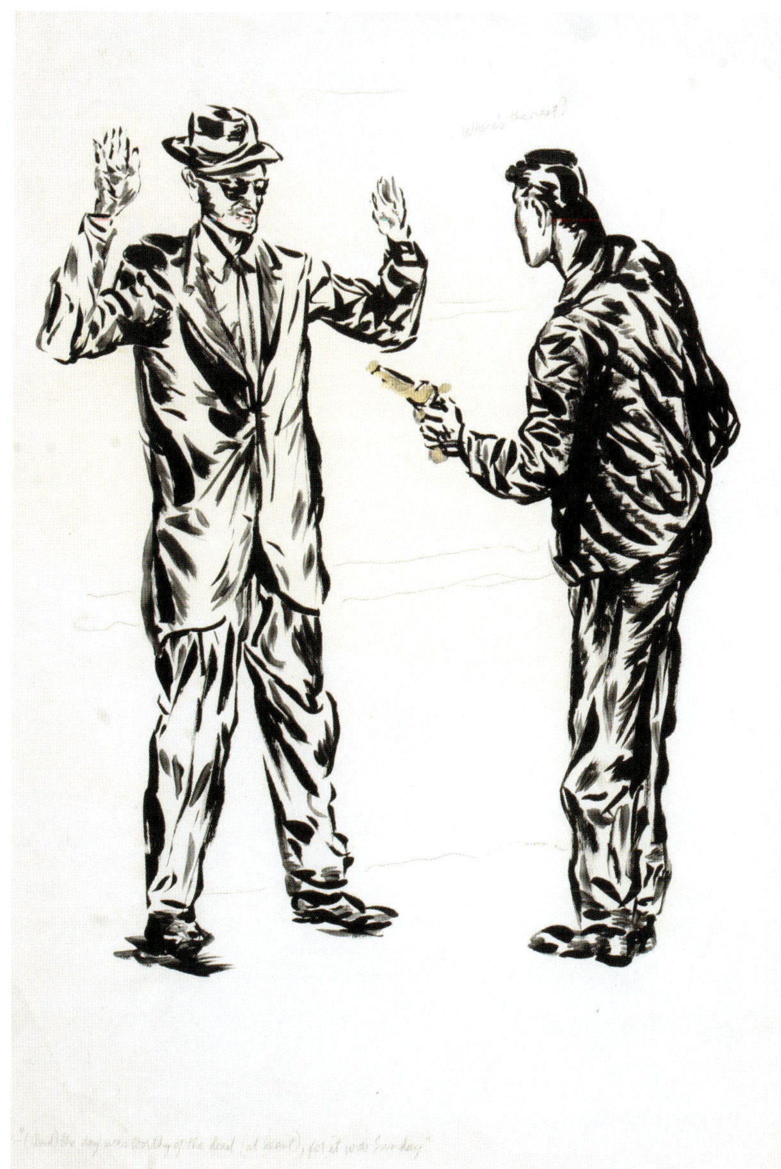

the dissolve

ROBERT **PRUITT**

BORN IN 1975, LIVES AND WORKS IN CHICAGO

Black Stuntman (Volumes 1 and 2), 2004

Robert Pruitt's *Black Stuntman (Volumes 1 and 2)* is a series of short, hand-drawn animations incorporating references to comics, hip-hop, and science fiction. Pruitt appropriates the genre of the super-hero to emphasize that *Black Stuntman* is an everyday hero. The character is an African-American male whose daily battles to successfully navigate multiple sociocultural spheres are portrayed as feats of heroic proportions. The narrative voice-overs play an integral role in the unfolding of the action.

ROBERT PRUITT
Stills from *Black Stuntman (Volumes 1 and 2)*, 2004
Video
Images courtesy of the artist

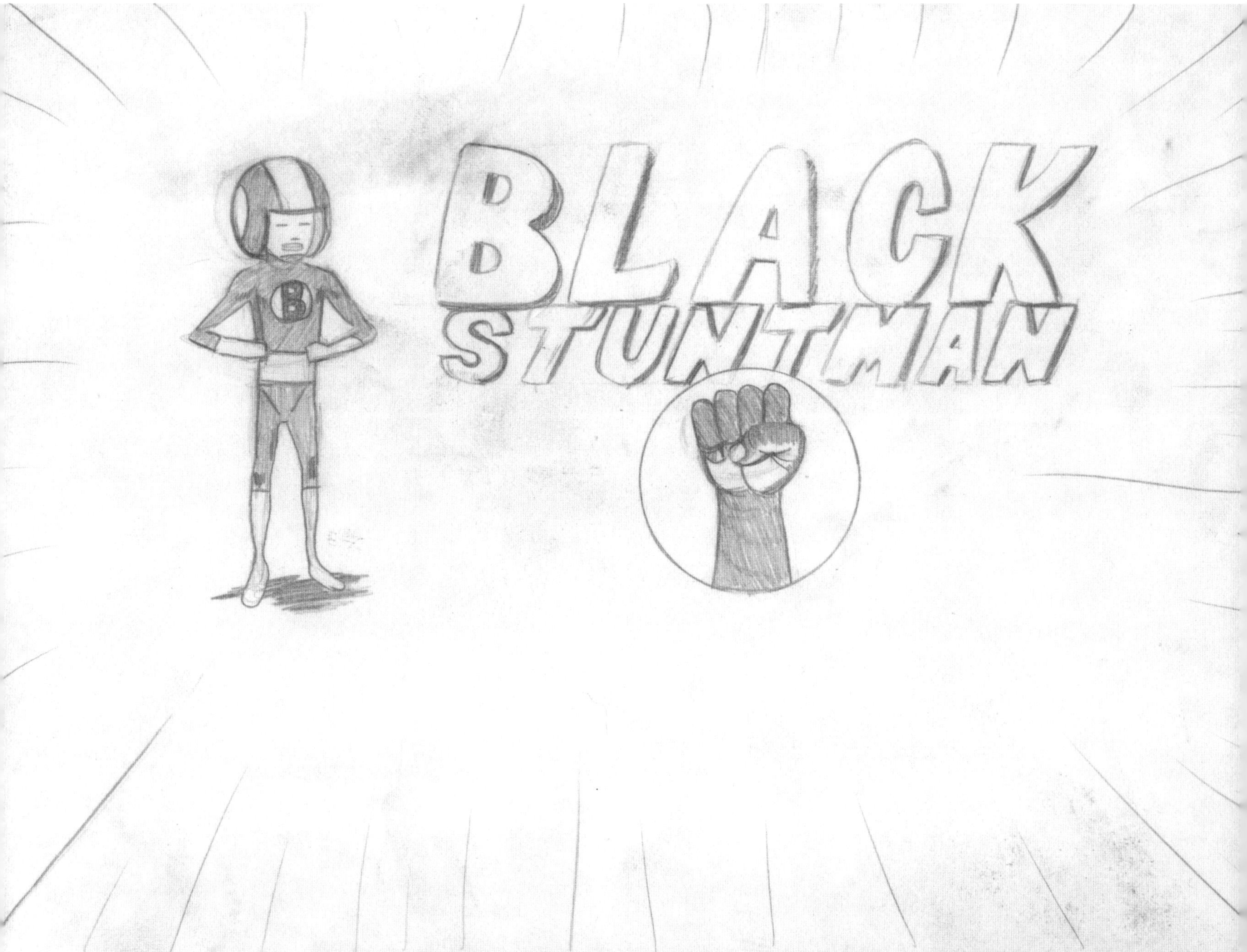

the dissolve

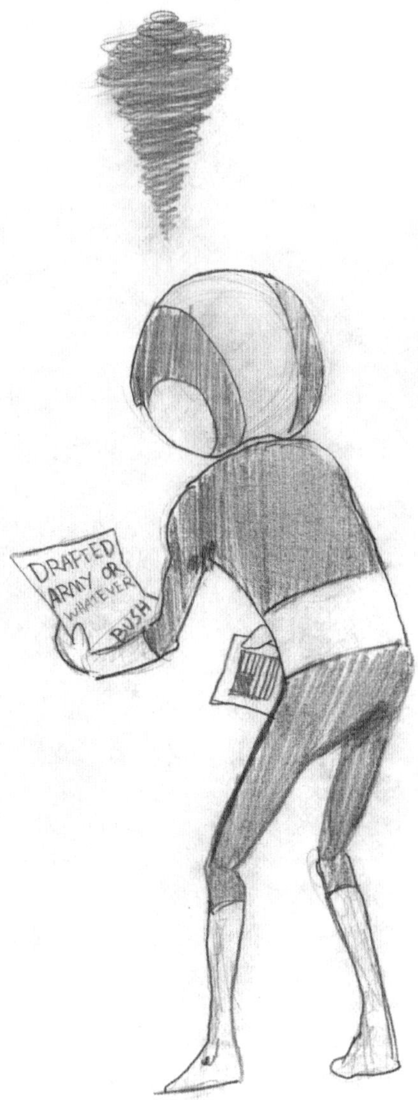

"For black people (and everyone else I suppose)
there is a blurry line between individual freedom and collective solidarity.
I make pictures with that line." — RP

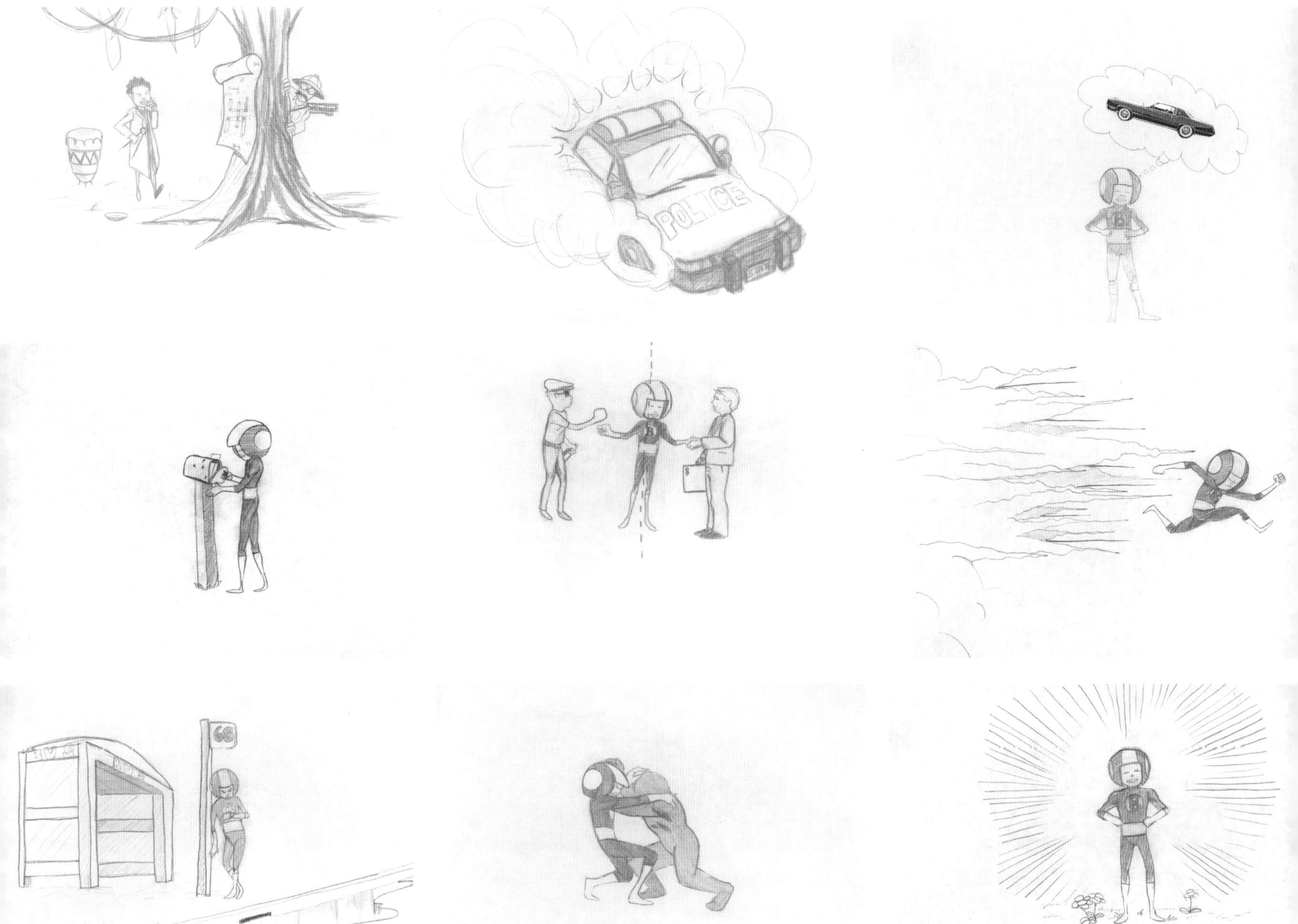

the dissolve

CHRISTINE **REBET**

BORN IN 1971, LIVES AND WORKS IN NEW YORK

The Black Cabinet, 2007

Christine Rebet's *The Black Cabinet* is a two-channel projection that simulates the experience of being in a Victorian parlor with a futuristic twist. In this installation's lower film, for instance, three men and one woman, in nineteenth-century garb, sit around a roulette table and subsequently engage in a series of parlor games that culminates in a séance. Rather than putting the characters in contact with spirits from their past, the séance prefigures the future twentieth century, characterized by despotic rulers.

CHRISTINE REBET
Stills from *The Black Cabinet*, 2007
35mm film transferred to DVD; two-channel video installation
Images courtesy of the artist and Galerie Kamel Mennour, Paris

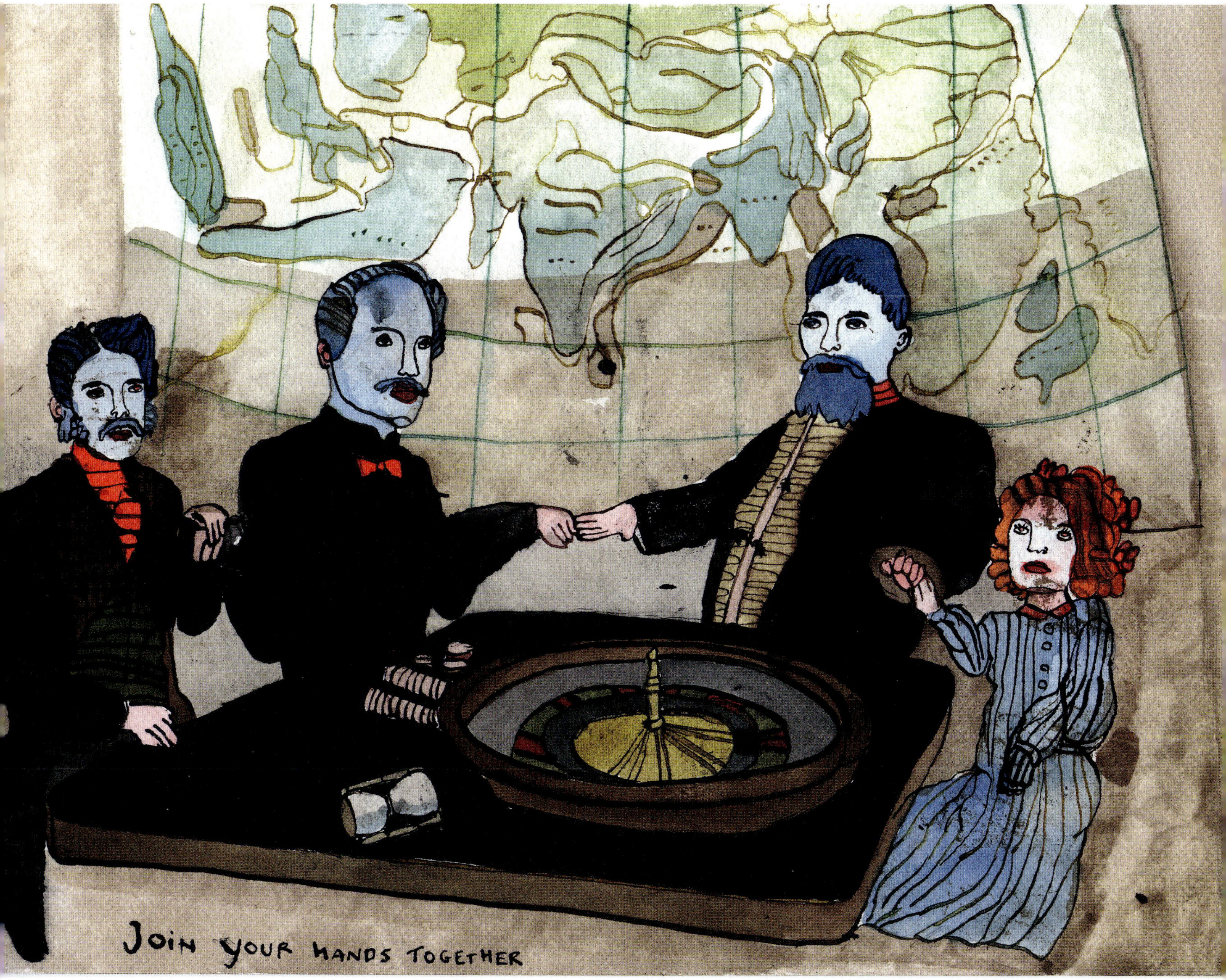

the dissolve

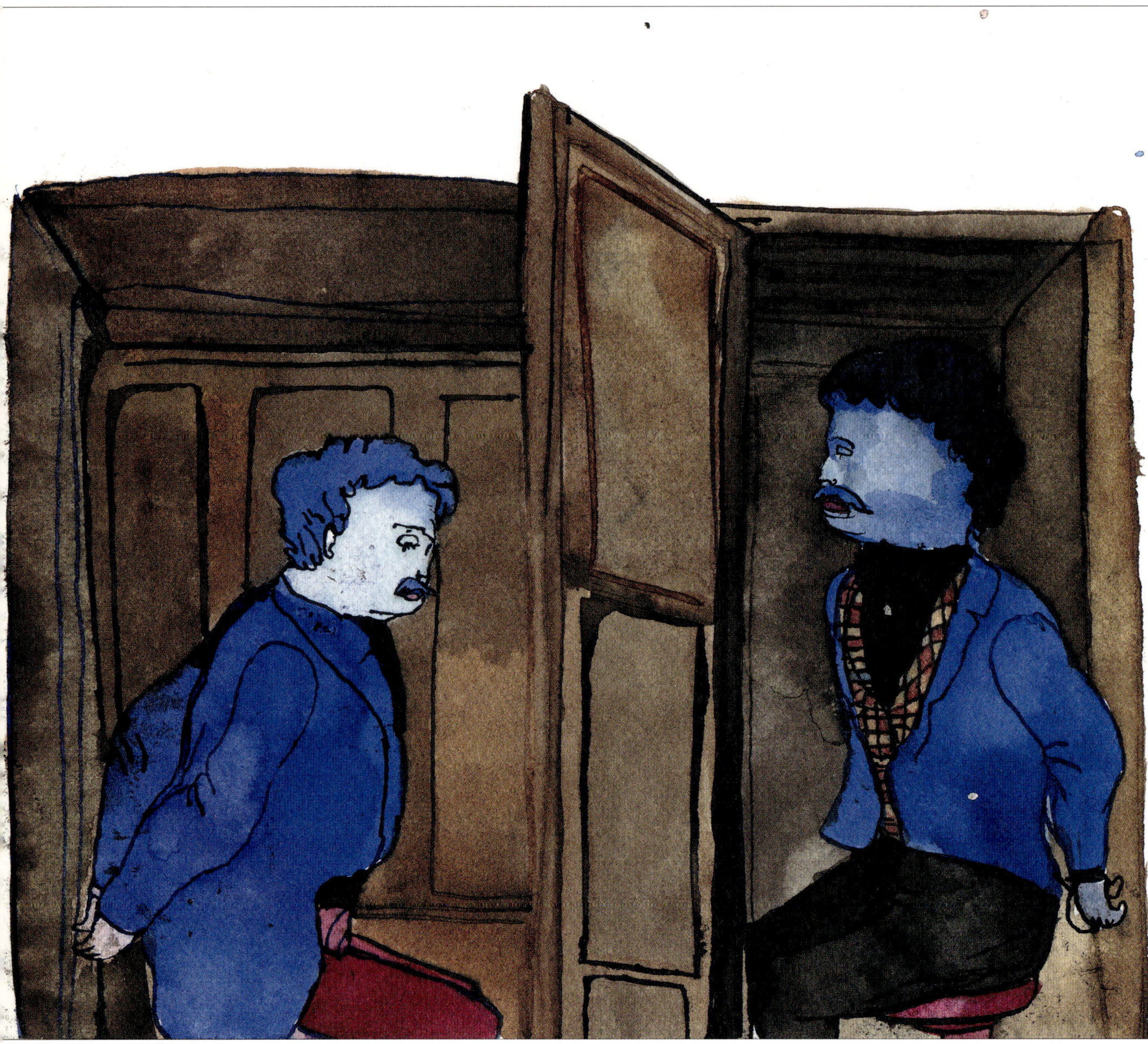

"Starting an animation is like a descent into an ocular crater where lay the wrecks and deposits of History. I rake their memories, backwards and forwards, reinventing their amnesic tale." — CR

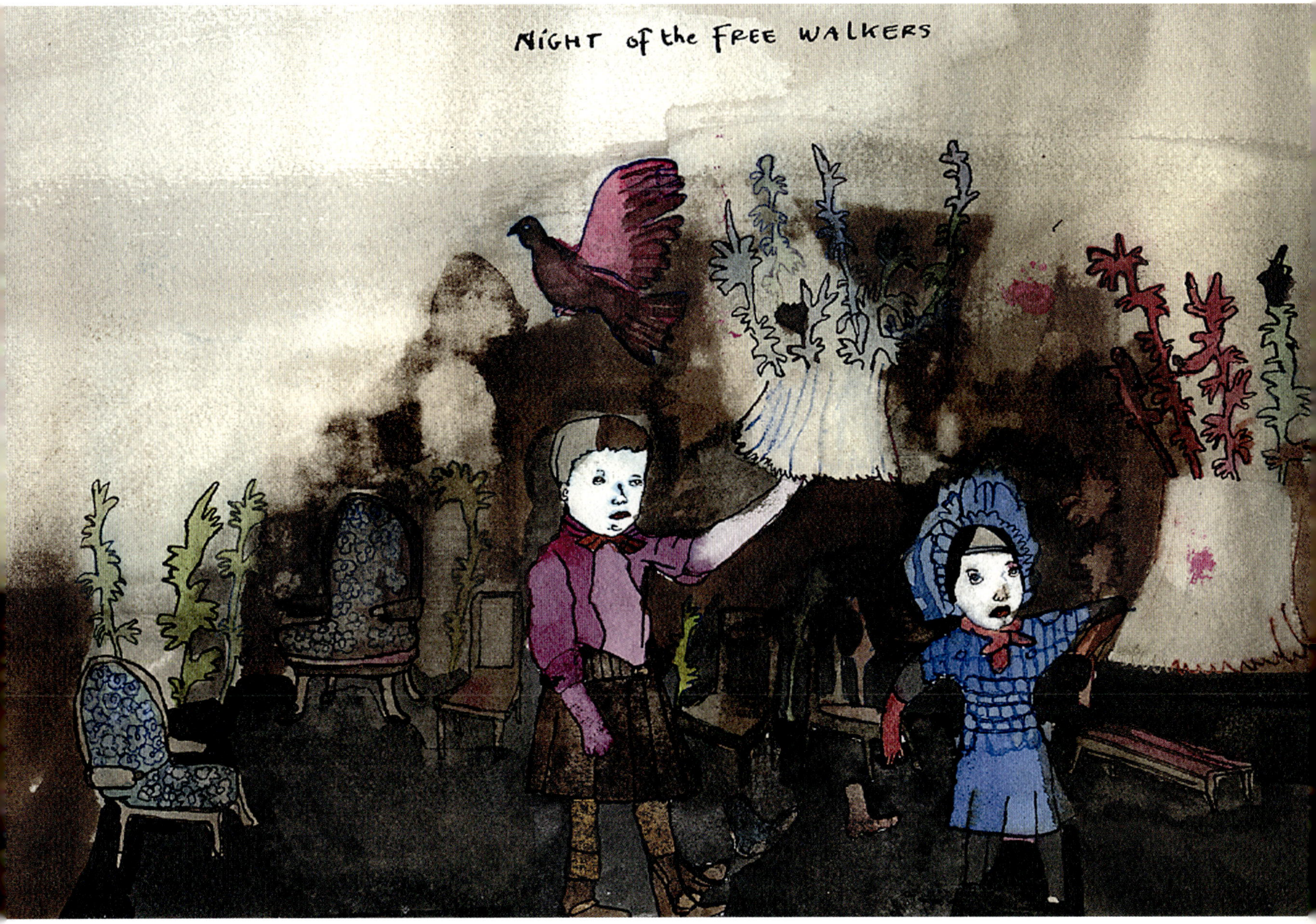

MARY **REID KELLEY**

BORN IN 1979, LIVES AND WORKS IN SARATOGA SPRINGS, NEW YORK

You Make Me Iliad, 2010

You Make Me Iliad, a video that combines live-action performance and stop-motion animation, is primarily set in a brothel in German-occupied Belgium toward the end of World War I. Mary Reid Kelley posits the brothel as a metaphoric space in which wartime exchanges and moral compromises, sexual and non-sexual, are explored. The main characters in this work, a Belgian prostitute and a German soldier, are both portrayed by Reid Kelley herself. Their dialogue is written in a style that evokes epic poetry and is saturated with puns, rhyme, and wordplay.

MARY REID KELLEY
Stills from *You Make Me Iliad,* 2010
HD video
Images courtesy of the artist

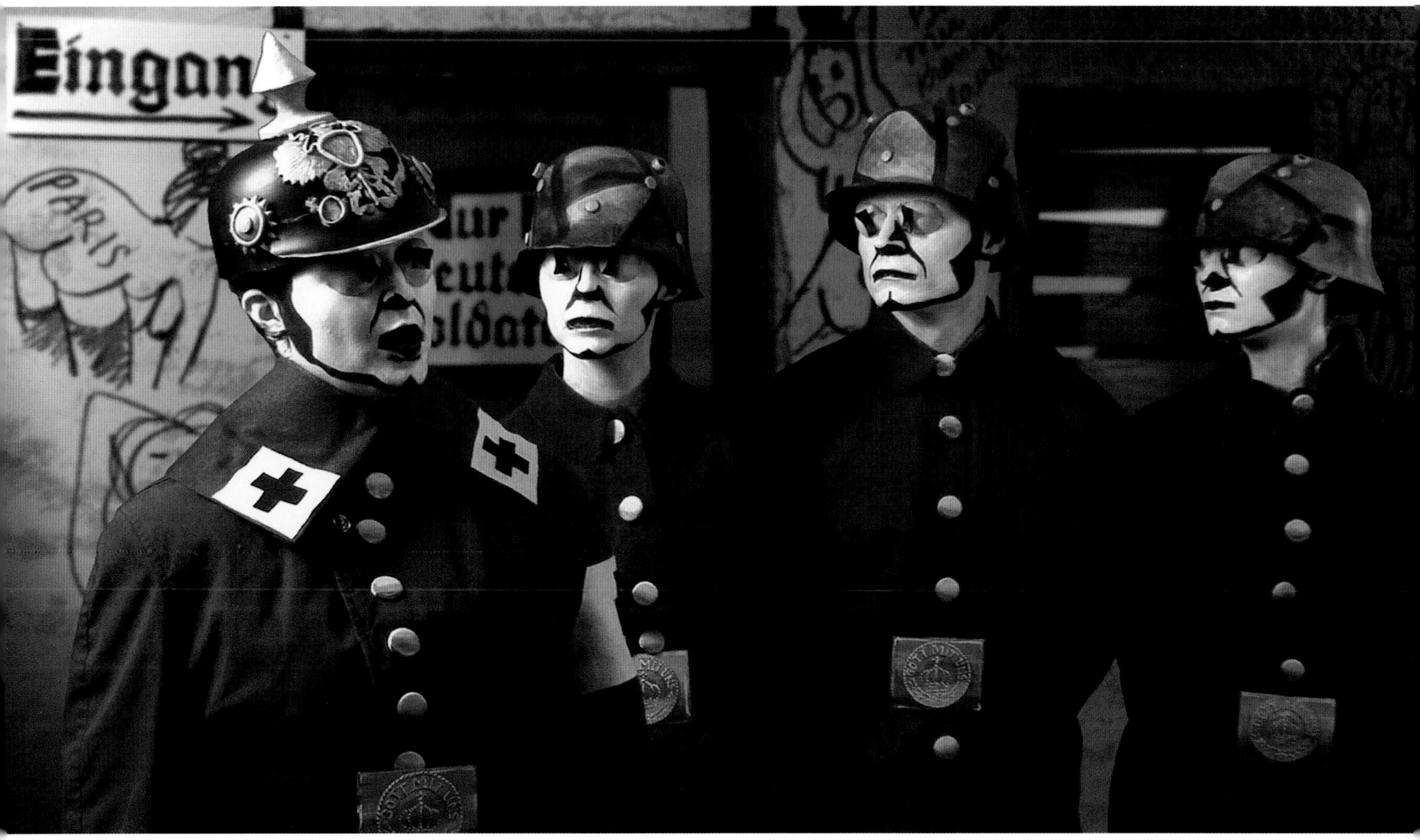

the dissolve

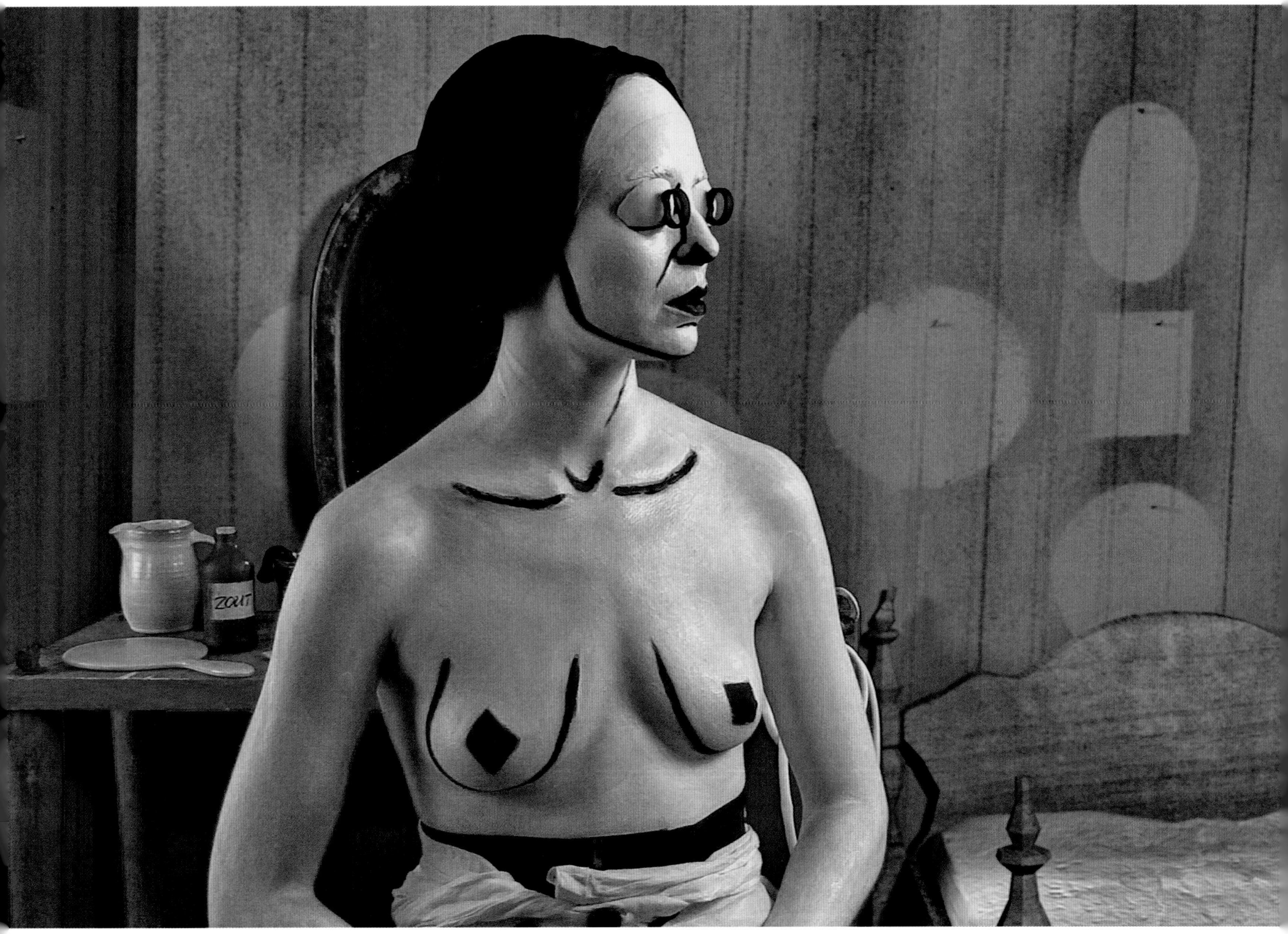

"What Ear disdains a Rhyme? This crucial word'll
squeeze a Listener in place, much like a girdle.
While she Absorbs its Meanings, then a Pun
Leaks out at oblique angles, and stains the Right one."
— MRK

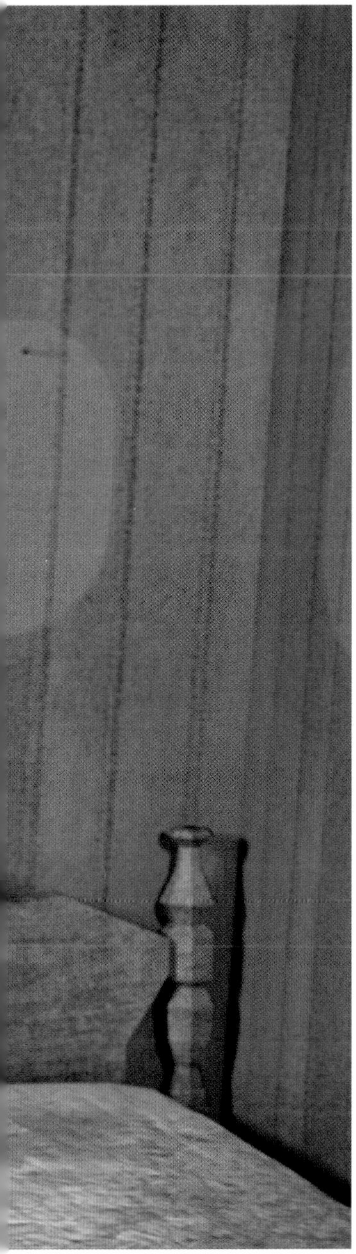

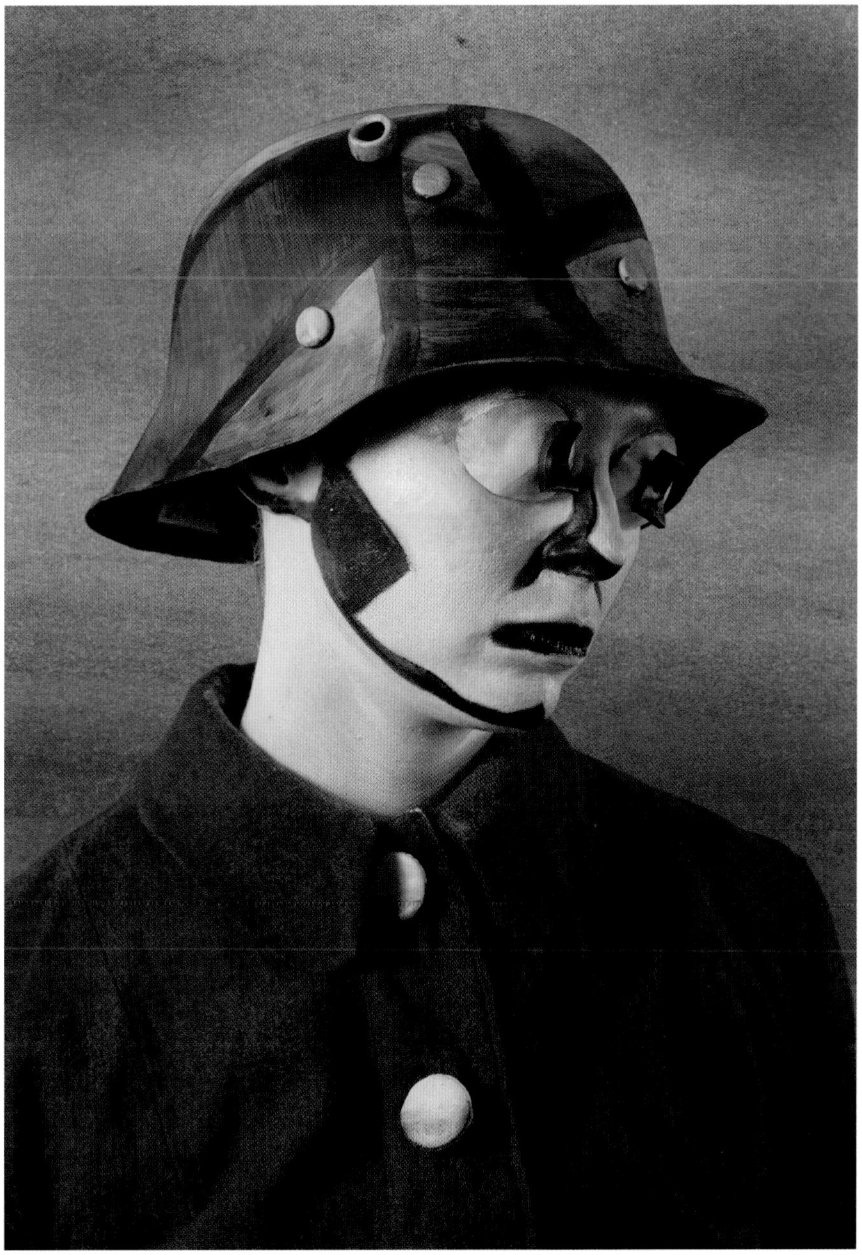

ROBIN **RHODE**

BORN IN 1976, LIVES AND WORKS IN BERLIN

Kid Candle, 2009

In Robin Rhode's *Kid Candle*, a live-action child protagonist silently interacts with a hand-drawn candle. The variously exposed film frames simulate the darks and lights of a flickering flame. *Kid Candle* recalls the innocence of childhood where one's fascination can be cultivated by something as simple as a candle, and playfully engages with the artist's childhood memories of boys' street culture in the South Africa of his youth.

ROBIN RHODE
Stills from *Kid Candle* from "Memories of Childhood," 2009
Super 8mm film transferred to DVD
Images courtesy of the artist and Perry Rubenstein Gallery, New York

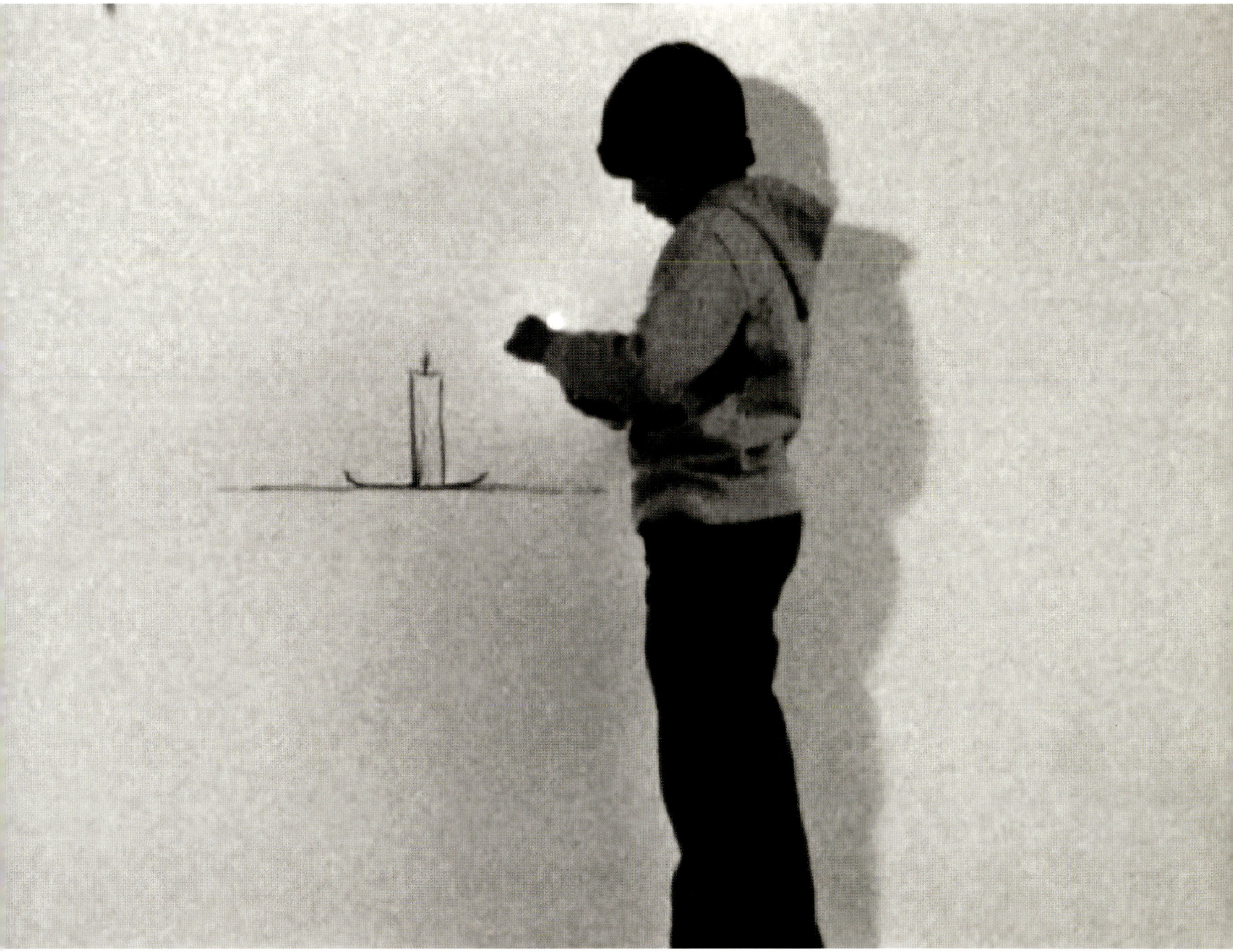

the dissolve

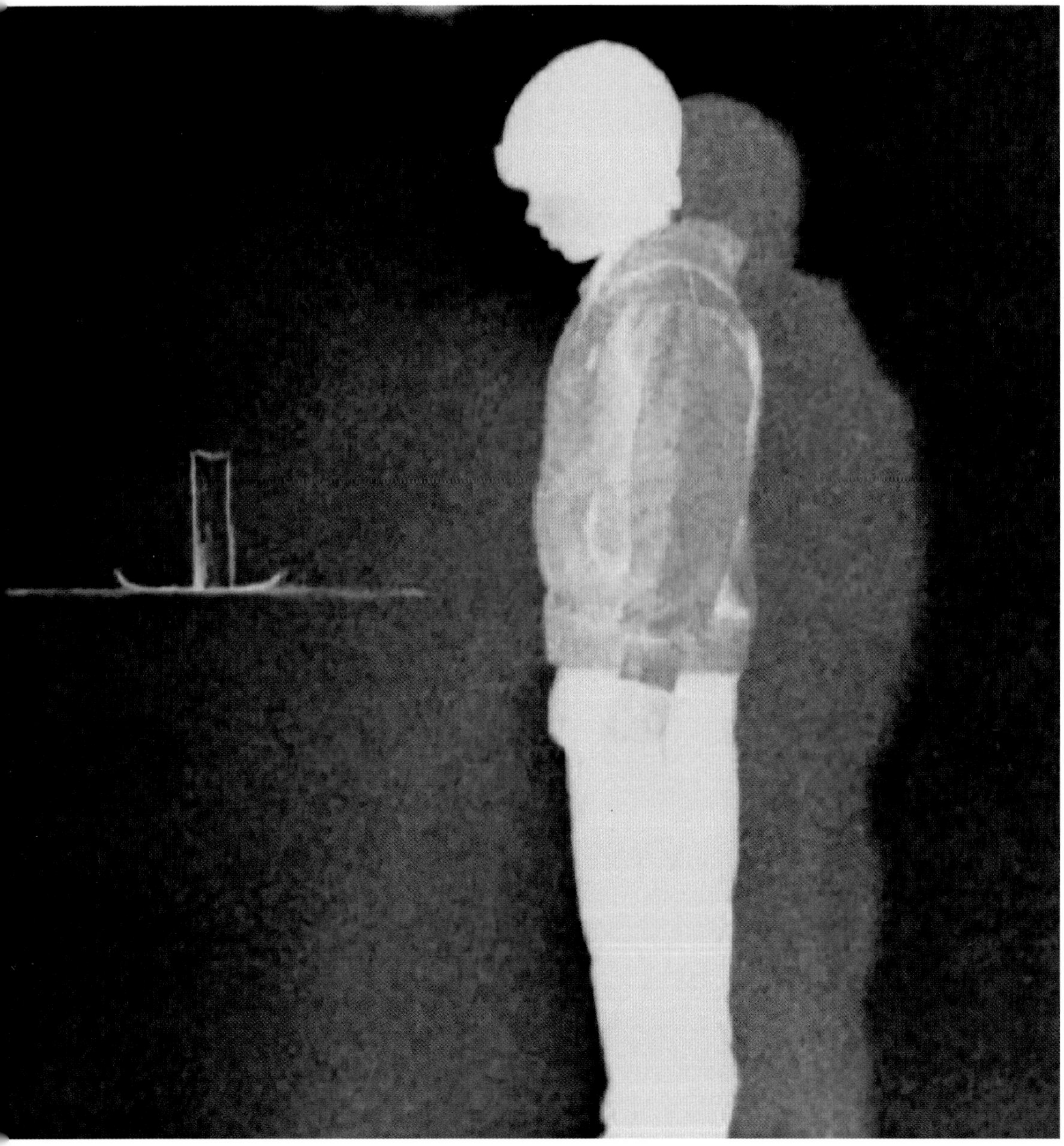

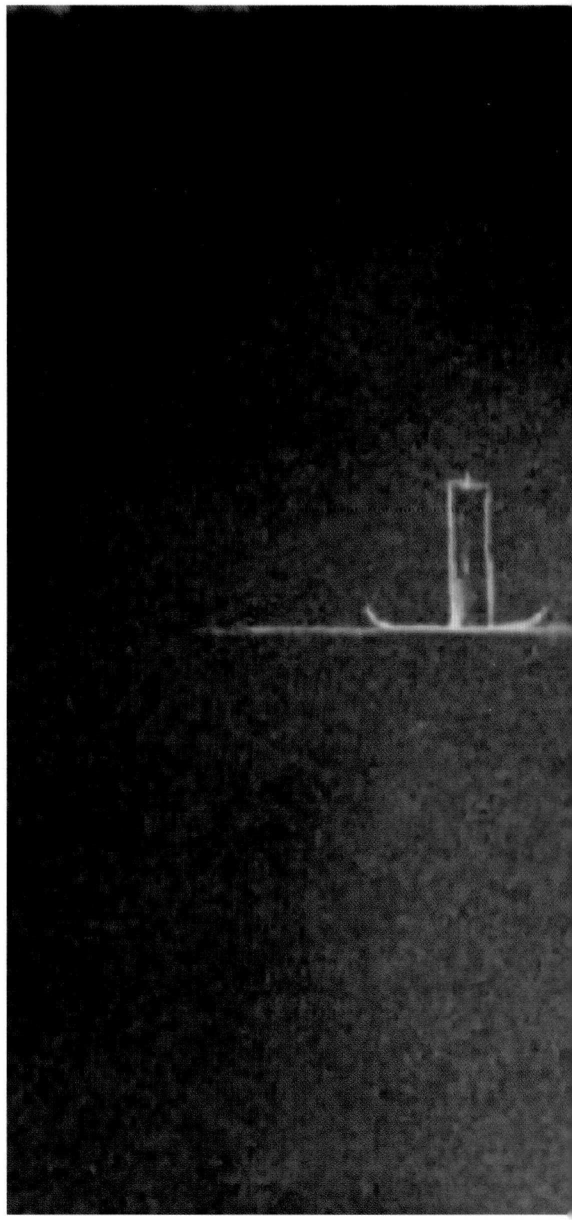

"One of the central themes in my work has always been childhood. In *Kid Candle* from 'Memories of Childhood,' I was able to zero in on this universal subject, capturing ideas about childhood through the simplicity of a single stationary camera, with the white wall as a stage, and a basic line drawing. It is my belief that any situation or struggle can be met with triumph and joy and that the imagination can make fantasy a reality." — RR

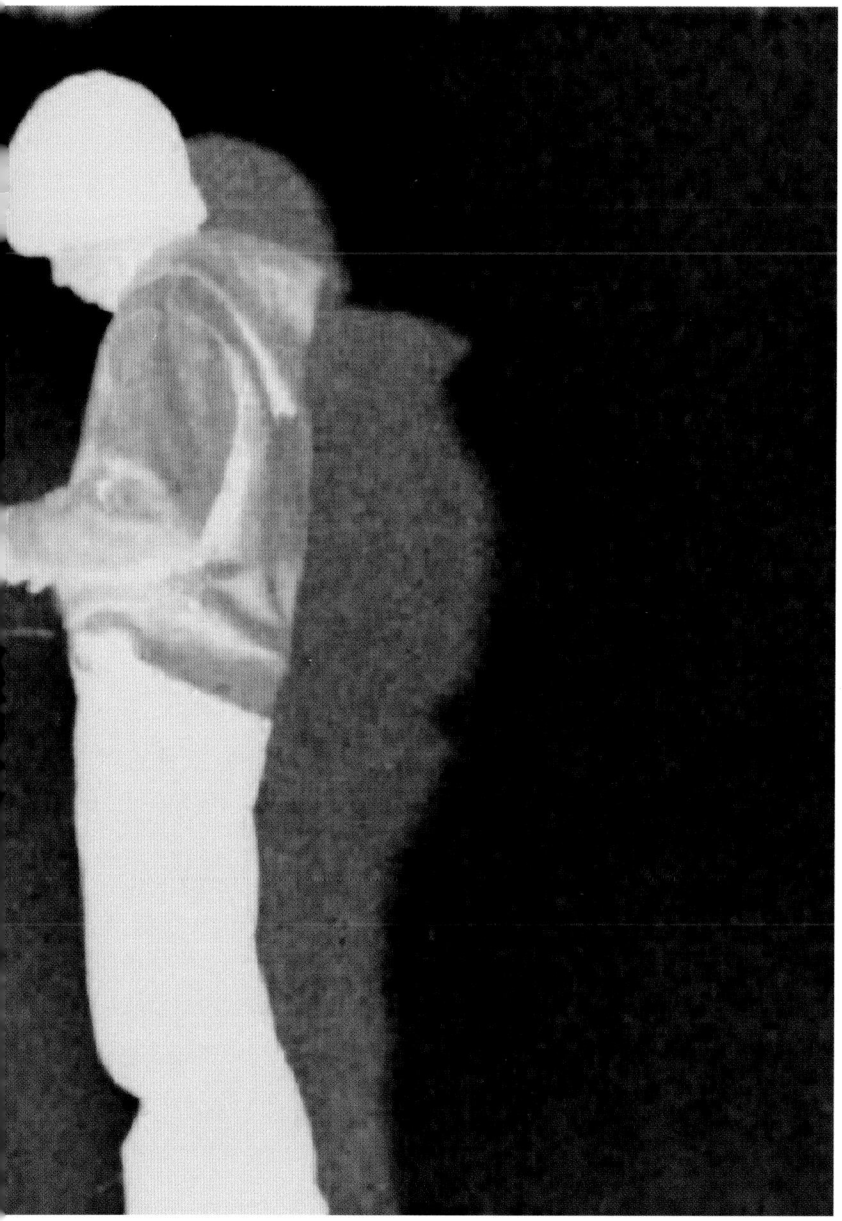

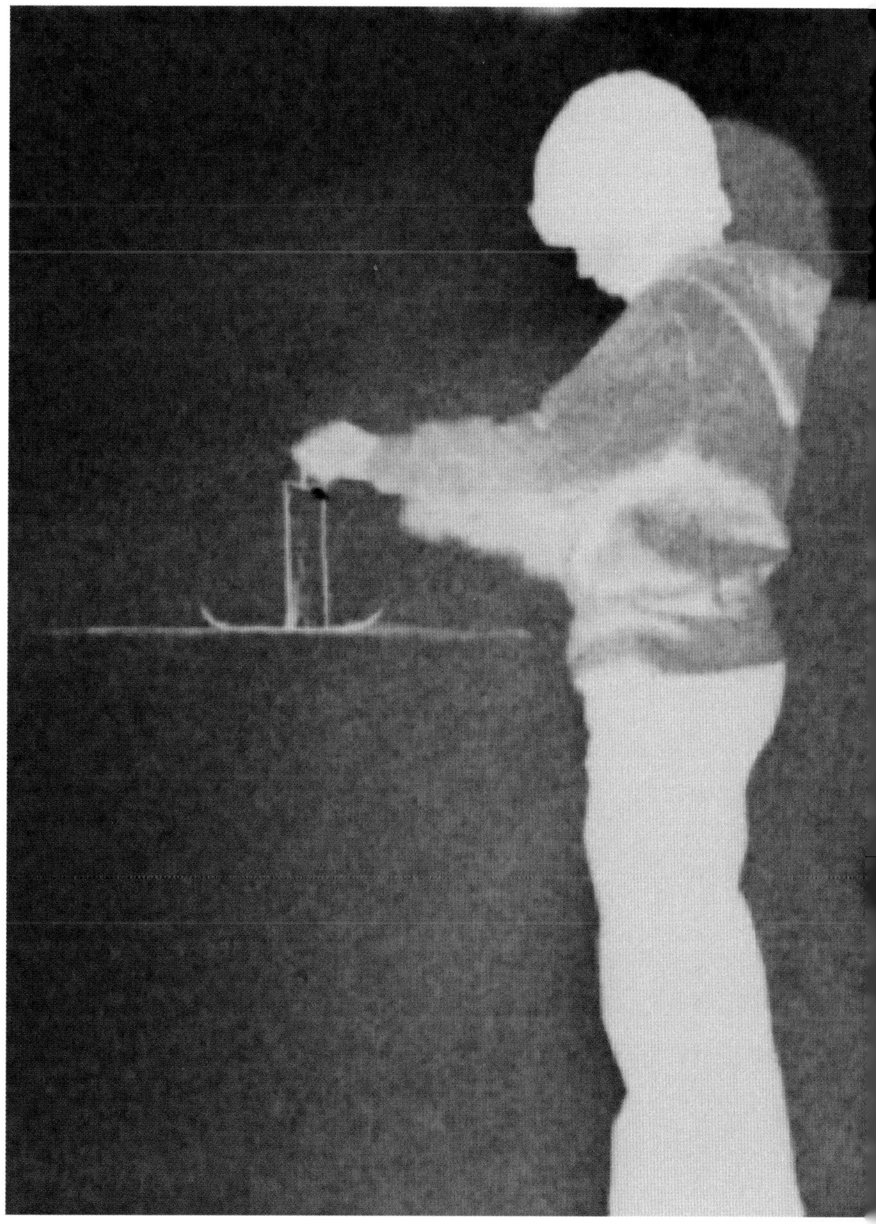

the dissolve

HIRAKI **SAWA**

BORN IN 1977, LIVES AND WORKS IN LONDON

Airliner, 2003

In Hiraki Sawa's *Airliner*, airplanes glide gracefully across the pages of an open blank book as a hand turns the pages at a varying speed. This action recalls a flip book, yet, in Sawa's work, the airplanes are digitally inscribed rather than hand-drawn. The density of airplanes and their continual movement suggest both global transit and ominous congestion. Yet, the fleet of planes also conveys the sense of an aerial show, layering Sawa's imagery with a sense of entertainment and play.

HIRAKI SAWA
Stills from *Airliner*, 2003
Video
Images courtesy of the artist and James Cohan Gallery, New York

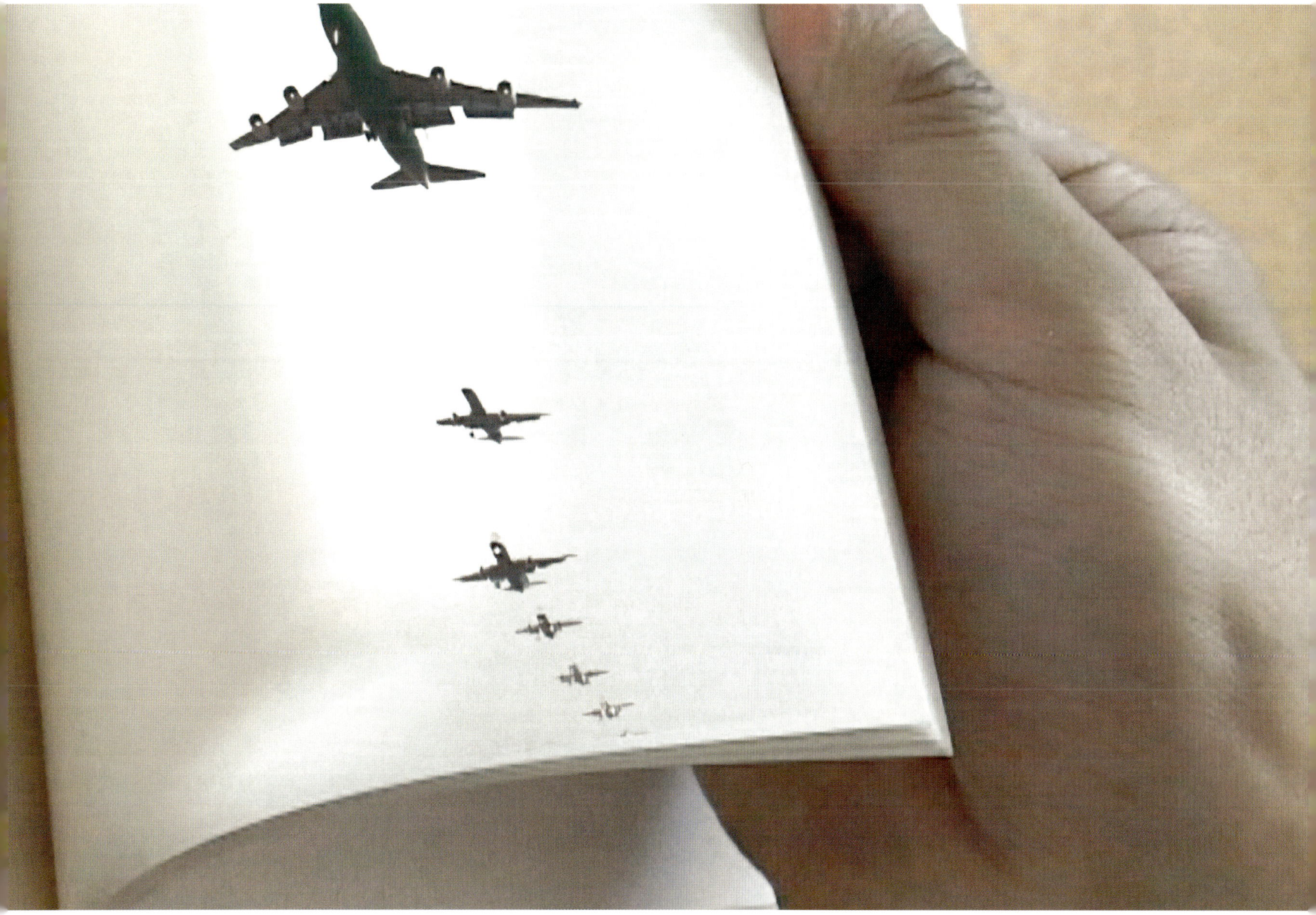

the dissolve

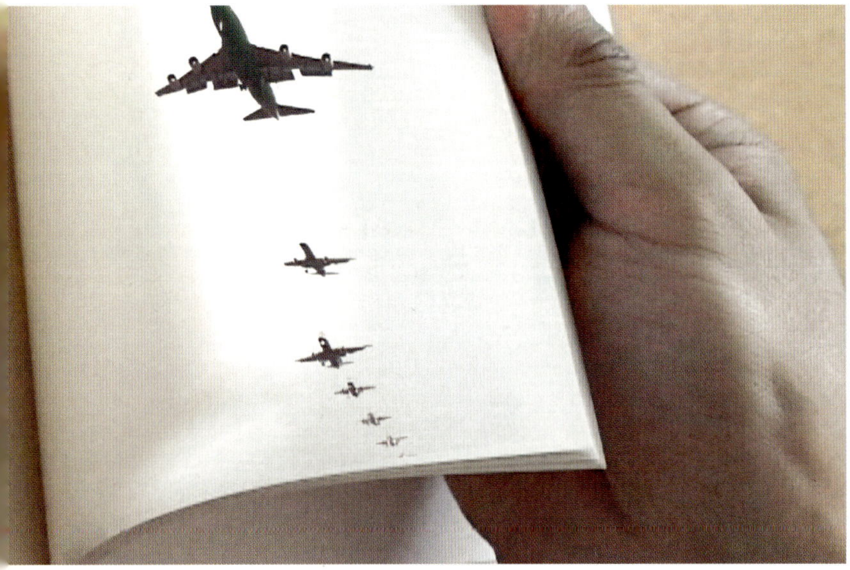

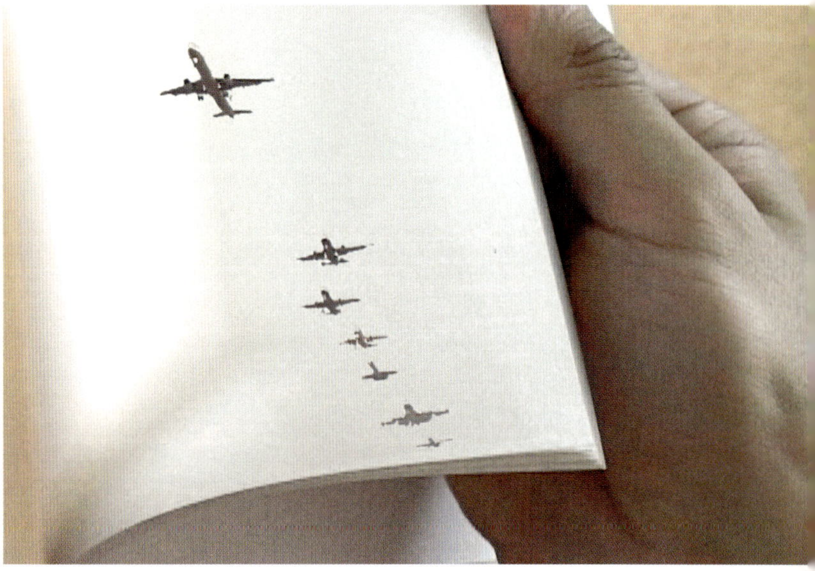

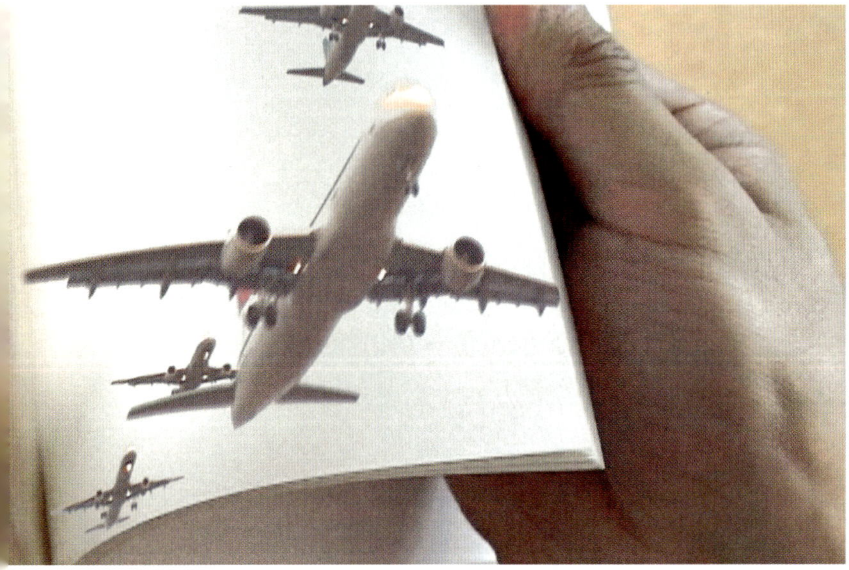

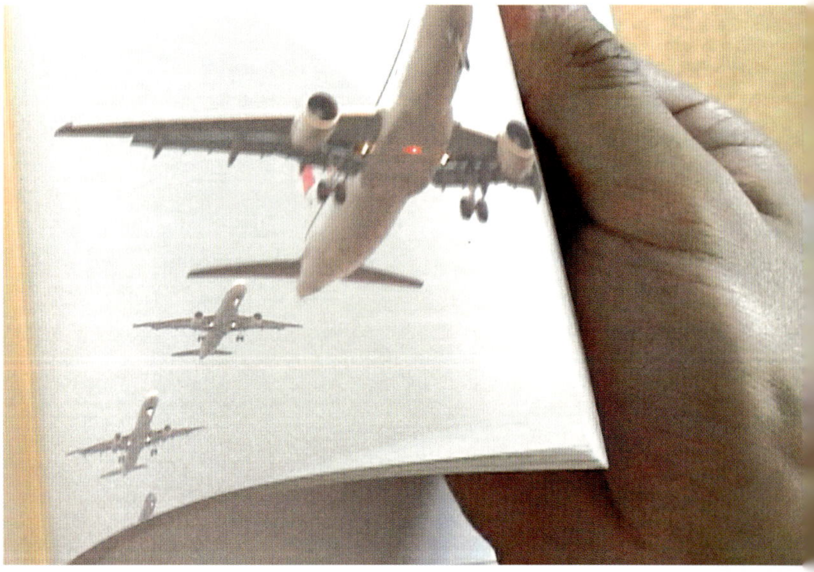

"I tend to be in limbo to start with, and insert lies in each piece as I go along." — HS

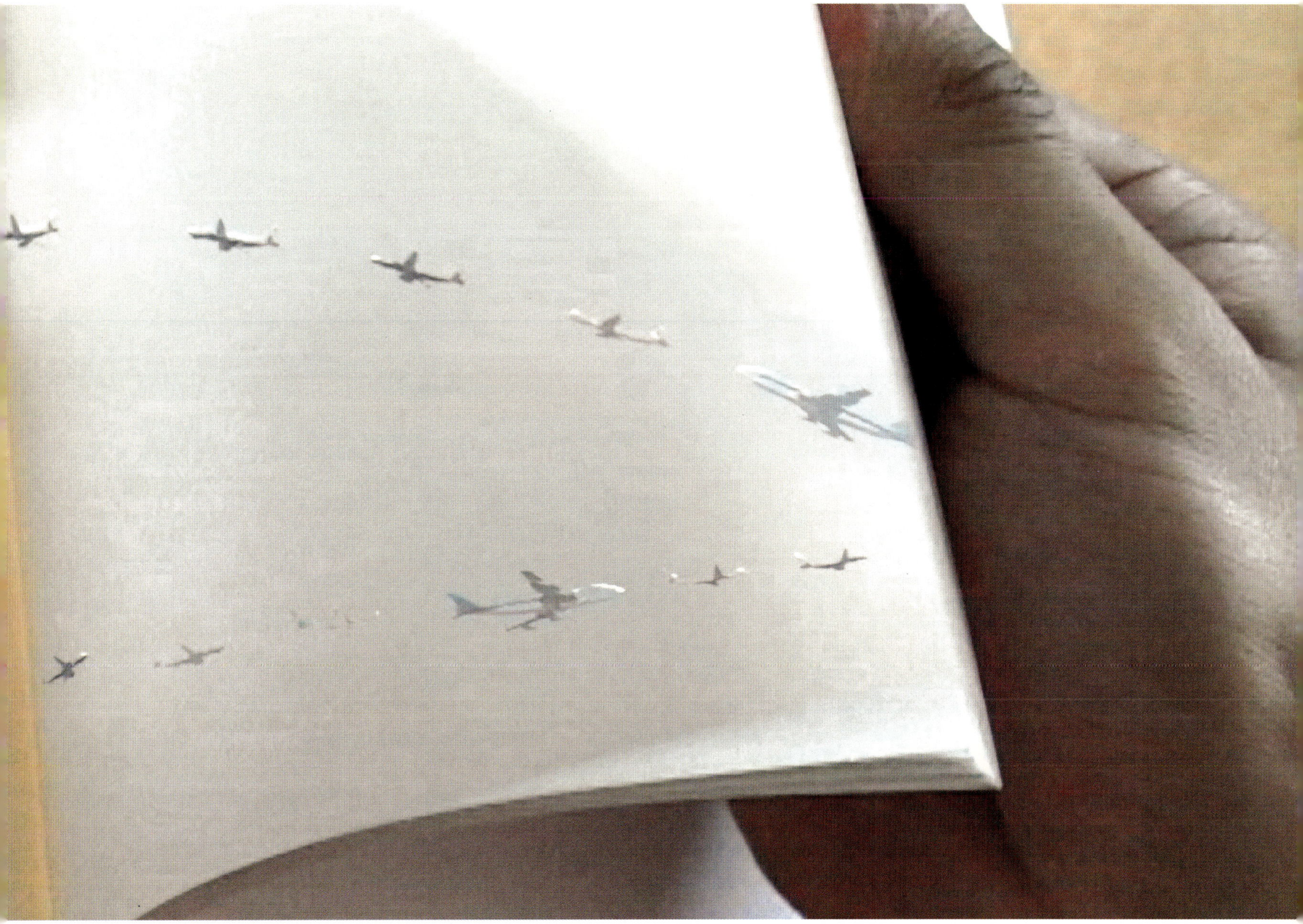

the dissolve

BERNI **SEARLE**

BORN IN 1964, LIVES AND WORKS IN CAPE TOWN

About to Forget, 2005

In *About to Forget*, Berni Searle transforms family photographs into a unified image by tracing the silhouettes of the figures onto one sheet of red crêpe paper. This action unites two generations of her kin, her grandmother and mother, who had been estranged for religious differences when her mother, a Muslim, converted to Catholicism for her marriage. As the paper is immersed in warm water, the ink bleeds, animating the images and providing a meditation on the transient nature of memory while calling into question the notion of connection through bloodlines.

BERNI SEARLE
Stills from *About to Forget*, 2005
35mm cinemascope film transferred to three-channel video projection
Images courtesy of the artist and Michael Stevenson Gallery, Cape Town

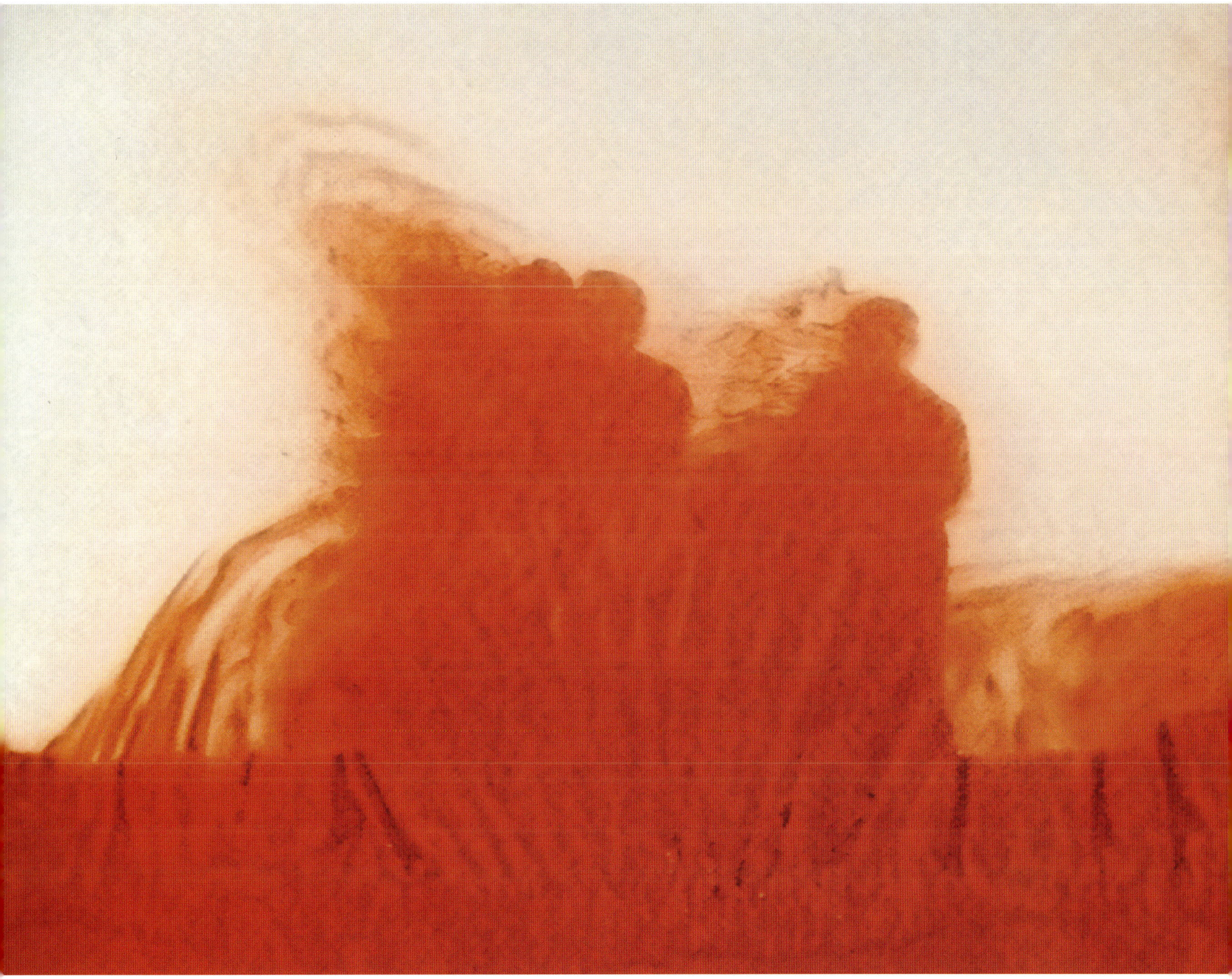

the dissolve

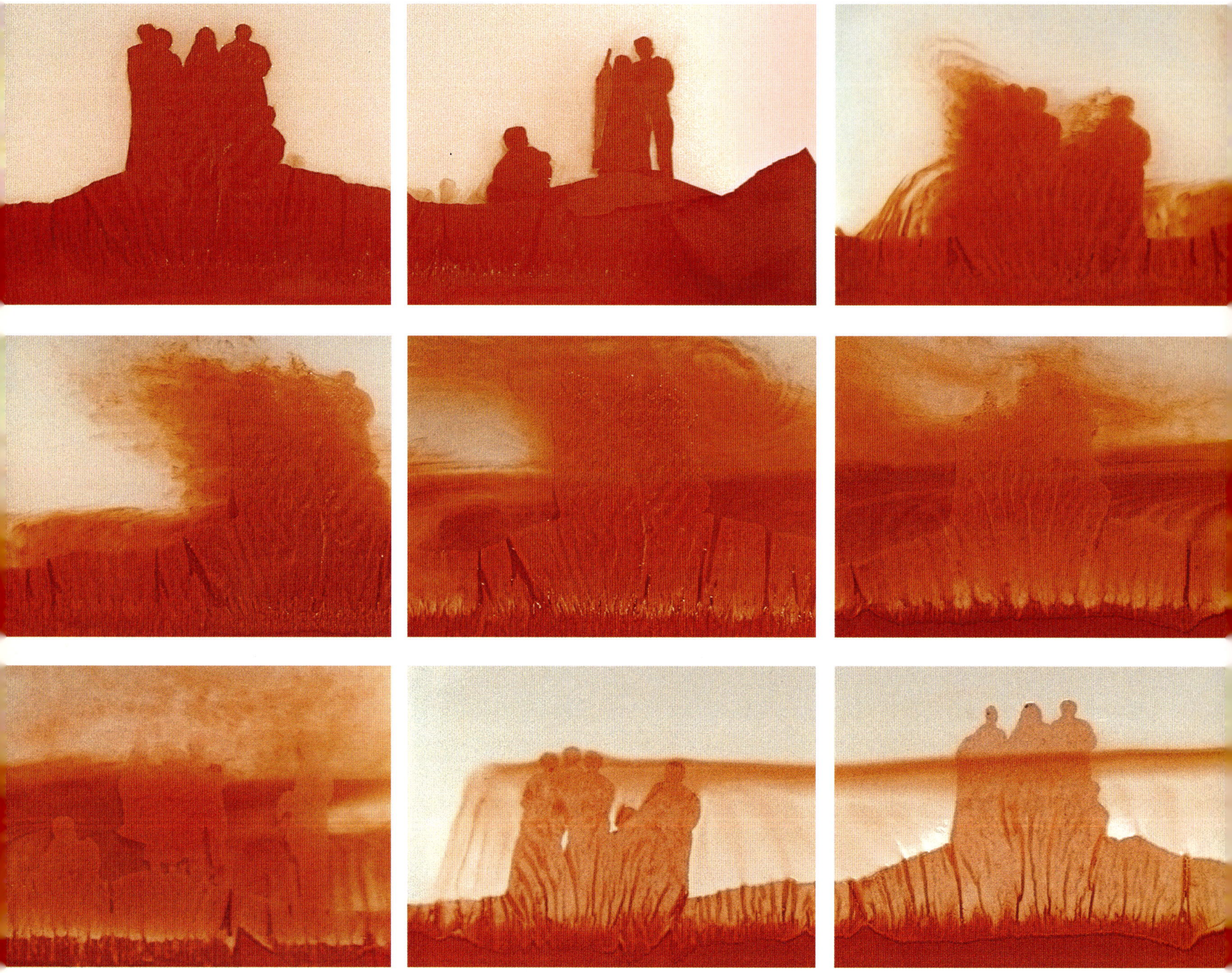

"Distilling the photograph into silhouetted forms adds both a sense of simplicity and monumentality to the image. Working with temporal dimensions and movement further activates the image to evoke or suggest a feeling or memory, which is fluid and constantly changing." — BS

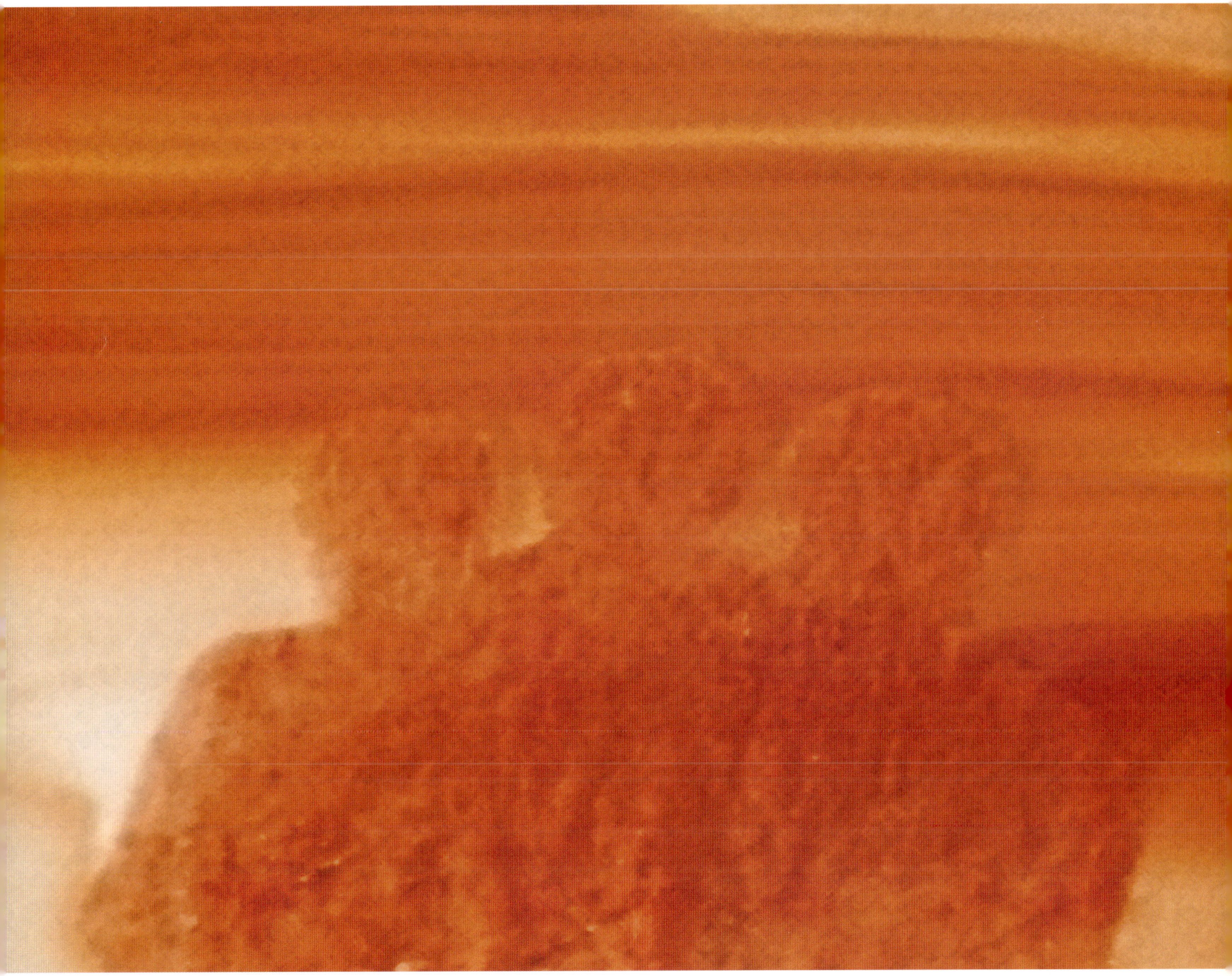

CINDY **SHERMAN**

BORN IN 1954, LIVES AND WORKS IN NEW YORK

Doll Clothes, 1975

Doll Clothes, the only stop-motion animation by Cindy Sherman, explores the construction of female identity. A paper doll, made in the likeness of the artist, peruses the fashion choices, with labels such as "casual" or "outdoors," available to her in an old-fashioned set. When the doll arrives at "dresses," she chooses an outfit and prances about the vanity, admiring herself in a make-up mirror. Her fun is spoiled when human hands pluck her up and put her back into her place within the paper doll set.

CINDY SHERMAN
Stills from *Doll Clothes*, 1975
16mm film transferred to DVD
Images courtesy of the artist and Metro Pictures, New York

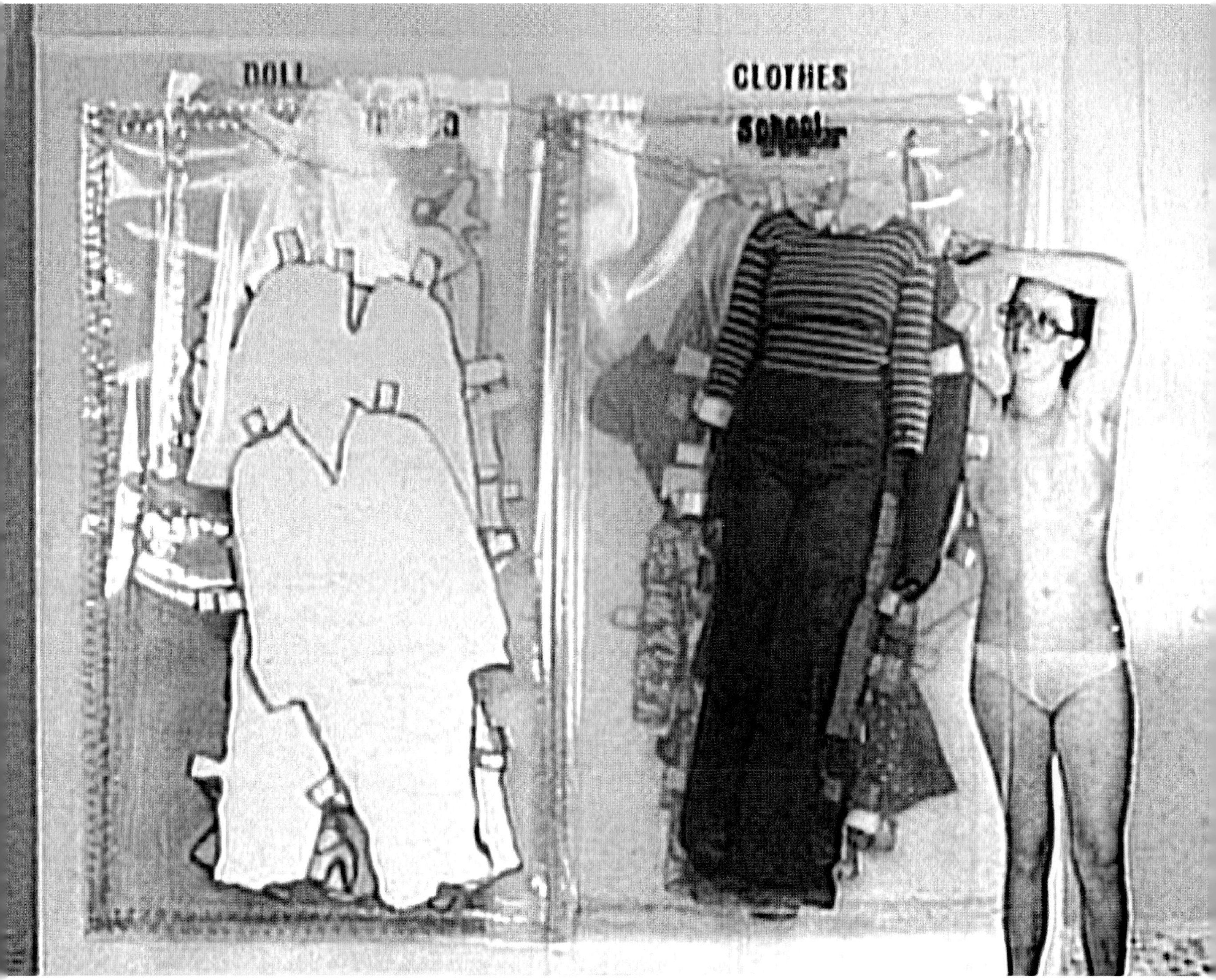

the dissolve

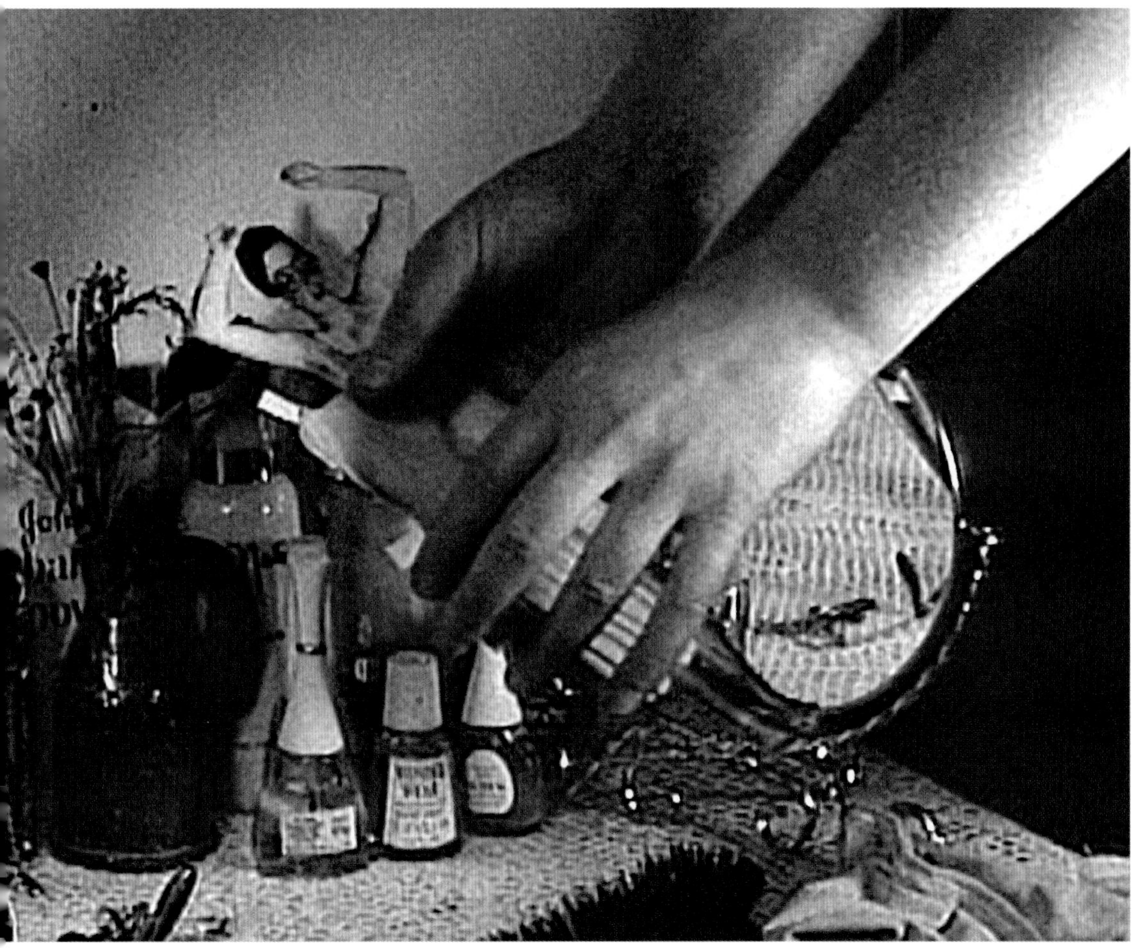

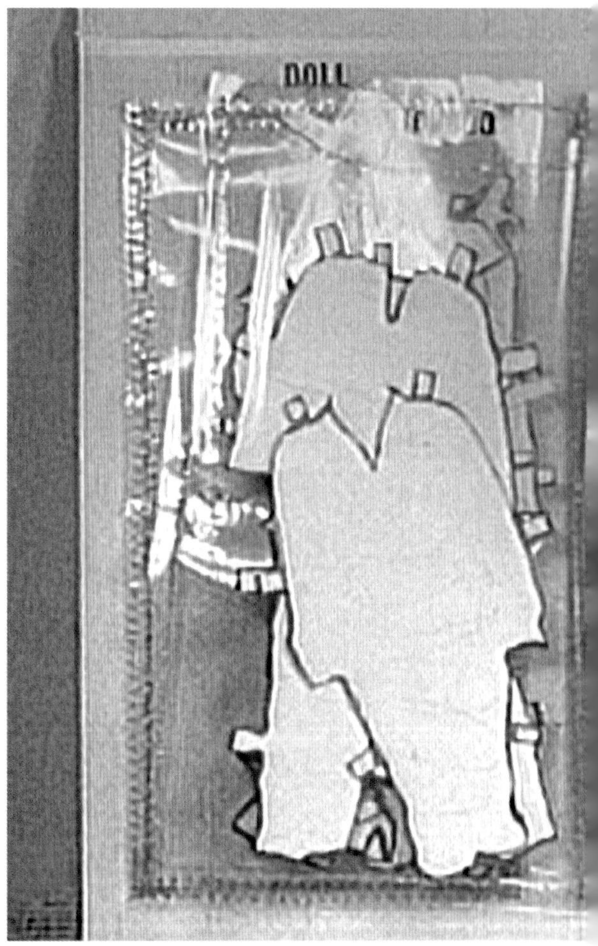

"This work was about starting out as a child and growing up." — CS

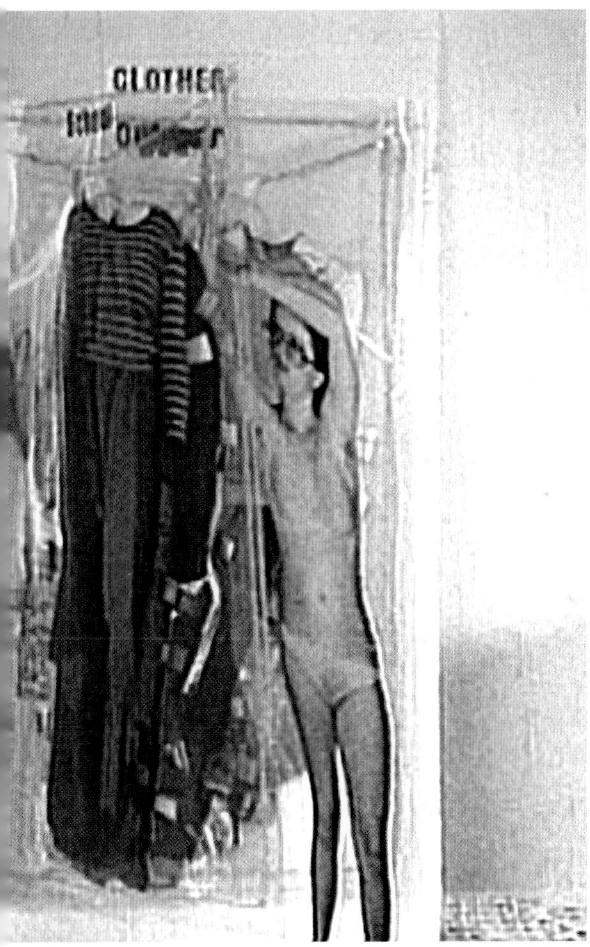

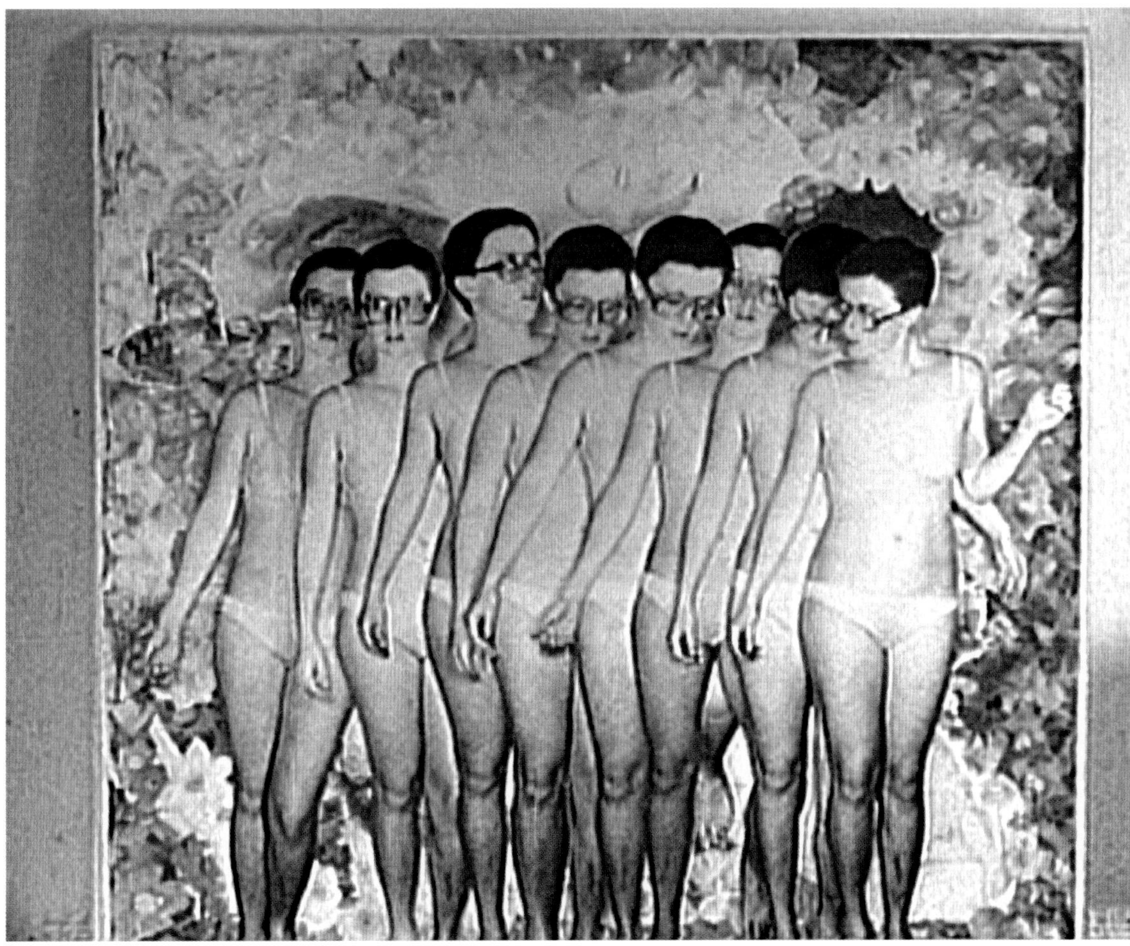

FEDERICO **SOLMI**

BORN IN 1973, LIVES AND WORKS IN NEW YORK

Douche Bag City, 2010

In *Douche Bag City*, Federico Solmi appropriates the format of first-person-shooter video games to offer a critique of corporate mentality. Dick Richman, the protagonist in his film, negotiates a landscape of urban decay that is populated with symbolic demons. Solmi's graphic style is based upon drawings that are digitally animated by his collaborator, 3-D designer Russell Lowe. These works also exhibit a kinship with graphic novels whose gritty narratives are mirrored in Solmi's work as well.

FEDERICO SOLMI
Stills from *Douche Bag City*, 2010
Video Installation
Images courtesy of the artist and LMAK Projects, New York and ADN Gallery, Barcelona

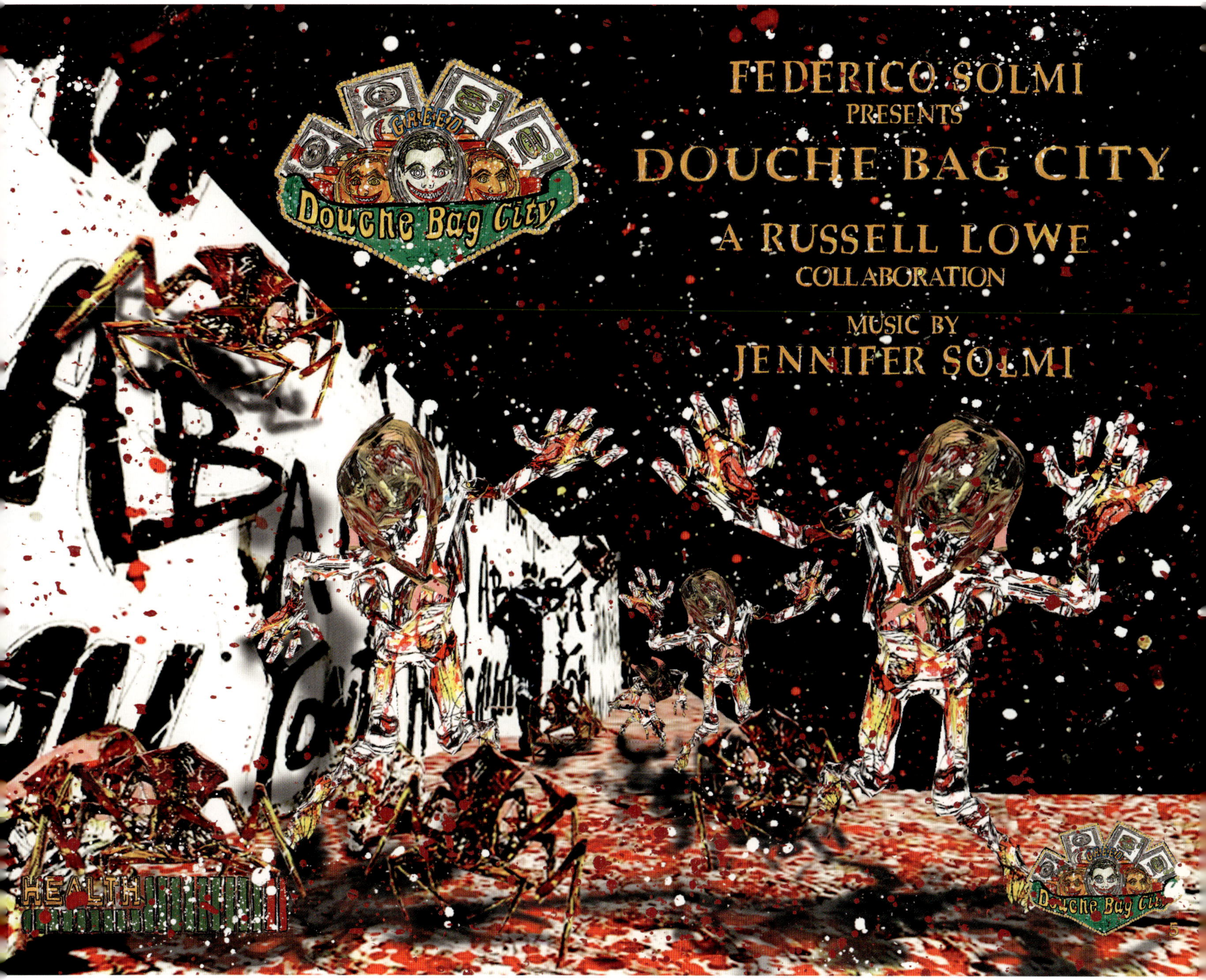

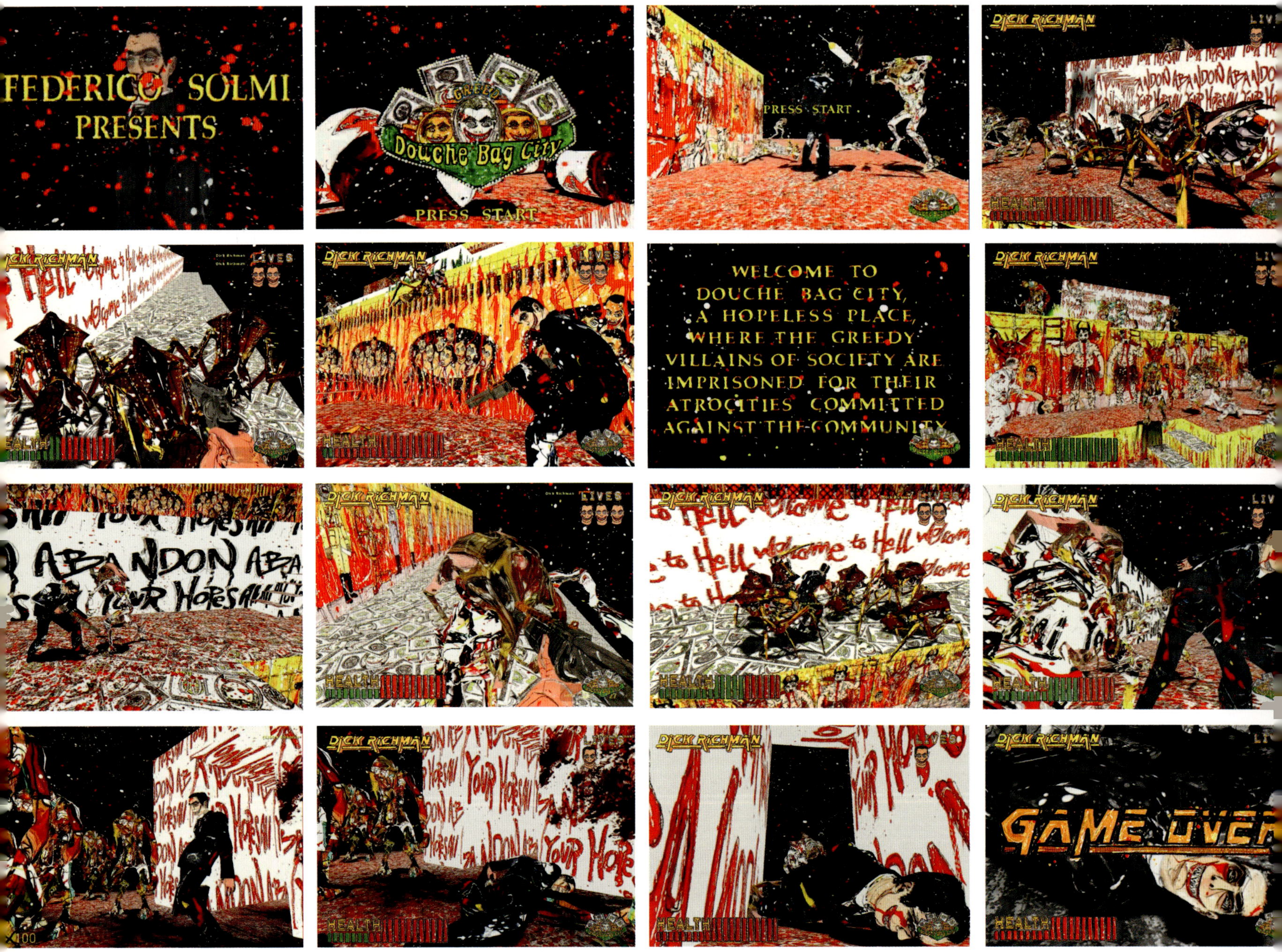
FEDERICO SOLMI
PRESENTS
GREED
Douche Bag City
PRESS START
PRESS START
DICK RICHMAN
HEALTH
LIVES
WELCOME TO
DOUCHE BAG CITY,
A HOPELESS PLACE,
WHERE THE GREEDY
VILLAINS OF SOCIETY ARE
IMPRISONED FOR THEIR
ATROCITIES COMMITTED
AGAINST THE COMMUNITY
ABANDON
YOUR HOPES
welcome to Hell
GAME OVE

"The universe that I like to represent is the exaltation of a present that is crumbling apart. The protagonists of my videos are typically lost characters—confused inhabitants of a hostile society in decay. *Douche Bag City* is a place where humans are trapped in a logic of rules, laws, and authorities, and where violence is the only possible reaction to a violence-based system." — FS

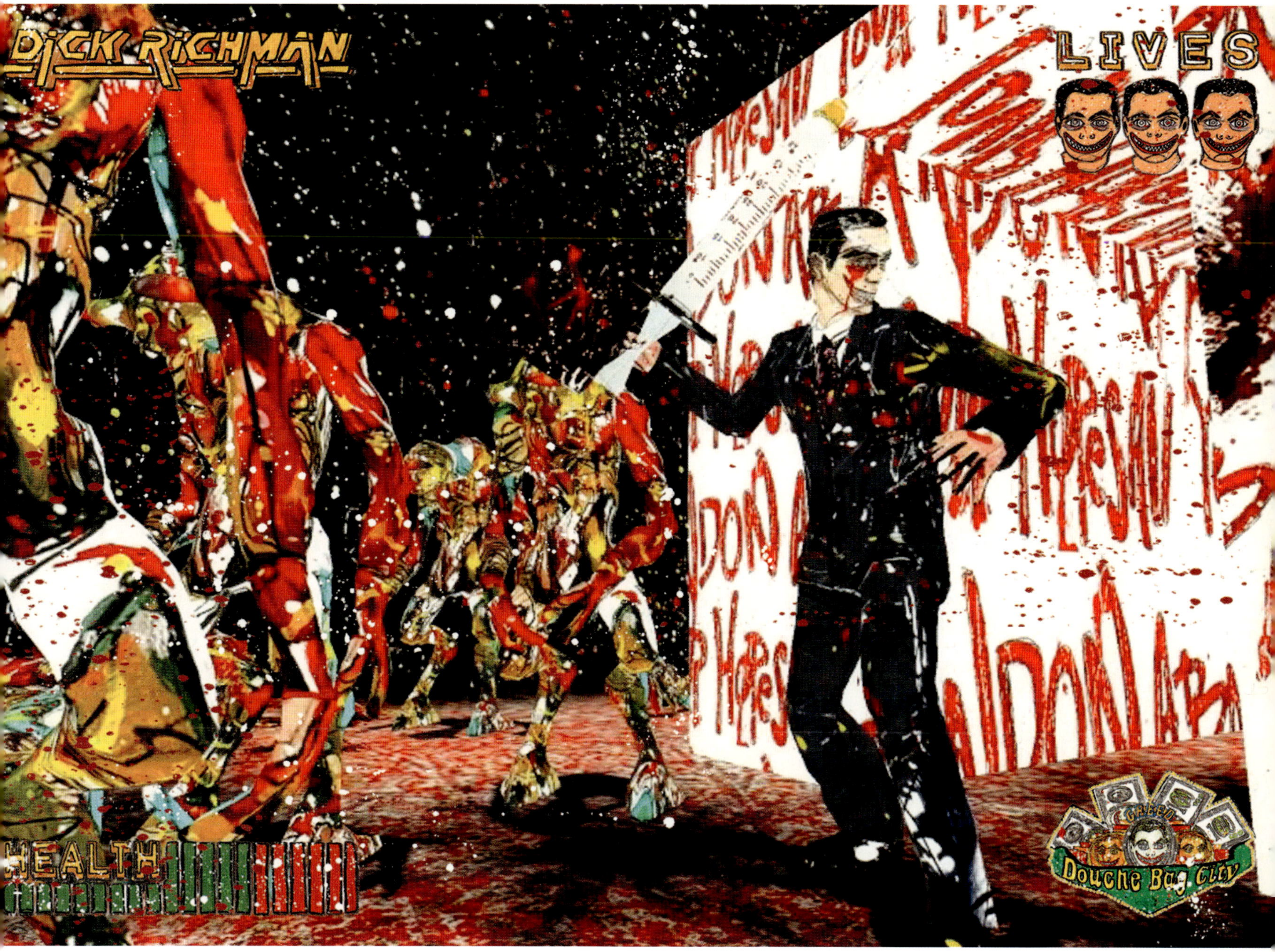

the dissolve

KARA **WALKER**

BORN IN 1969, LIVES AND WORKS IN NEW YORK

National Archives Microfilm Publications M999 Roll 34: Bureau of Refugees, Freedmen and Abandoned Lands:
1) *Six Miles from Springfield on the Franklin Road,* 2009
2) *Lucy of Pulaski,* 2009

Kara Walker's recent films take their titles and narratives from documents in the archives of the Freedmen's Bureau, established in 1865 to assist African Americans with the transition from slavery to freedom, and operational until 1872. The artist employs her signature black-silhouette cutout figures to depict extreme emotions in a shadow puppet theater-like space. The presentation is deliberately self-referential, with shots panning behind the scenes to reveal the human actors.

KARA WALKER
Still from *National Archives Microfilm Publications M999 Roll 34: Bureau of Refugees, Freedmen and Abandoned Lands:*
1) *Six Miles from Springfield on the Franklin Road,* 2009
2) *Lucy of Pulaski*, 2009
Video
Images courtesy of the artist and Sikkema Jenkins & Co., New York

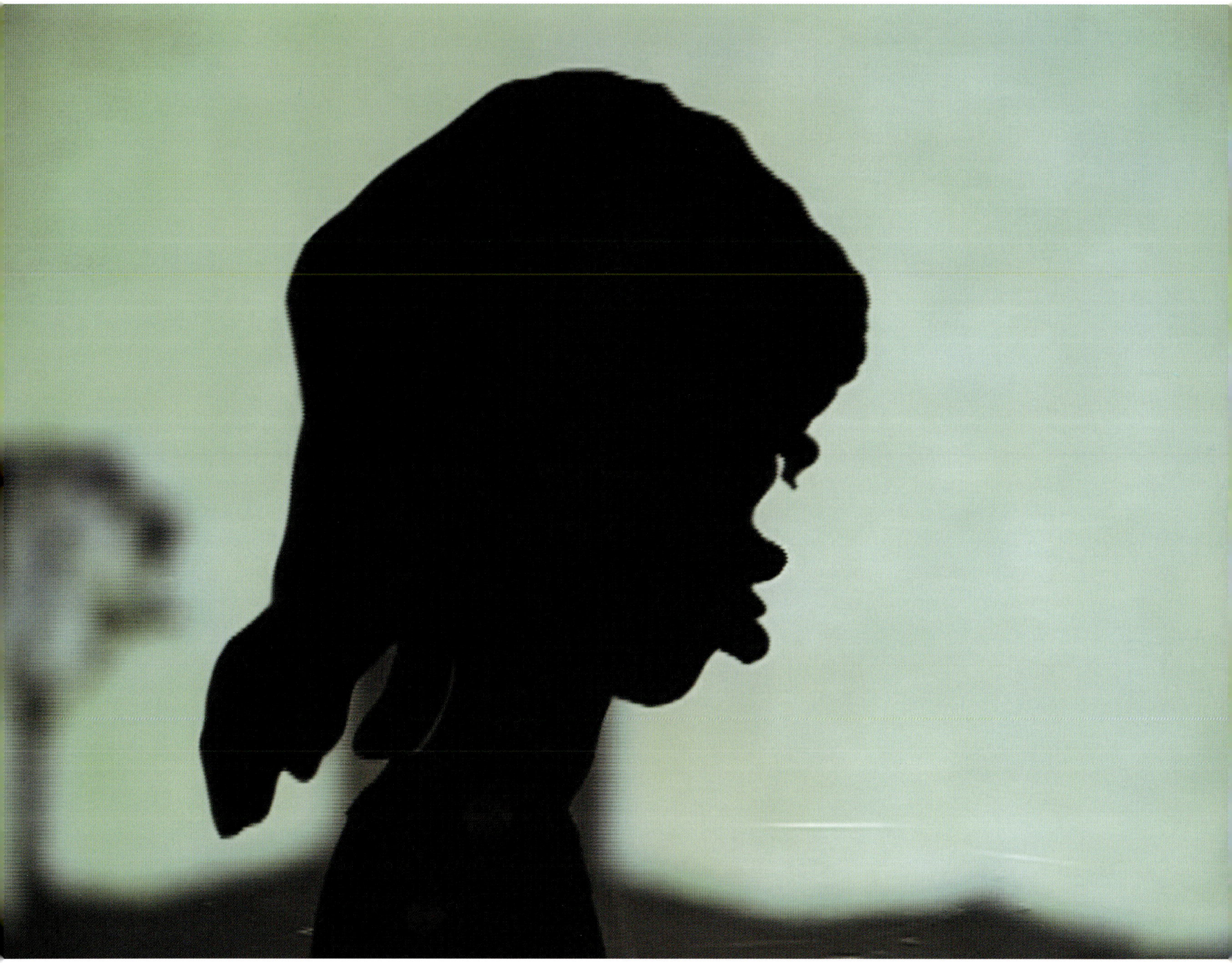

the dissolve

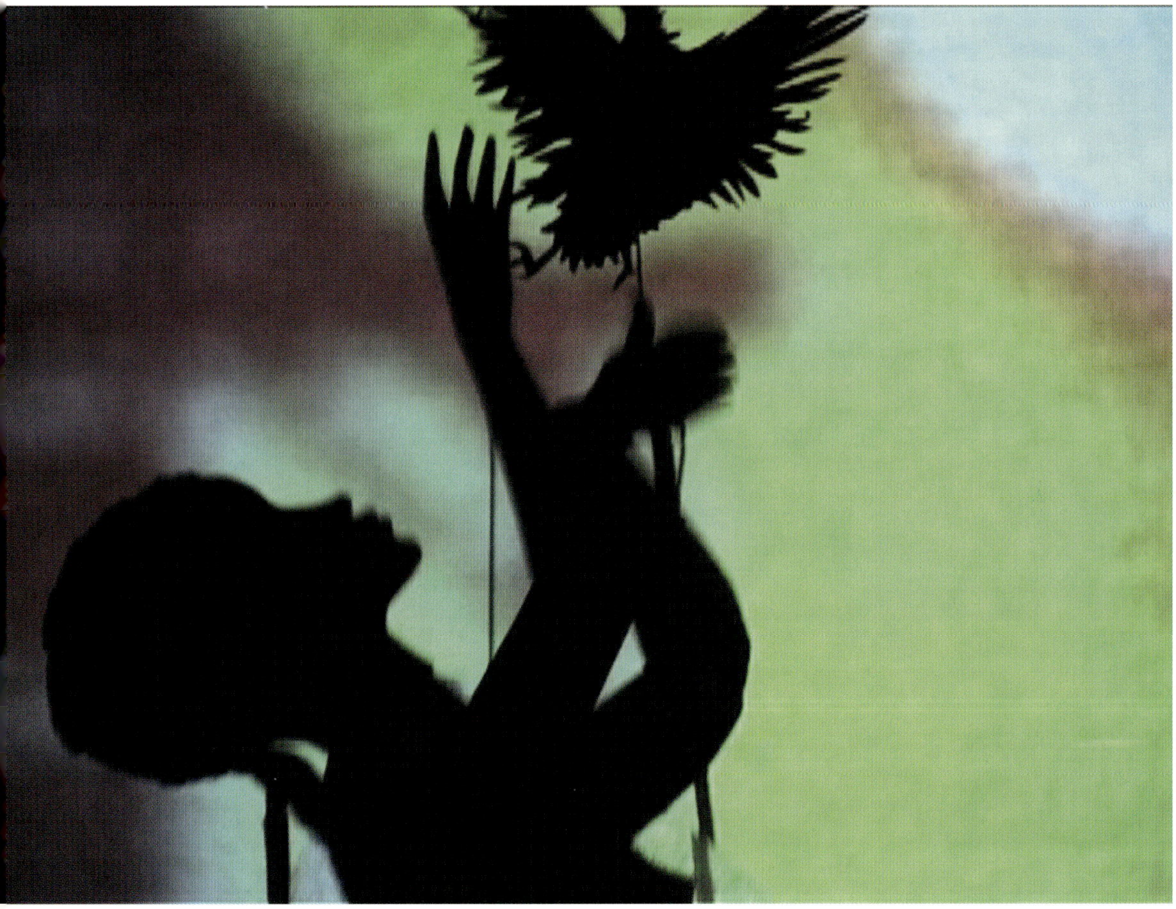

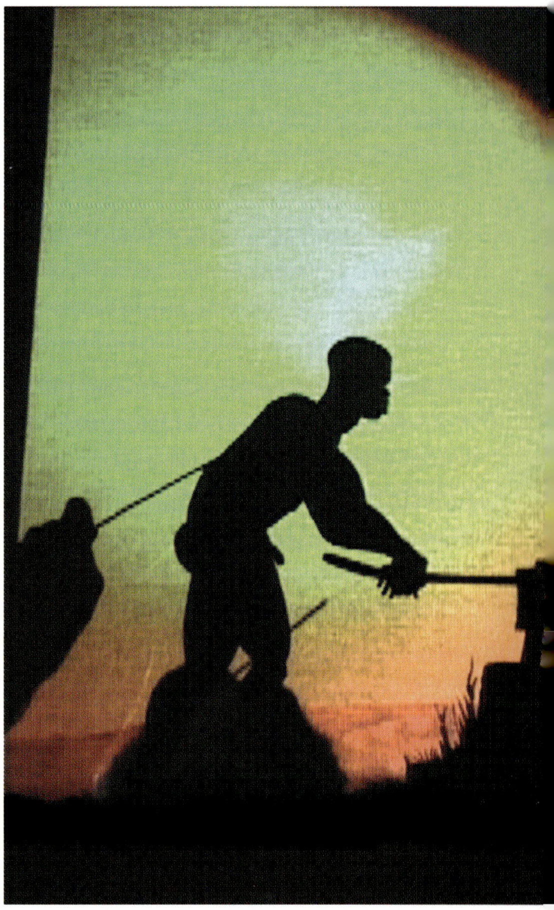

Before me personally appeared this day Amanda Willis and having been duly sworn deposed and says:

"My name is Amanda Willis. I live on the Springfield and Franklin road about six miles from Springfield. On or about the 23rd day of October 1866, I saw three men at mother's house and after putting all of us out of the house and our clothes, one of the men got me by the arm and told me to follow him. He brought me down into the woods and had forcible connection with me. They all left immediately afterwards. They burned up father's house."

Signed Amanda (X) Willis
Sworn and subscribed to before me this 26th day of November 1866
(signed) Michl. Walsh, Capt. V. R. C., Chief Superintendent, Nashville Sub. Dist.

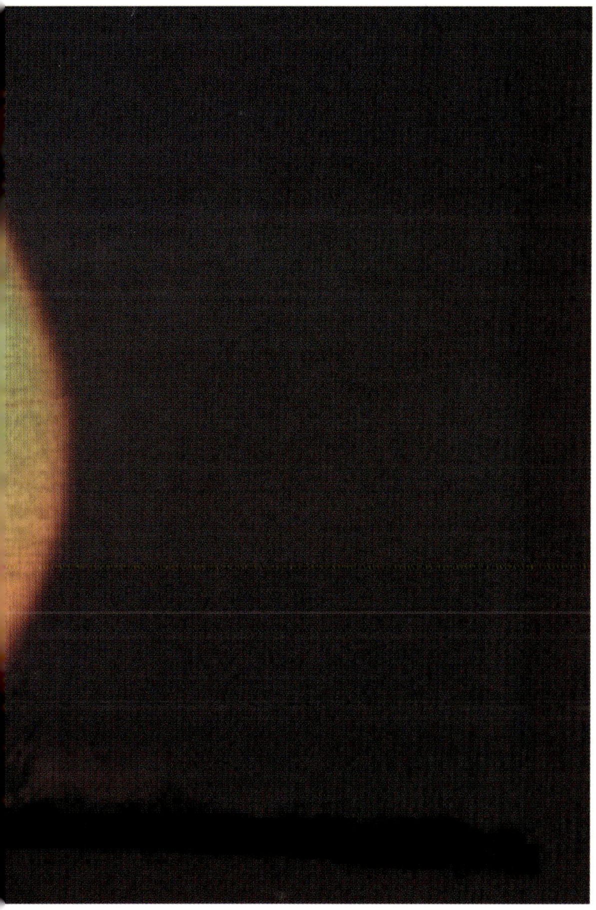

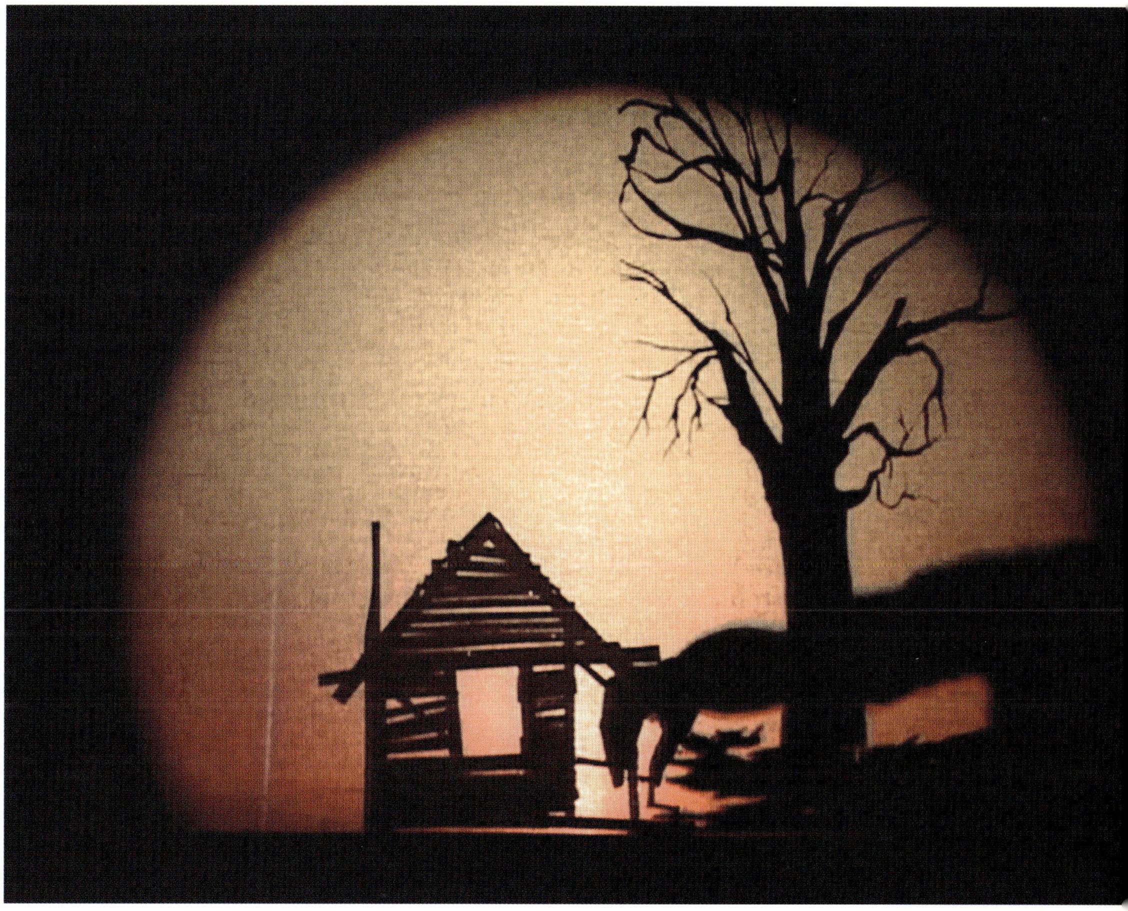

the dissolve

EDISON MANUFACTURING COMPANY

ACTIVE IN NEW YORK AND NEW JERSEY, 1894–1918

The Enchanted Drawing, 1900

Produced by the Edison Manufacturing Company, *The Enchanted Drawing* is a pioneering example of the use of stop-motion animation techniques. Combining live action and animation in this work, a lightning-sketch artist, portrayed by the filmmaker J. Stuart Blackton, is able to bring to life the objects he draws on a large sketch pad, including a top hat, a glass, and a bottle of wine. In this humorous piece, a fully animated caricature of a man's face interacts with and responds to Blackton's pranks.

EDISON MANUFACTURING COMPANY
Stills from *The Enchanted Drawing*, 1900
35mm film transferred to DVD
The Library of Congress, Paper Print Collection, Washington DC

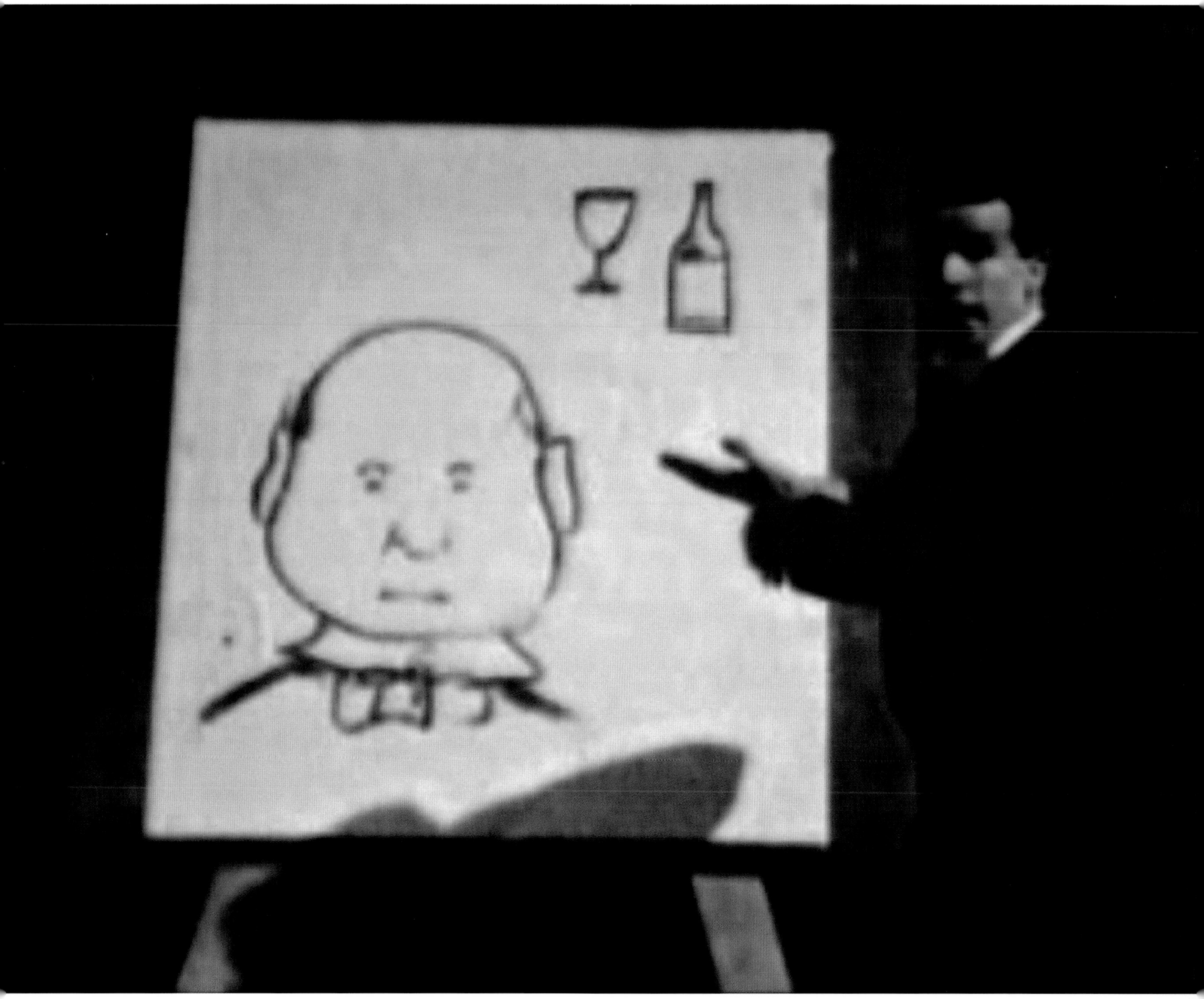

the dissolve

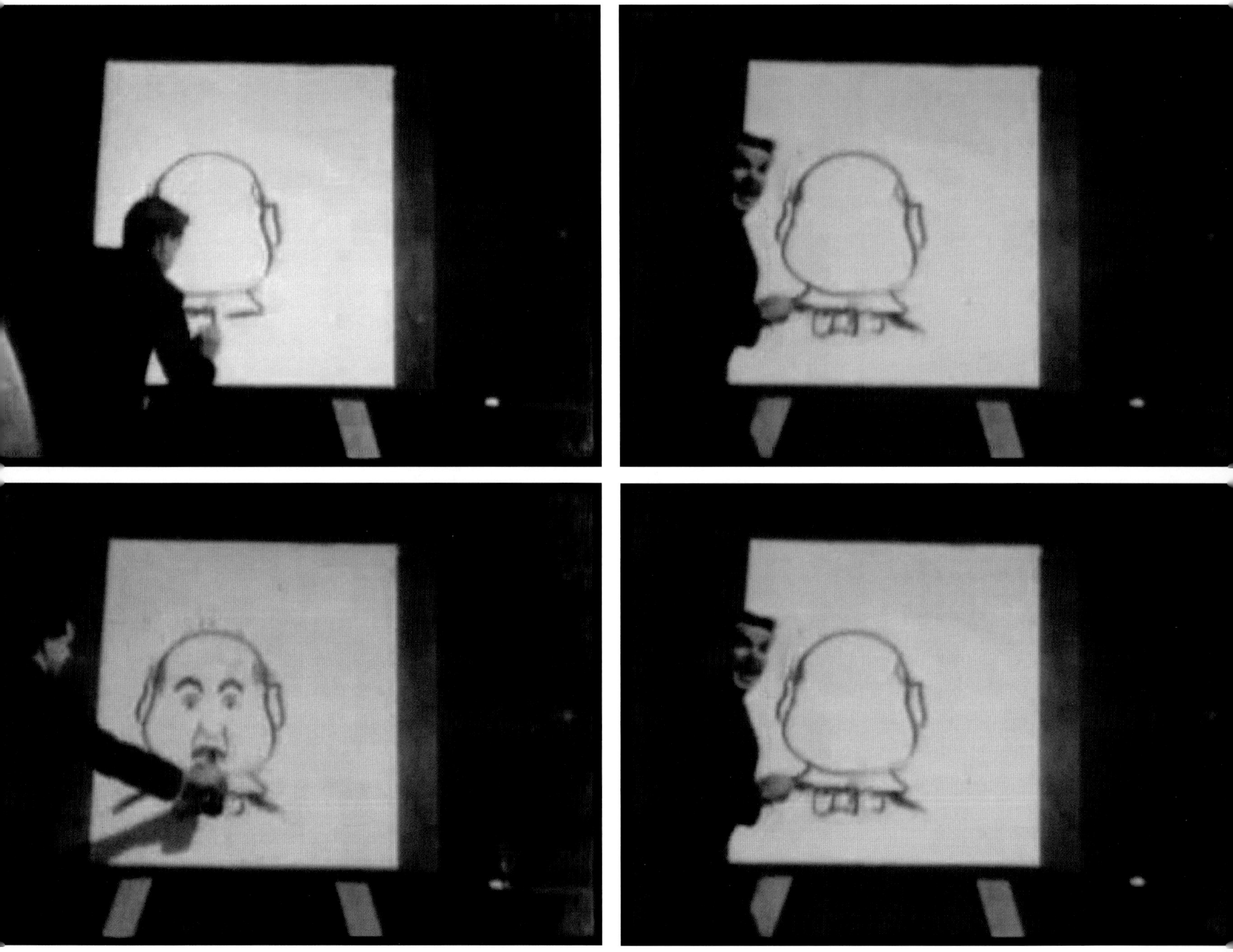

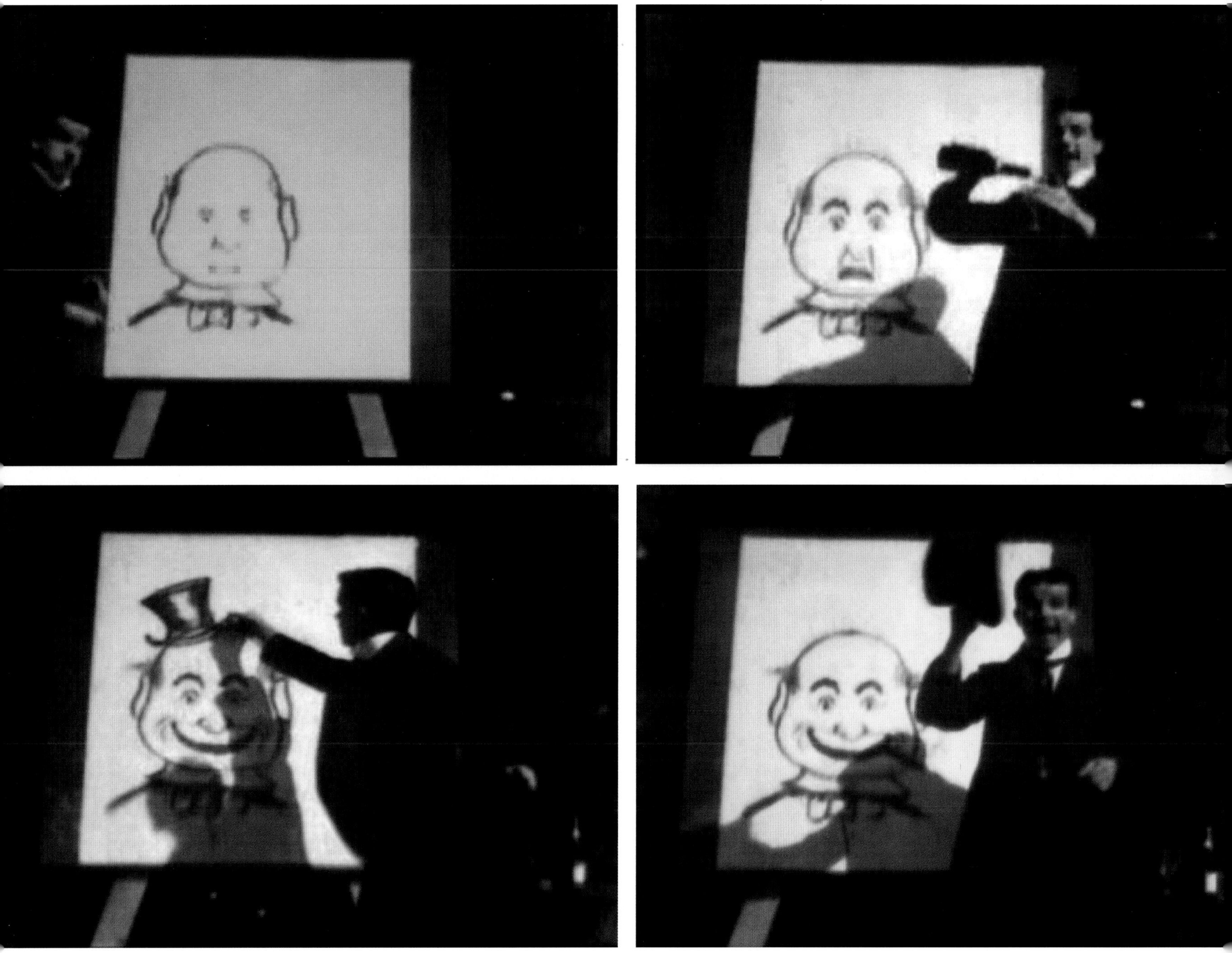

the dissolve

FLEISCHER STUDIOS

ACTIVE IN NEW YORK AND LOS ANGELES, 1921–1942

"Big Chief" Ko-Ko, 1924

Ko-Ko the Clown was a signature character of Fleischer Studios' cartoon repertoire. In *"Big Chief" Ko-Ko*, the animated clown competes with a Native American artist for the attention of cartoonist Max Fleischer setting off a series of misadventures. Although rife with stereotypes that were prevalent in cartoons of this era, *"Big Chief" Ko-Ko* is a prime example of Fleischer's technical innovation. It features rotoscoping, a technique Fleischer developed in which the movements of a live-action figure are traced and converted into animation.

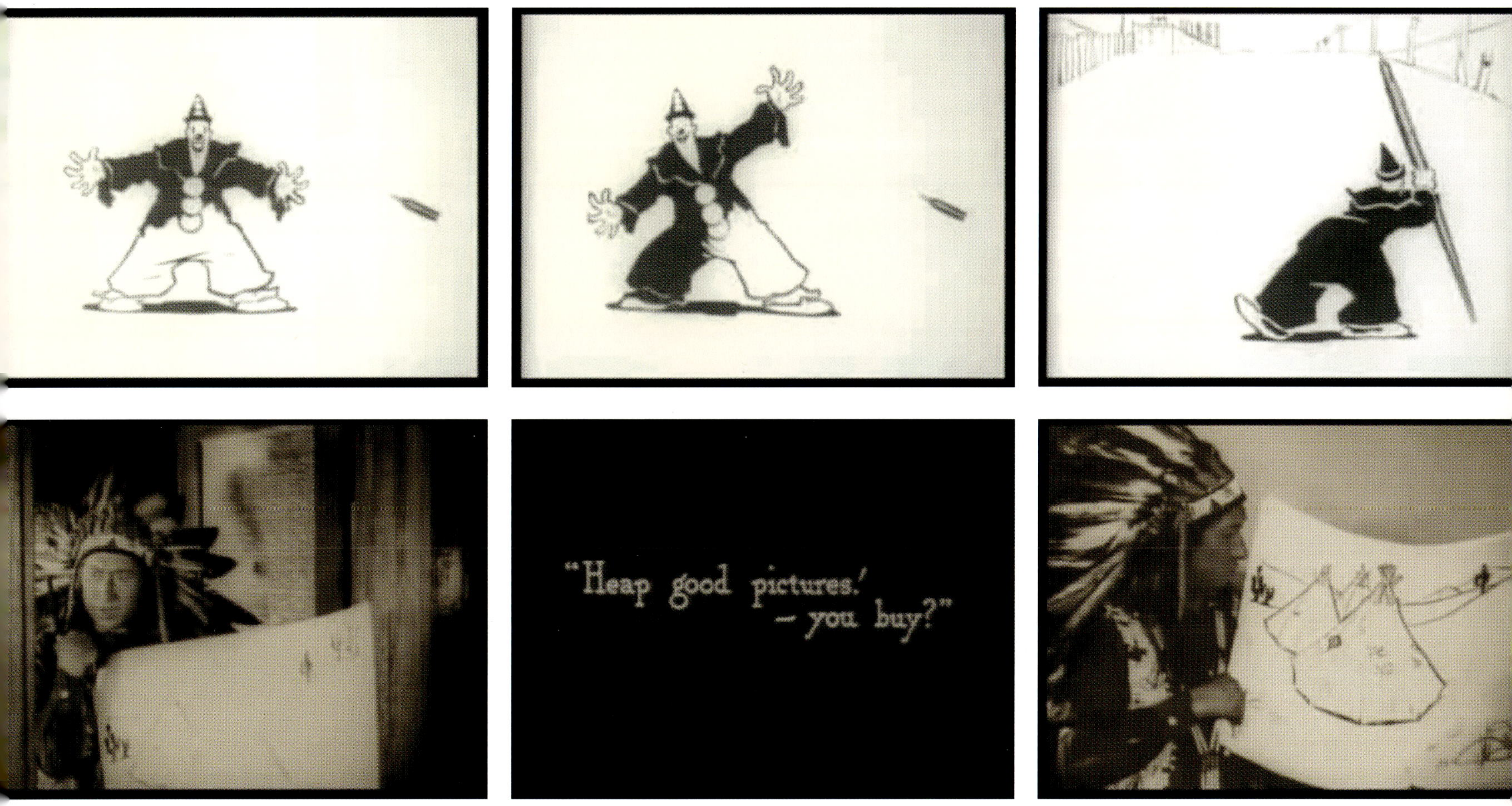

FLEISCHER STUDIOS
Stills from *"Big Chief" Ko-Ko,* 1924
35mm film transferred to DVD
Images courtesy of Inkwell Images, Morley, MI

the dissolve

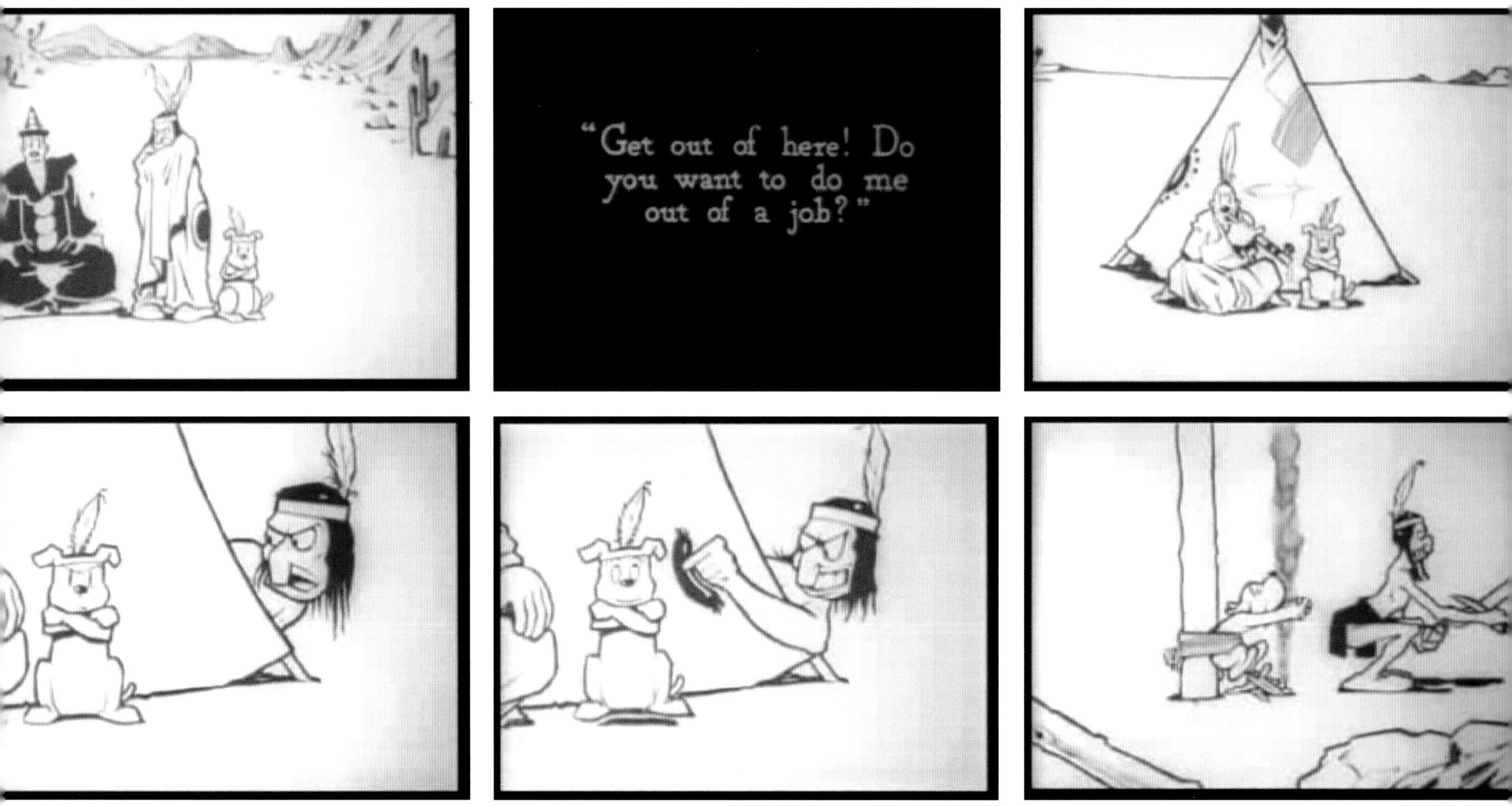

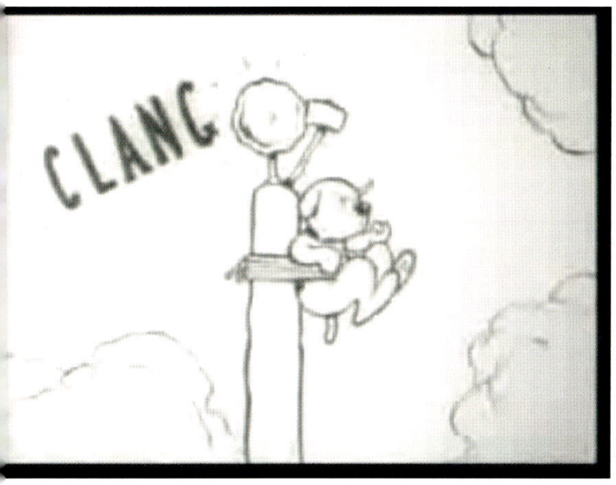
CLANG

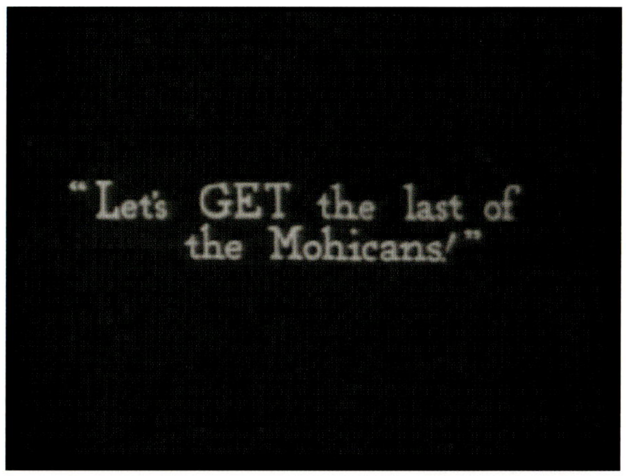
"Let's GET the last of
the Mohicans!"

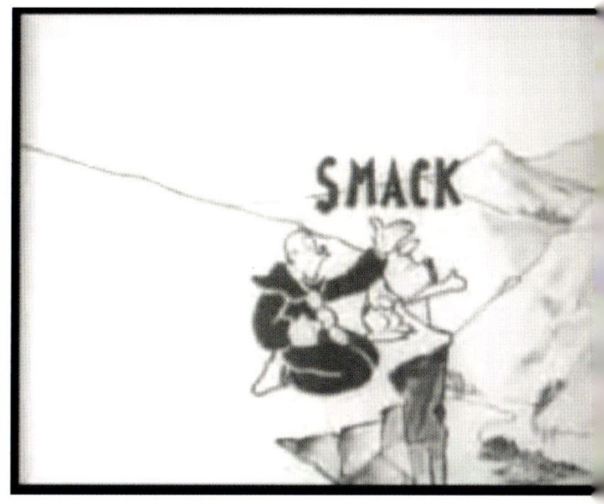
SMACK

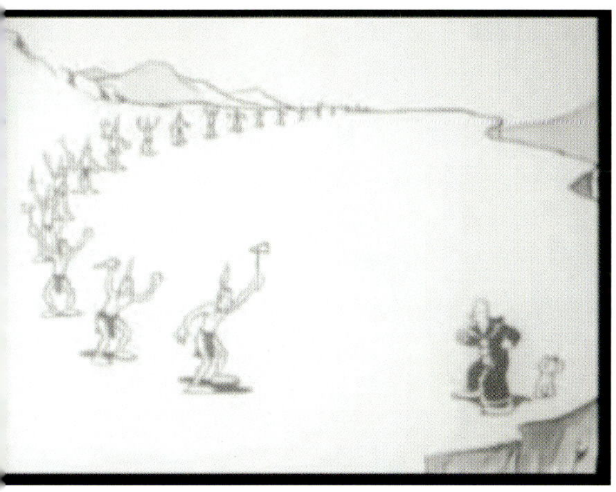

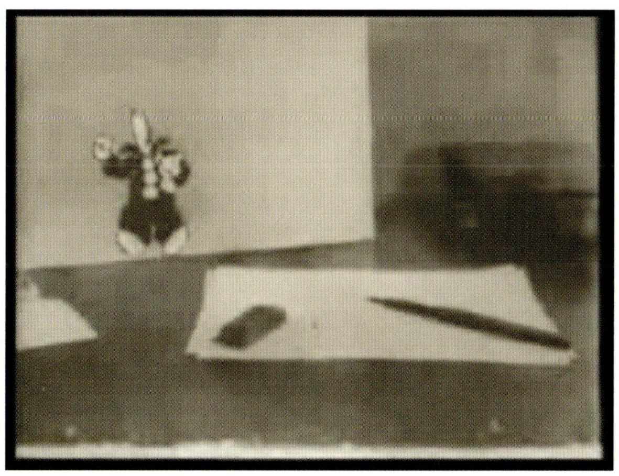

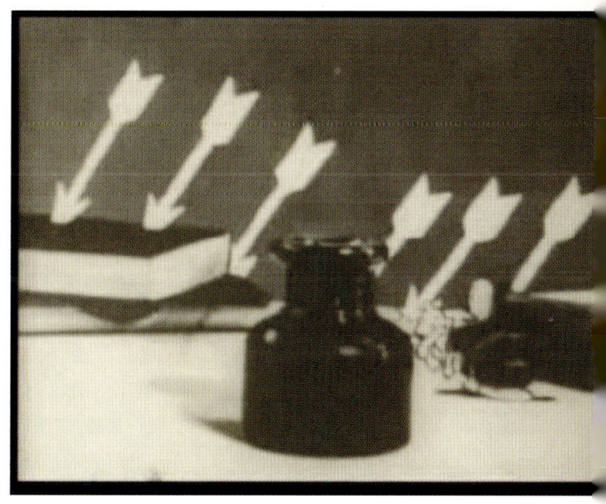

LOTTE REINIGER

1899–1981, LIVED AND WORKED IN GERMANY AND BRITAIN

The Adventures of Prince Achmed, 1926

Lotte Reiniger's *The Adventures of Prince Achmed* is widely believed to be the oldest surviving feature-length animated film. The film's narrative is based on episodes from *The Arabian Nights*, and Reiniger took advantage of animation's ability to represent the imaginary by focusing on some of the more fantastical elements of these stories, such as Achmed's flying horse. Reiniger used shadow puppets, which she meticulously crafted by hand, in concert with stop-motion techniques, to create a film of technical complexity and haunting beauty.

LOTTE REINIGER
Stills from *The Adventures of Prince Achmed*, 1926
35mm film, black and white/tinted, transferred to DVD
Images courtesy of Milestone Films, Harrington Park, NJ

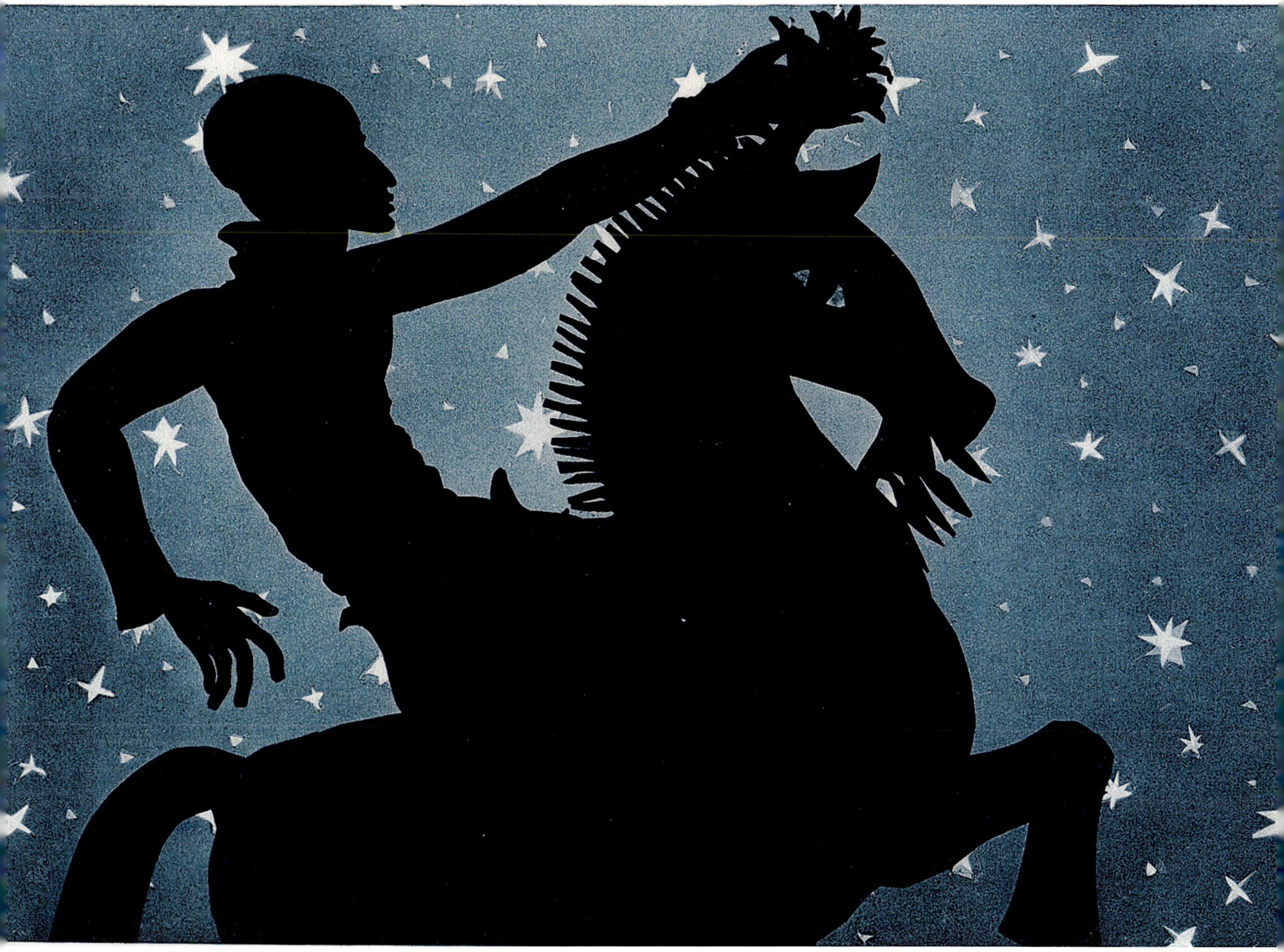

the dissolve

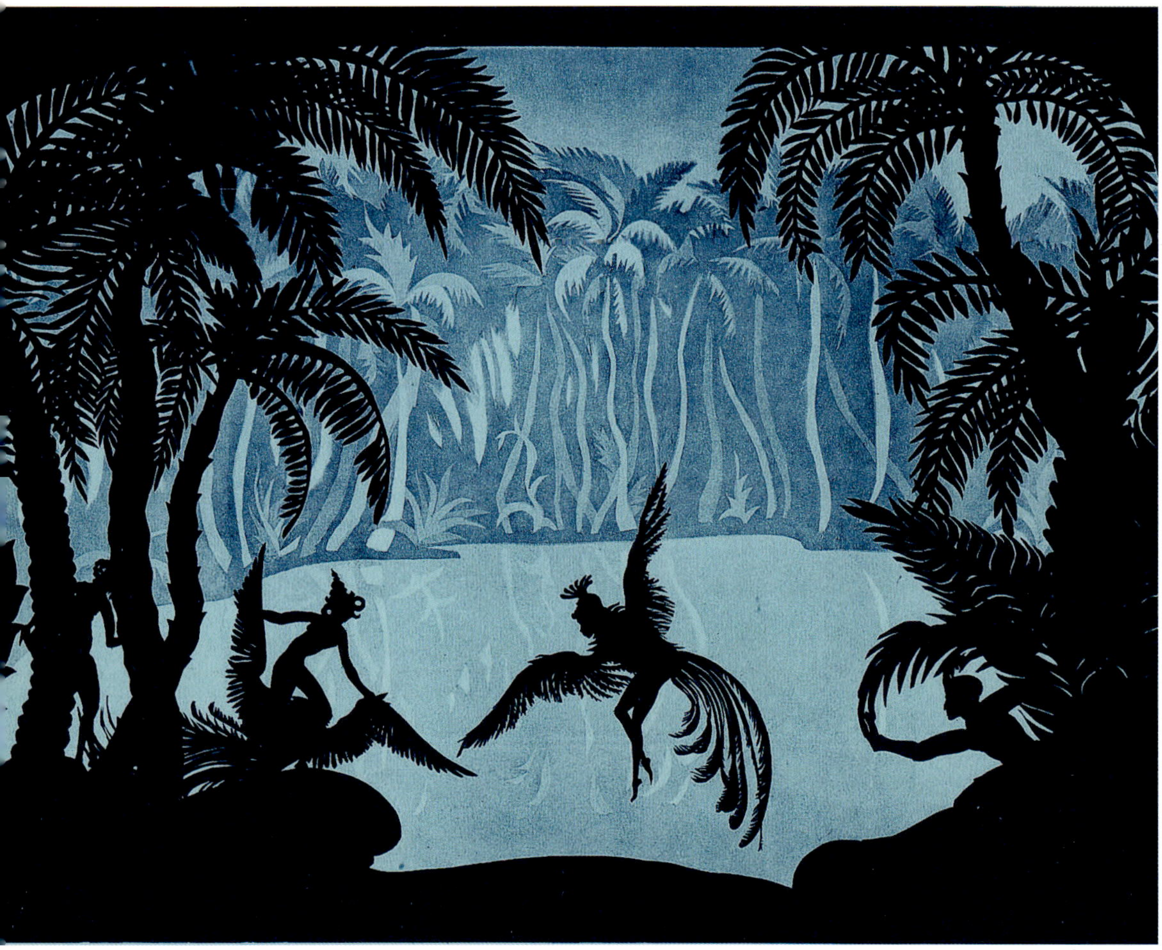

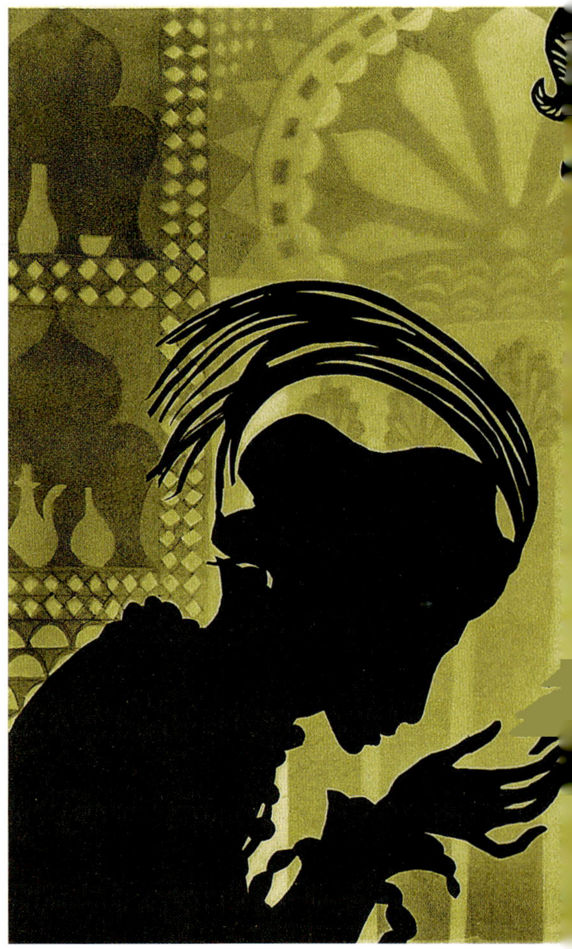

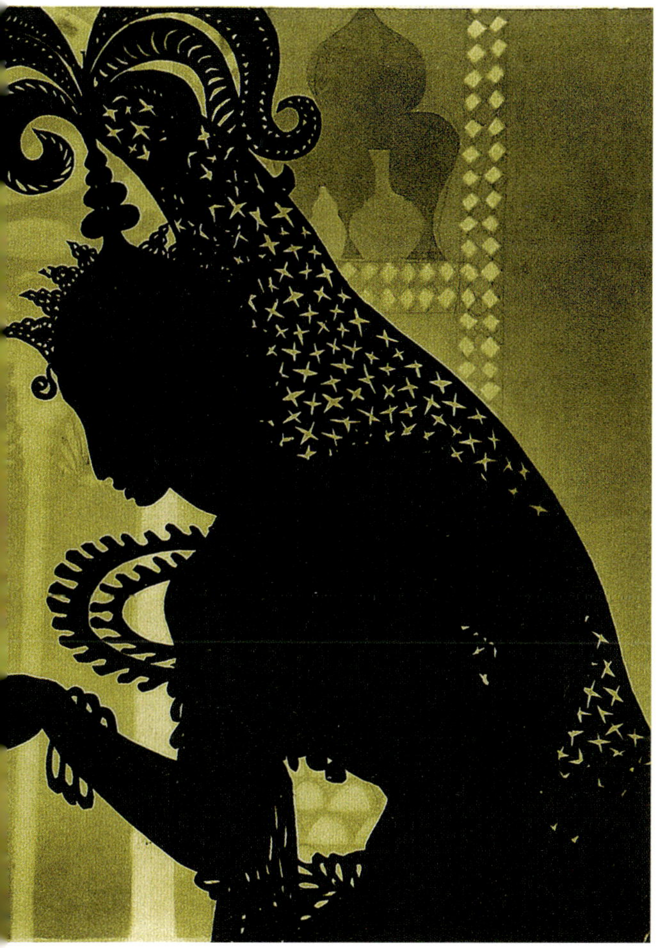

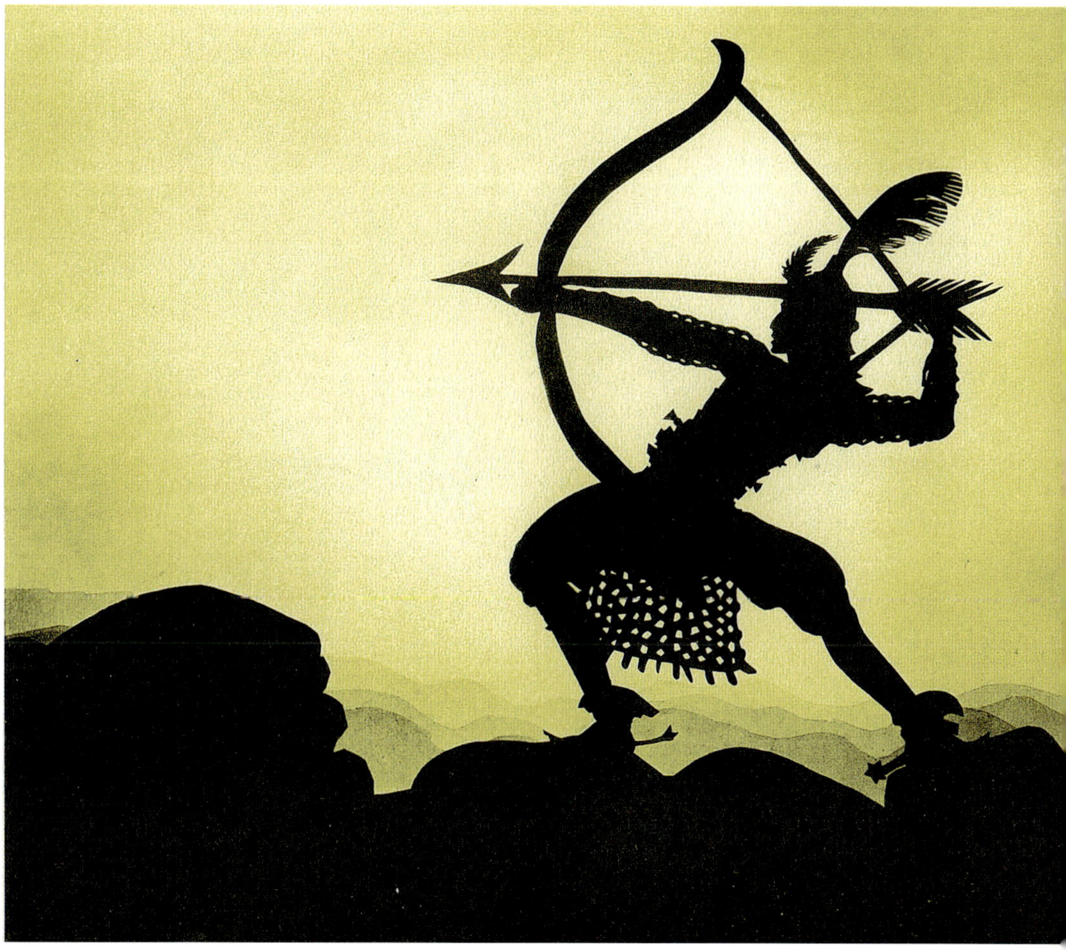

the dissolve

DZIGA **VERTOV**

1896–1954, LIVED AND WORKED IN THE SOVIET UNION

Soviet Toys, 1924

Soviet Toys is the only animated film by Dziga Vertov that survives in its entirety. Vertov used a combination of stop-motion animation techniques and employed a style reminiscent of Soviet political cartoons. *Soviet Toys* critiques the New Economic Policy (NEP) enacted in 1921, with the aim of bolstering the Soviet economy by allowing some private ventures. The figures symbolize different groups in Soviet society. For example, the NEP Man, portrayed as a glutton, represents those who disproportionately benefited from the NEP at the expense of the working class.

DZIGA VERTOV
Stills from *Soviet Toys*, 1924
35mm film transferred to DVD
Images courtesy of the Yale Film Studies Program

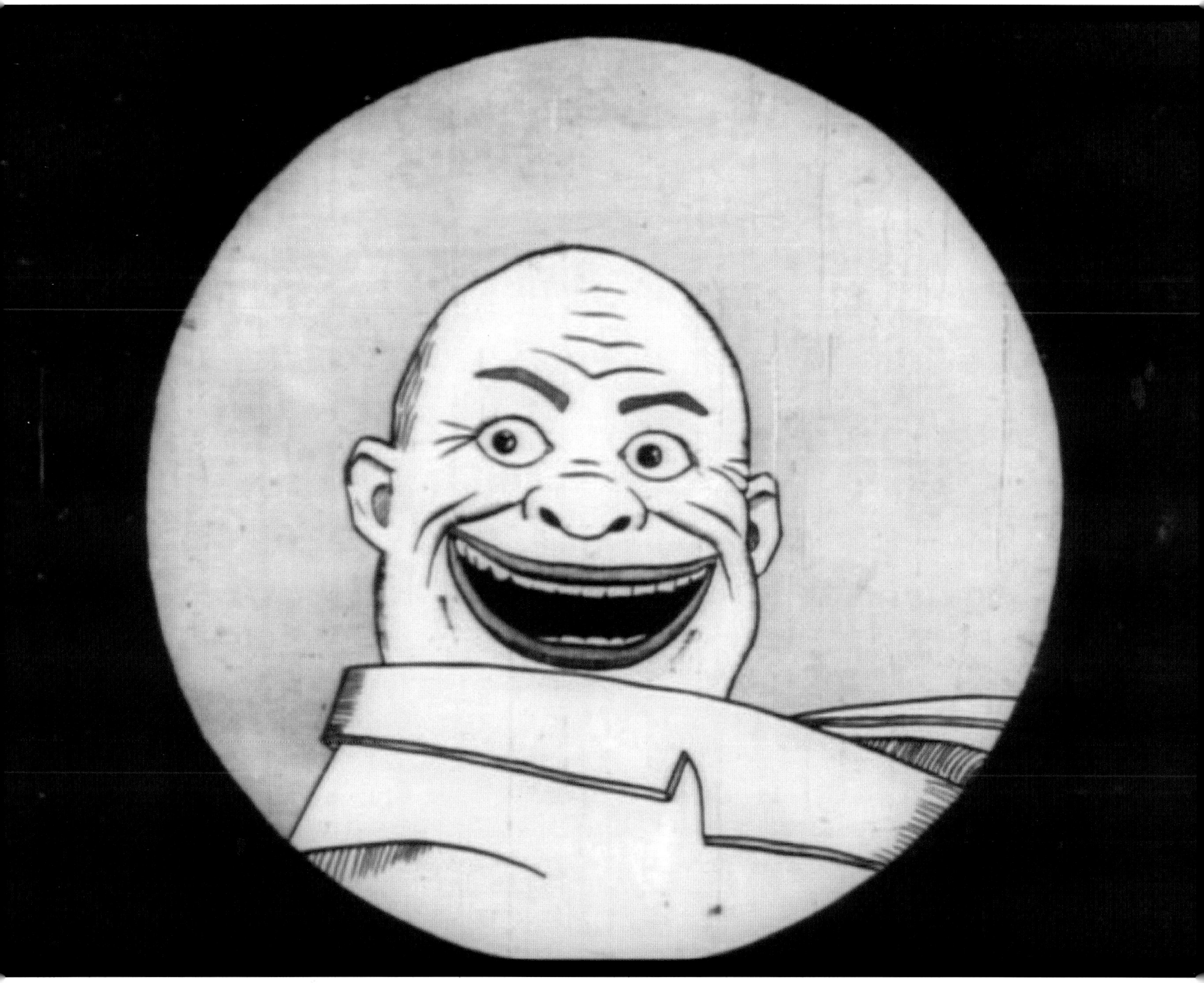

the dissolve

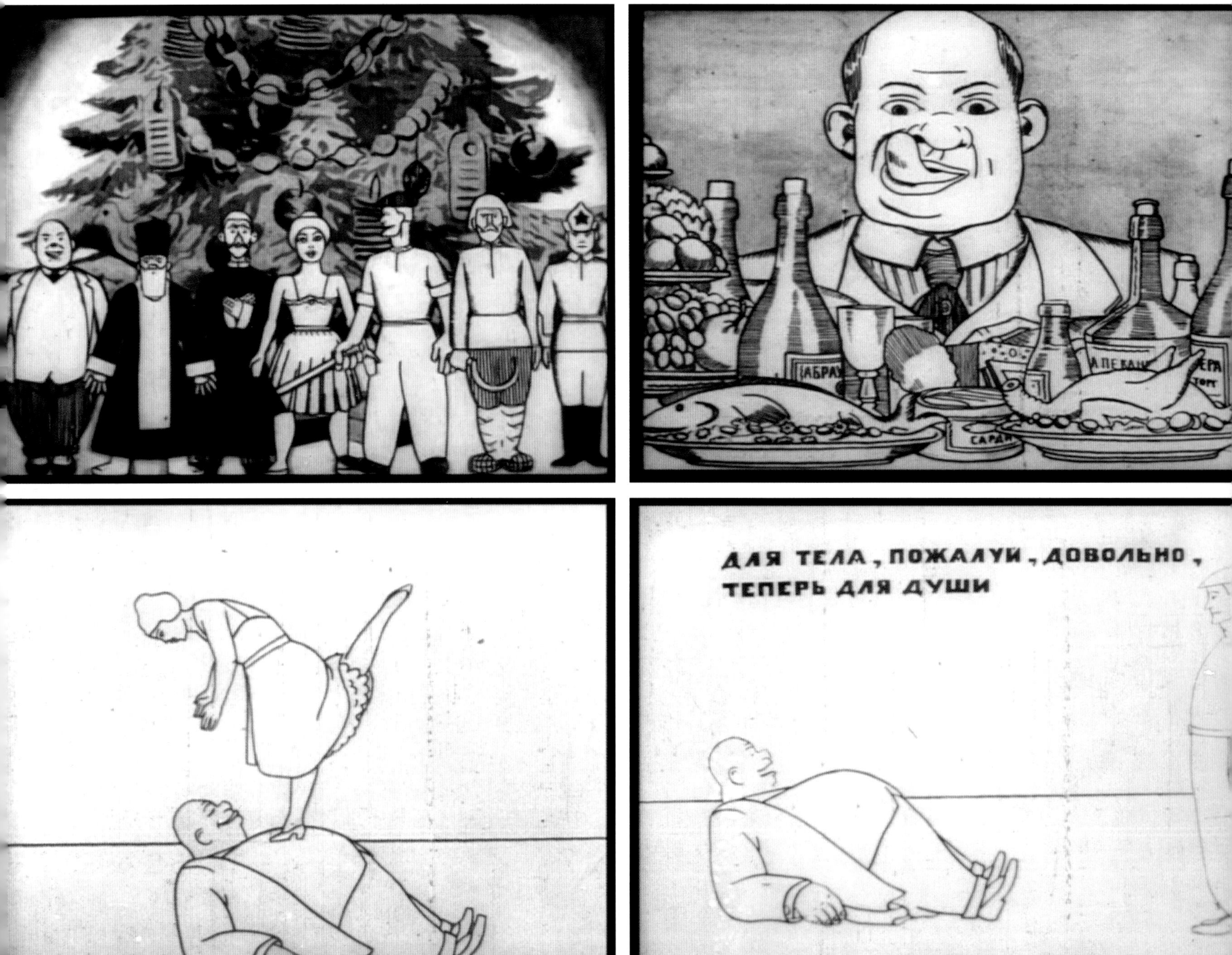

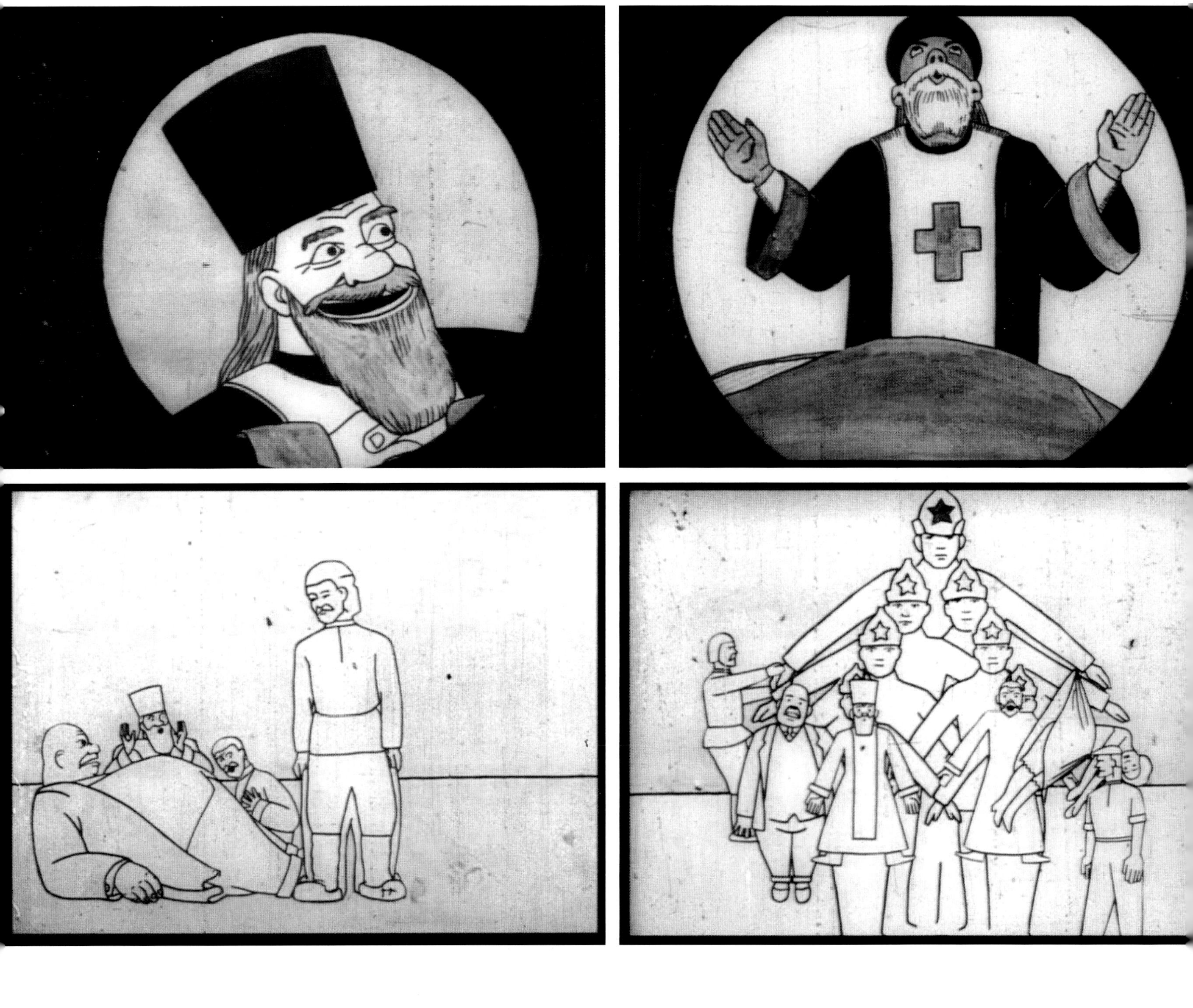

the dissolve

artists' roundtable discussion

BIENNIALS CAN CONVENE WORKS IN ELEGANT DIALOGUE in a given space, but often do not offer the opportunity for the collective of artists themselves to engage in direct conversation. On October 5, 2009, we created a forum for nine artists included in *The Dissolve,* SITE Santa Fe's Eighth International Biennial. Because of their availability and location, they are here to discuss the Biennial's pertinent questions and claims, conceived as they are from the artist's own working practices: why has animating diverse media become a signature development in contemporary art of the last decade? Why are artists fascinated with older animation techniques, even those that predate film itself?

The panel consisted of a group of established and emerging artists working in varied media: Martha Colburn, George Griffin, Ezra Johnson, Avish Khebrehzadeh, Jennifer and Kevin McCoy, Joshua Mosley, Christine Rebet, and Federico Solmi. The conversation, moderated by Daniel Belasco and Sarah Lewis, took place in Martha Colburn's studio in Long Island City, New York. Our sincere appreciation goes to Martha for hosting this discussion, and to everyone else for bringing their enthusiasm, curiosity, and hard questions.

DANIEL BELASCO: I find that people are often more interested in what artists have to say than what curators have to say. And so, with this roundtable we'd like to give our audience a direct insight into your individual practices and your work, as well as, ideally, glimpses of a shared commonality that overlaps, even contrasts, in interesting ways. We were inspired to do this by the New York School of Abstract Expressionists which organized "Artists' Sessions at Studio 35 (1950)." [1] The "Artists' Sessions" was a very open and honest opportunity for artists to talk, and that's what we're hoping to do here. As an icebreaker, let's go around and introduce ourselves. You could either say anything you want, or talk about the first animation work that you made. We'll start with my left and go around.

JOSHUA MOSLEY: I work in Philadelphia on projects that involve animation. So far, each has included a long period of time where I've done some drawings, and some research, and figured out what my primary question or curiosity was. Then I find some techniques that somehow relate, or function on another level, or give me the instinct that I am going in the right direction—and a lot of times it involves animation, and this has become the pattern. Over the years, more and more of the projects have included physical objects, which I've created, that integrate themselves into the work as a type of character or location. Those physical objects have been serving as Phase One of the process, because it's difficult for me to envision the final result at this stage—it's not like typical animation that's produced in a studio where the concept is completed before the animation starts. I like the process to be open until it's done, and Phase Two is figuring out how this world of objects will evolve and what the relationship between the elements will be.

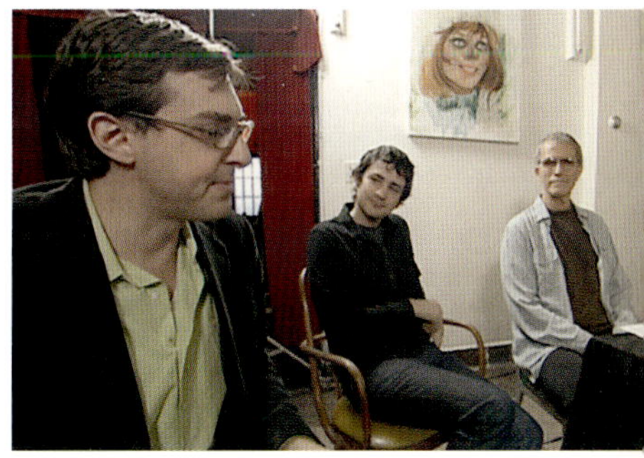

Daniel Belasco, Joshua Mosley, George Griffin

GEORGE GRIFFIN: I've been making animation since the late '60s. I came to New York after having a short life of drawing clandestinely. With animation, however, I discovered that the drawing could bloom on the front page. I learned at a cartoon studio, so probably I'm the most traditional of all of the animators here. I learned how to animate the human form, and I ran truant into an experimental zone making my own films while earning a living at it. "What is animation?" I argued with many of my friends back in the '70s, and we never really satisfactorily answered that question. I think the concept of Frankenstein is more like it—make something spring to life that wasn't alive before, and that still works for me. One of the things that I found through the years, and, actually, what I'm doing now—returning to earlier work and rethinking it—is that I'm using the computer to re-digest it. It's sort of a ruminative way of making art, which I find very satisfying. I use flip books in my work, so having the original drawings is kind of nice—I can rethink them.

MARTHA COLBURN: I've been working in film since '94. I'm self-taught and although I went to art school, it didn't really interest me. The critical aspect—I didn't understand. Basically, I am an Appalachian girl. So, I went to City Surplus where I found an old projector, a splicer, and old films and started cutting up the found-footage films. I found myself getting an education by going to the library where they had 60,000 film prints—you could take home Hans Richter and Len Lye and that's where I discovered Stan Vanderbeek and the Italian Structuralist filmmakers. And so, it began with this very physical, hands-on approach with film, and then I literally started filming in Super 8. I went on to make what I'm making now which is very complicated: multipaned glass and mirrors and other homemade special effects. I developed my own trip technologically. My idea of making progress is advancing something that was started in the teens or twenties that I feel was dropped and replaced by computers. There's a lot of experimentation in stop-action—in working with what you have in the room and a camera. And my work takes both political and personal directions.

CHRISTINE REBET: I started animation around 2003. I was in Berlin at the time. I had a theater background and was doing choreography. I got a grant from an East German filmmaker to try animation and the grant's requirement was that I had to work with a very traditional animator. I had worked with a studio in Berlin with DDR political animators and I did this type of animation with them where I would see very simple movement being animated. So, in the first fast animation I did, called *Soul Hunter*, I used my imagination to try and create narrative. And the more I practiced animation, the more I looked back to the "society of entertainment" taking place at the beginning of the twentieth century. I used a lot of sounds made in the studio such as recording the rustling of paper, the movement of the camera, the click of the camera—to create a mechanical narrative that is reminiscent of that time.

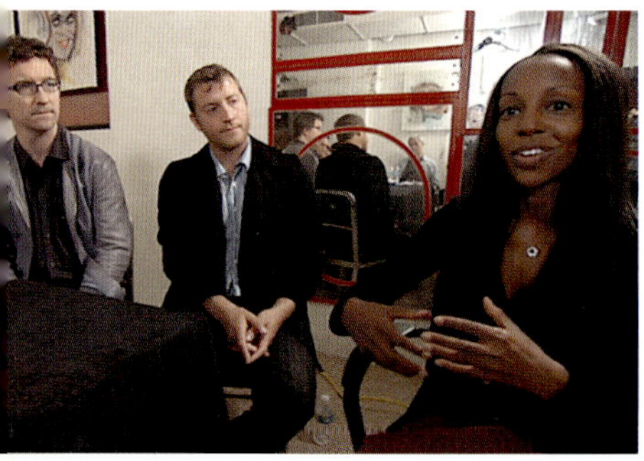

Kevin McCoy, Ezra Johnson, Sarah Lewis

FEDERICO SOLMI: I never planned to be a video animator. I was just interested in making drawings. However, I was very interested in making a narrative work of art because I was always interested in telling a story—no matter real or fictional—and little by little, I found that the best way of telling a story was by switching to animation. Five years ago, I started to go deep into this media and I combined drawing with 3-D animation. This was for me a turning point; I was introduced to this new world of unlimited possibilities through an expert in the digital animation field: Russell Lowe, an Australian university professor, who, today, is still my closest collaborator on all of my projects. Ever since, I've been stunned by this media and I keep experimenting.

AVISH KHEBREHZADEH: I also have a drawing background and my first experience with this medium was helping Nafiseh Rahi[2] make her animations: I was doing "in-betweens"[3] and I hated it—it was very difficult. And then when I progressed from there into the narrative aspect of animation, I liked it better. My first animation was called *Aleph*—my interpretation of a Borges story—and the point was that you can see everything in the world. So, from then on I started using animation as a tool for my narration.

JENNIFER McCOY: Kevin McCoy and I work as a team. We aren't essentially animators: we work with video and sculpture and we have projects that interrogate the filmmaking process—that kind of divide it up. Some of it is about the casting process—like recent work—and some of it is about the set design. We've always been interested in unusual tools so there's a kind of technological underpinning to a lot of our work. And I think in terms of animation, it comes out as animatronics—the idea of having something live in the room, like a performative object, is important to the work. For this exhibition, the work that's on view will be a project that is a restaging of a cinematic moment in our life.

KEVIN McCOY: I studied philosophy in school and I didn't have the drawing background that is one avenue into animation, but for me the artistic awakening was this experimental film that was an integration of artists dealing with sounds and visuals in this open-ended experimental holistic way—something that I found exciting and still do. And so all of our work has this wide focus of orientation to it. With filmmaking, collaboration isn't as unusual as it is in a more fine-art oriented mode of working. And one concept I think is applicable to this idea of animation has been some live or real-time aspect to our work. With many of our pieces, we are both concerned with their making as well as with paying attention to what is happening in the space, and having all aspects of the production of the images happen live in front of the viewer so that it becomes a re-animation—you know, re-animating things that would otherwise be static and have the whole experience be about what the art/object is.

EZRA JOHNSON: My first animation came directly out of my paintings, motivated by a state of frustration with painting. I was looking for a way to push the medium, expand on it, and I started experimenting with animation. One thing led to another, and I was amazed by the process and this whole bigger thing started to form and I couldn't stop.

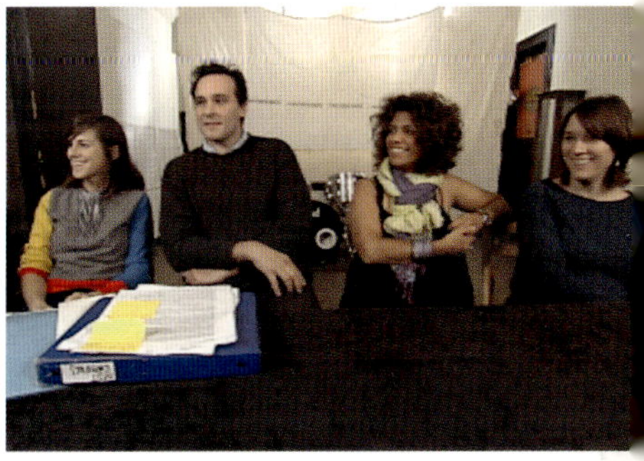

Christine Rebet, Federico Solmi, Avish Khebrehzadeh, Jennifer McCoy

MC: Your first film?

EJ: My first film was called *What Visions Burn* and it's a twenty-two minute animation about these art heisters stealing paintings. There's a convoluted narrative that goes back in on itself because the whole thing is painted—it's a moving painting—and ironically they are "moving" paintings.The piece has this *film noir* inspiration behind it. Since then, I've explored animating three-dimensional objects, and more abstract things.

DB: Okay, that's everyone. Now let's continue this as more of an informal conversation. Does anyone have any questions or comments for each other?

JM: Maybe one thing that is consistent, or similar, in the ways we all work is that the work remains open enough in its final state so that it reveals the activity of its creation—how you made the thing itself—there's no closed package. Animation might be—not that it's important to resolve this or come up with a definite answer—a pointing back to an activity like painting, such as when you look at painting, you can see the top layer of brushstrokes, and the middle and bottom strokes. Some animation work is like that—where you see the process unfold.

MC: Unfold in two minutes when it took you like eight months! It's time-based, maybe that's somewhere to start.

GG: It's synthetic time. It's constructed. It's not something that exists outside of that. But this whole notion of process involves a push-back toward narrative and a very personal approach as opposed to the dry analytic self-referential, or the process-oriented stuff. When I started doing self-referential animation in the early '70s, I thought, oh my god, this is great! But then I realized that this had already been around—the earliest animators did the same thing: the quick-sketch artists. They would exclaim: "Here's my drawing and I'm making it move!" This has always been in the DNA of animation, and I think that points to the essential use of technology—that there has always been a machine that makes it go. And this has also been our burden, our handicap, because the art world has historically denied fine art status to animation. That's now changed, but early in his career, a prominent critic told Robert Breer, "If it moves, it's not for us."

FS: Immediately, I see one thing that is common for all of us. Going back in time for me is going back to a labor-oriented practice. In fact, I think no matter how different we all are, what we have in common is that we can spend a month or years to make an art piece. And this, I believe, is something we all acknowledge. I, myself, spent two years to make a four-minute animation comprised of 1,200 paintings working with different helpers. I think this exhibition is important because it shows the labor behind our practice.

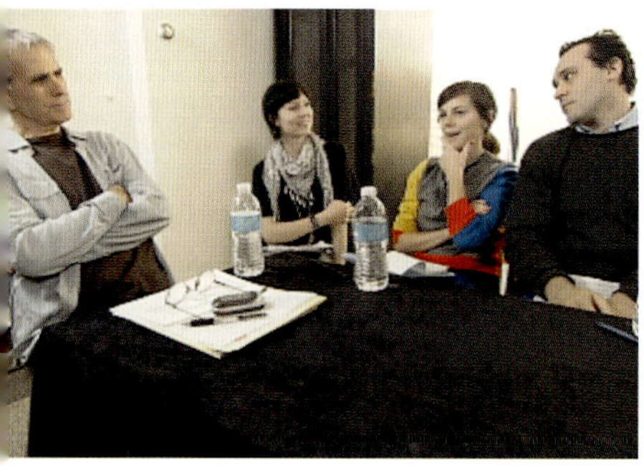

George Griffin, Martha Colburn, Christine Rebet, Federico Solmi

AK: For me, the moving image comes from the narration. When I have an idea I always think a minute before it, a minute ahead, and of how it existed a ways back. I have even thought of the painting by Piero della Francesca *The Baptism of Christ*, and of his characterization of Christ in the act of taking off his shirt as very magical. Even at that time, the artist was trying to suggest movement in that painting.[4]

KMcC: For me, the idea of time is just a part of how I think about any kind of media—photography, or music, or an image put with a sound—there has always been a time component, either with the viewer or in the succession of images. I never had an interest in an art that wasn't solidly time-based in some way.

JMcC: I have to agree with the idea of something that transforms a room or a space. What is this thing going to do in a space? The collage of time can happen in a film or any time-based work where the viewer is there, each with his/her own experience of time. This is especially relevant with projects like Carl Dreyer's film *The Passion of Joan of Arc*, a long silent film. What's happening on the screen, and then, what's happening in your chair? What's happening in your mind? What's happening in the space? All of those things coming together makes an interesting space for a viewer to be in. It's hard to imagine having everything happen with just one shot.

DB: I think the tension between craftsmanship and spontaneity is interesting. And also, narrative being the rubric that ties together craftsmanship and spontaneity. That's not really a question, more of an observation. Is it something that anyone wants to respond to?

MC: I like what Daniel said about a window through craft and through the process into some sort of space of the maker.

CR: I use a lot of my accidents as the narrative. It creates a tension between what you're drawing and the timing. Often the timing is wrong, and so I always end up being as spontaneous as I can be within a calculated frame.

FS: The great thing about animation is that no matter what great plan you may have, you're always getting into something that is going to develop into something different—something you know will take a lot of unexpected turns that probably wouldn't happen in a painting. Technology, especially in the last fifteen years, with all of these new digital sources, has really opened up opportunities for trying new techniques. I feel fortunate to live in such a period where you can combine traditional craftsmanship and new technology.

GG: I don't see the distinction between spontaneity and craft. Maybe it's formula and craft. Charlie Parker had great craft but he was also spontaneous. It's a balancing act. But you've got to combine the two, or else it can become formulaic craft.

KMoC: For me, going back to the narrative thing, it's almost like the formula is what interests me about narrative. I like the genre consideration, thinking about things as a weird little distillation of some situation down to this A plus B equation, kind of boy meets girl thing. There are all of these formulas out there that you can pick and choose from and recombine different kinds of operations visually through software. I like these endless recombinations and short-hand forms of signifying these different ideas. For example, the reduction of those weird little Facebook profile pictures into your Twitter captions. All of those seemingly stupid little gestures and images evocative over time or through accumulation suddenly become really interesting.

MC: It's like bricks in a building, or words in a poem, or notes in music.

GG: Formulas within formulas, it's fun. Narrative formulas—doesn't it add up to parody of parody? So much of what you see on television is interesting because it is parodying television. That's sort of one dead end. I like the myth of something unique and new and spontaneous.

MC: Invention is still possible?

GG: We try.

AK: I'm just curious: Why do animation? Or why do other artists do animation? For me the narration part is very interesting. I wonder if, for everyone else, it is the narration aspect or if there is some other reason artists choose this medium?

FS: I jumped into animation because I wanted to make something narrative. And I also want to make possible a visual language for people who are not involved in art—a visual language that is universally understood.

CR: I do a narrative constructed by orchestration because again I think animation is pushed by music. It's about visualizing the rhythm as it is heard or how it was written. And I like to think of narrative as a timing that keeps extending to another screen or another place. And within the orchestration you are still very free—a word can be expressed, an idea can be expressed, and it's a wonderful exploding framework going back to a linear form.

JM: I think narrative is inescapable—it's the way that people perceive whatever you make, even if you're trying to work outside of it. I think that it's probably something that's more biological and it's good to be aware of it as you're making things. You would have to concentrate a lot to make something that was not narrative or to set up a certain kind of situation where the viewer wouldn't perceive it as such.

AK: I don't think an animated work needs to have a beginning and an ending. I think it can be just be about an idea.

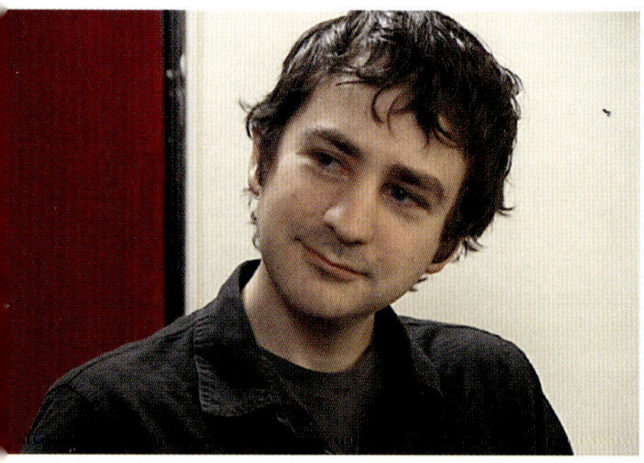

Joshua Mosley

JM: But it always projects into the future...

AK: Whenever you remember a work, your imagination inevitably projects the time after the sequence; or the time before it; or the context that it was made in. And what's left for the viewer to imagine is whatever they would like to envision as the end, or what came before or after. That is what I like about this art form.

DB: Taking the part of the viewer, what interests me about this idea of animating is the visual richness within the frame of the work that has a sense of surprise and excitement, and also a sense of cultural specificity. Somehow, I feel that when things are animated, and you see the materials from which they're drawn—often with histories of their own—these works set themselves apart from traditional video art. Does anyone want to even remotely address issues dealing with culture and politics through these layers of time and narratives?

KMcC: One aspect that's come up with the work we're doing, especially with the projects that are being shown in this exhibition, are sculptural dioramas. They are filmed by miniature cameras and edited together on the fly. The construction of these dioramas, resembling types of doll houses or train sets, triggers all sorts of parallel histories that are implied by these objects. The dioramas themselves are made up of a combination of things that are found or bought from hobby stores or that are made in the studio. Often times, there are all kinds of points of entry as well as different roles and individual associations—different trajectories—that the viewer takes on or makes in relationship to the objects that are in front of them.

JMcC: One personal triumph we had was with this little plastic grim reaper, which was so cheesy. After about six years, he worked his way into a sculpture, and it was the perfect thing! He had been just sitting around, and you're like, "What am I going to do with a grim reaper if I'm doing autobiographical work?" And all of a sudden—one drug trip visualized later—how to use him became clear.

KMcC: Silhouetted against a harvest moon.

CR: I think that the process of drawing so much, repeating small movements in between the frames, twists the brain in a way—it eliminates something in the back of your mind/head. I feel that sometimes in the process of working you almost have an antenna inside your head that simultaneously transmits and receives different themes, and extends a personal narrative into a more collective consciousness.

AK: My work is not about politics—there is nothing in it about politics. Because where I'm coming from, our life and family is consumed with politics and what is happening back home. By this, I mean I want an escape and I don't want to take advantage of what is happening there. So, I think I'd rather talk about the human condition than politics.

GG: I think that the structuralist and conceptual animation that I did, and others did in the '60s and '70s, was a kind of reaction to politics. People didn't want to deal with politics directly so they went into game theory or sets and structures. That was rewarding to me, but then it became a dead end because it didn't really lead to an emotional kind of response or connection to the art—and that's what I really think is important for me right now. How can you dredge up feelings in your work and also make it honest? It's hard to do.

AK: I don't understand. So you're saying you can only do it through politics in your artwork?

GG: I was talking about a historical thing that I was involved with—very structural and minimalist animation for a while in the '70s, and it really just petered out, it was a dead end for me because it didn't offer this emotional connection with the art.

MC: Well, animation is mathematical, it's almost scientific. Isn't it?

GG: Well, what I was doing was. But now I think that anger is a very important subject for me and I'm dealing with it in my projects. It works for me! But you know why one animates? It's a calling and, it's temperamental too.

AK: It's very meditative.

CR: Yes, meditative.

GG: [to AK] You talked about the "in-between" drawings you did as a young person—I think that it's a very mechanical thing but it's also meditative.

AK: Well, it was a long time ago and I was very young and I had to go to an office and I didn't want to do that—the story wasn't mine, so I had to do whatever they told me to do and it wasn't creative because they wanted a certain movement done in a certain way. That was difficult.

the dissolve

GG: The idea of an "in-between" is very interesting: you're in between two slices of time. You ask yourself: "Where will I go?" "Am I in limbo?" and "How will I make this frame be like that, or this, or a third frame?"

CR: I think it goes back to the idea of "the dissolve," which I think of as the "in-between."

DB: And its potentiality to think about this idea of animating as a metaphor, really, for contemporary art practice in general. Maybe that's where ultimately Sarah and I are interested in pushing this conversation and the Biennial: Proposing that animation is not a genre or a subset of filmmaking or a subset of anything, but in fact all art forms are moving into animation. With digital media, everything can be manipulated—every pixel can be deleted, recolored, enlarged. In terms of drawing, I think people are not even content to draw—they draw and then they scan; they do something and then they print it out again. And that's still drawing... And so these multiple practices and multiple procedures are often done for an artwork that is inert. Contemporary artists feel like they have to work hard. A number of people have mentioned the idea of labor, and the idea of craft, however we happen to define it. There's an urge to not have idle hands, but to keep doing things, so maybe that's the animating element that potentially can bridge a lot of your practices.

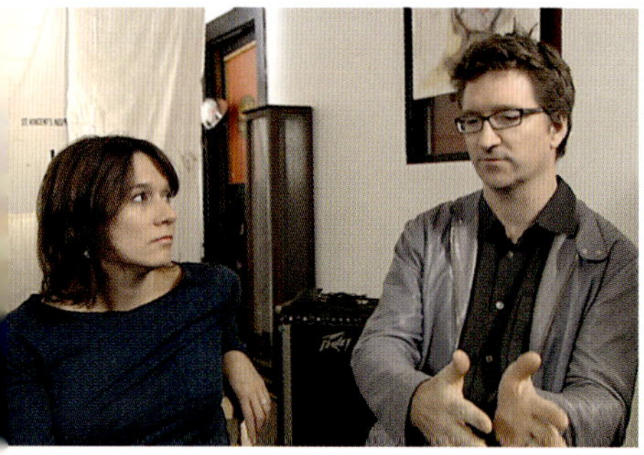

Jennifer and Kevin McCoy

FS: I think that in my case animation became an obsession, because when you basically have to deal with tons of drawings you really realize, once you've started, you're dealing with something you can't control—at least with my method. I think that probably some of us must have an obsessive personality because we tried to push a media that once wasn't of interest to the galleries. And so I feel very lucky to be here.

EJ: In contrast to painting which is often obsessed with the idea of one object—a perfectly finished object of sorts—animation adds an honesty through its sequences of images and sometimes awkward parts. And when taken as a whole, it creates an energy that is not about that individual perfect object, but about the process.

MC: I try not to think about the process. I don't want to be considered an animator. I feel like I want to make things that are more like songs, or an experience, or a political statement. Forget about talking about how much work it is, how much time it took, or how it's done. If I could, I would work with just a solar camera with no electricity, with just a table and my ideas, and make it more like a poem. And I want people to feel that weightlessness, like an easing into something that seems so difficult. That's the big challenge—to let all of that meticulousness just fall away, to let it become a vision, an idea, or something that people don't stumble over.

DB: Are there any historical antecedents that you would want to talk about, because we will be showing a couple of very early animations in the Biennial? In these older works, the process is very legible and there's a self-consciousness about what's real and what's constructed. Early animations have this materiality to them and an open process and they generate a sense of wonder. When some of you started animating, were you inspired by other artists in particular whom you would like to mention, whether you knew them from your immediate surroundings or whether they came from centuries before?

AK: I think my drawings come from the pre-Renaissance artists, whom I really like, because of their simplicity.

MC: Well, cave paintings could be seen as the first animation. Any Animation 101 book is going to tell you to look at cave paintings.

AK: Well, in the pre-Renaissance artists' work, emotions are expressed with simple lines—that's very valuable for me.

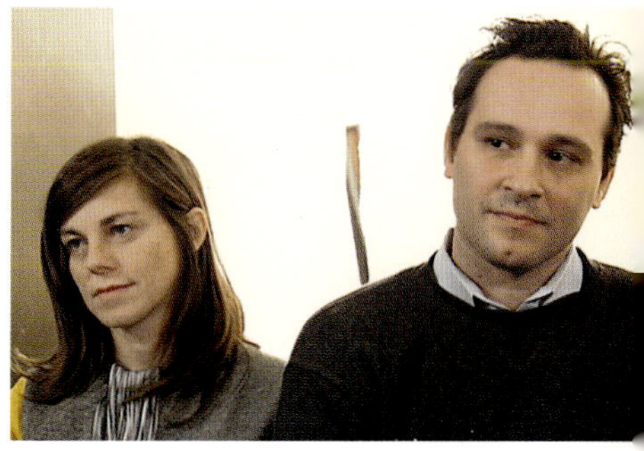

Christine Rebet and Federico Solmi

KMcC: I've been thinking about what you've been saying about cave painting and also about technique falling away. A couple of summers ago we were down in the south of France in Dordogne and I went to visit Lascaux, and its replica Lascaux II. It's a reconstruction—a theatrical remake—in an old mine quarry that they roofed over in the '60s and meticulously recreated from scratch. You can't go in the real cave anymore because of the contamination from people breathing, and it's sealed air tight and you can only go in if you're a researcher or scholar with some sort of underwater-like suit. You go to Lascaux II, which is the tourist thing, a Disney-like world. But then you walk in and it's so amazing, it's so compelling and you're in this space, in this world, and you're looking at this 25,000 year old painting that was re-created in the 1960s—and you're like wow! I have this whole new understanding of cave painting because of visiting this remake. And you don't even think about the fact that you didn't see the actual soot and berries that were there. It was an amazing experience.

CR: This summer I went to the pyramids and I had a very similar experience. There are many drawings—depictions of the afterlife. I found a very strange guide who showed me only scenes that I wouldn't have expected—like orgies. It was amazing, just to see that everything that was drawn was imagined, and erotic, and very fascinating.

KMcC: As I was saying earlier about re-animation: the Lascaux II replication has re-animated the idea of Lascaux itself. Or these ancient things, made new, that by some way come back to life for you.

DB: Any questions about emotion? And when you've been talking about emotion today, are you talking about your personal emotion, or are you talking about a more generalized emotion, one that the viewer might have?

AK: I think it's common.

MC: I portray some pretty heavy emotions, a lot of death and a lot of violence in some of my recent films, and they're politically motivated too. I made a film called *Triumph for the Wild.* It's five hundred years of war in ten minutes. But I think people should see it and be alert to the fact that there's a great deal of pain, be sensitized to it, think about it on a deeper level somehow.

FS: I think that at least for me there is always a hidden message, a personal one that I decided at one point to share with the viewer. Sometimes you can leave some open questions but...

AK: I don't offer any message, but I like to leave it open because I don't think I can give you a message.

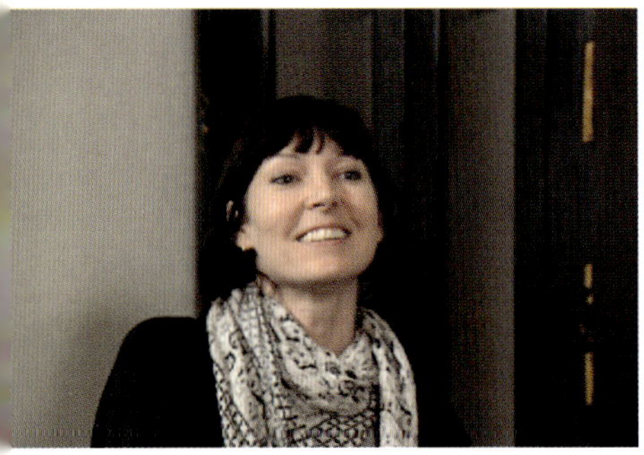

Martha Colburn

FS: You mean make a statement?

MC: I like to pose things that people can put together, so it's up to them really. It's not a message—it's an idea. And you grapple with: What does it mean to me?

CR: It's a treat, like a little piece of candy that you eat.

MC: But, it's not easily digestible. Animation can contain many layers of meaning.

GG: Going back to historical antecedents, one of the people I admire is Saul Steinberg and the other is Robert Breer, the animator who made me exclaim: "Yes, this is the spirit of liveliness and of experimentation that I want to do, I don't want to do traditional cartoons." Another painter who is a cartoonist in a way is Philip Guston—and talk about dealing with the underbelly of American life, and doing it insightfully with just very simple objects, but with a cartoonish quality.

KMcC: As a kid, I looked at Raymond Pettibon's drawings on Black Flag album covers and listened to "Slipping In" and "My War" over and over again and stared at these drawings—that integration of what's depicted, the way it's depicted, the attitude in which it's depicted, and the soundtrack of these intense albums was one really singular integrated moment.

CR: Theater is a good place where I like to observe movement under light as well as narrative.

DB: It's interesting you mention Robert Breer because at the time he was making cartoons, he was also making kinetic sculptures. And so, obviously Jennifer and Kevin's art is kinetic at heart and Ezra has been moving in that direction recently. I'm wondering if anyone else has found that the flip book maybe even has a sculptural quality itself?

FS: I have been actually in the studio working on a mechanical sculpture for about three years. The crazy thing is that it comes right out of a scene from one of my first video animations. I'm obsessed with movement and the idea of an exhibition that combines animation and drawings and mechanical sculpture has been a dream of mine.

CR: I go back to animation because of its performative elements.

GG: Do any of you do live performance with the animation?

MC: I do. It's my favorite thing.

JM: Are you animating during performance? Or projecting?

MC: No, my animation is performed with musicians. I use hand-filters and multi-projections. I'm not dancing, but they still call it a performance. So whether it's shooting, or dying, or dancing—you get to participate vicariously in some way, which is a thrill.

KMcC: In the mid '90s to '99, we did tons of live video performance, now you'd call it VJ stuff, but it didn't really have a name back then—it was just live video mixing with musicians that fed a lot into a live real-time way of working, which is absolutely the backbone for the sculpture work we're doing now. But even then it was about cobbling together programming—live video, mixing tools, using animation and flip-book logic, layering loops and colorizing them on the computer. It was all live improvisational performance.

SARAH LEWIS: So, this show is not an animation show; that's not an accurate descriptor for what you all are up to with your varied and pioneering practices; yet your practices are still caught up with this idea of animating as in offering movement... And as you are nodding over there, I'm interested in hearing you articulate what is behind those nods, how does that operate for your work?

AK: Well, when you refer to animation, do you mean only drawings? Because I think animation can also refer to animating many other things.

EJ: It's an impure process. I do not know whether to submit my applications under painting or video categories, and that's sort of attractive I think.

SL: Great. Can you tell me more? How is that attractive for you?

EJ: It is because you break out of the parameters of how a medium has been defined—in my case, it's the filming of my paintings and following this tactile process. Other ways of reading things come up that I couldn't have had before. I'm interested in impure areas—it's something that comes out of a desire not to make pure formalist art.

AK: I think that at some point you want to mix materials as one can get tired of only painting or only drawing. I was doing animation separately, drawing separately, and painting separately until I started projecting animation on top of my drawings.

JMcC: There's a great Marshall McLuhan quote that says, "I don't know who discovered water but it wasn't a fish." I'm pretty sure that's why we ended up in visual art more than in filmmaking or screenings per se, because it just seemed like you had to interrogate film from a neutral standpoint, although in the visual art world, nobody thinks of us as visual artists. It's from this "in-betweenness" that we find a good place to stand to look at these other forms. The content and the narrative is there, invigorating everything, and completely embedded in it, but the shifting of the form and throwing away one format for another art form has been a very open strategy.

FS: The word animation is not really defined so that allows you to play with everything, to discover territory, especially with new digital technology and, probably, this is what attracted me to the medium.

KMcC: It's a new genre.

MC: Its limitations turn themselves into my inventions. You have to make do with what you have and make something really spectacular out of something simple.

GG: I'm concerned with people who want to expand the word animation to include everything because I think you then lose its essential meaning. I consider myself an animator first and it's okay, but I think the idea of "image eating" is a wonderful thing that animation can do.

KMcC. It's definitely true that animation, even in the most traditional sense of just images drawn on paper, provides a density of information that creates all of these incredible transformations that can happen in ten seconds. You see that in *South Park* where these weird, quippy little references condense so much of culture into this little package that's right there in front of you. I really like that about animation.

GG: Animation used to consist of frame-by-frame applications—if it wasn't made that way, then it wasn't animation. But I think the frame has given way to some other mode of thinking about time-based media so I'm not sure if it has validity anymore.

MC: Well I do stop-action, so it does to me.

GG: To you, yes, and film.

MC: But some people work with the computer and video, and it's totally different.

GG: But with the computer, earlier methods of animation seem to be losing their distinction: the idea of the single frame as a slice of time.

MC: I have wondered why I was so attracted to rectangular shapes or configurations like horse stables and the drills in the square, or even insects wedged into square cases. There is something about the frame, you have to be interested in blocking life into a frame, be it square or round.

SL: Well, on that topic of the importance of fashioning a viewing environment that harkens back to historical ones, how important is the viewing environment to you?

GG: Well, I just made a digital mutoscope with the computer. I think the revolution is in production, but I think about presentation and of course delivery and distribution. A film I did over thirty years ago had a little figure in it who was cranking a little mutoscope and I said to myself, "Well this is a perfect set of entropy or metaphor for self-reflection." The mutoscope that I built is based on a computer but it does let the viewer stop and control the flow of illusion which is something I've always wanted to do but wasn't able to until figuring this out, this toy. It presents itself as a sculpture and in a way, it is a kind of apparatus, and allowing the viewer to control it is something rather exciting.

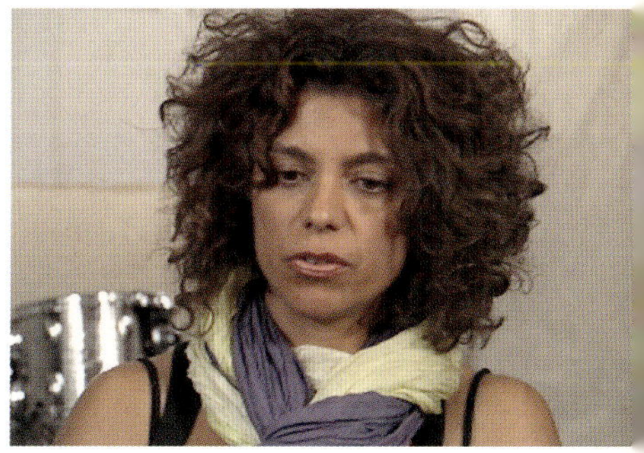

Avish Khebrehzadeh

DB: I am wondering about the space of viewing and the difference between showing your work in a film festival format versus a gallery, if any of your work can even be shown at a film festival, or a three-dimensional environment, or can it only be shown in a gallery, and how that becomes factored into your work?

AK: I think there are some works that you cannot show in festivals, works that have to be viewed more than one time. I do not think many festivals offer experimental videos.

SL: Just for the record, what is gained in the multiple viewing for you?

AK: I think because it generates more perceptions and layered meanings, I want the viewer to imagine things and I think with just one viewing you can't grasp what is happening.

SL: Absolutely.

MC: I like how democratic film is, working in moving-image media. I lived in a Baltimore ghetto for ten years. It was a dangerous area. There was no contemporary museum, but there is no limit to what you can see on film and what you can see on video, and now with computers, it's very expansive and extensive.

CR: I think that multiple viewing spaces is like multiplied time—how you can be in different spaces at the same time. It's a wonderful addition to your narrative if you have this possibility. And the differences between an installation and showing it in the cinema offer you different audiences.

JM: The kind of response you get with a big group is so different than what you get in an art venue, especially when it's shown in a different country and there are language translations. But then there's not that much critical writing associated with festivals. There's not as much of a critical response though they have sessions that are like a discussion after the screening where all of the filmmakers who have showed up are there, and that's a great experience. So I think it's kind of nice to be on the edge of the two worlds and to see what the reactions are to the same piece. I also know that when I'm constructing an installation with a loop, I don't have to make it resolve quite the same way it would have to resolve in a linear piece that would show once.

AK: I think also in festivals, it's impossible to have an installation.

CR: Entertainment as in cinema is flat. By contrast, in the gallery as the viewer you contour the story, you keep re-experiencing the story.

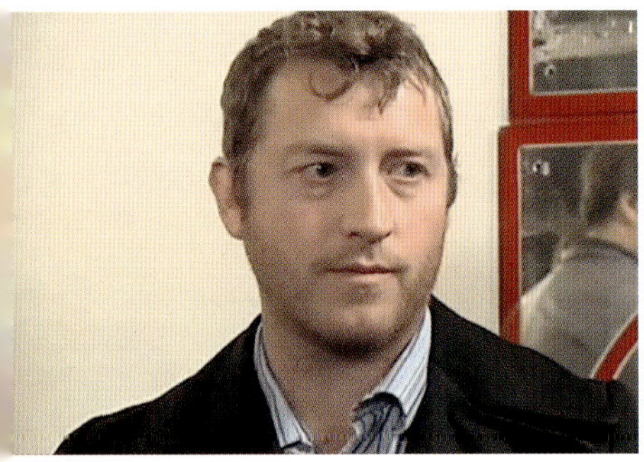

Ezra Johnson

GG: There's some festivals, one in particular called Platform in Portland. They have a whole section on installation that's rather interesting. I love private voyeuristic relationships between the viewer and the art object so the mutoscope can be seen by one person at a time and that's rather interesting for me. It's very intimate.

SL: I think this is a good opportunity to ask something that Daniel and I have been mulling over in terms of the exhibition design and it's the ironic arc of collective viewing processes. First, we started out with this personalized mode of viewing—from the hand-crank to the glorified cinematic experience where we all sit gazing. Now, we're back in many ways to this individualized one-on-one engagement with the computer. You know, I wonder if that fits into some of the desires some of you hold for individualized, personal viewing, for example, as in George's case.

EJ: The way the art world deals with time-based media is a bit frustrating—you walk in to see a forty-minute film or video, and most of the time, after two minutes, you go, "Okay, I kind of get the gist of this," and leave. But at my first ever film festival, it was amazing to have people sitting there from start to finish, hearing the audience shifting, laughing, or whatever. In that context, you get their undivided attention—so I think how to solve that problem within a gallery space is important.

KMcC: There's definitely a pressure on the work to modify or meet those needs. I personally found that working in the gallery context liberating in a certain sense—moving into this space that's much more undefined.

JMcC: Well, it's definitely a place where you can look and talk about the work at the same time, which in the cinema is obviously frowned upon. But that kind of intimacy in a gallery with a conversation going on in front of a piece is a great moment.

FS: I never had this feeling of frustration with the gallery setting because my animations are between one minute to four minutes. At the same time, they always fit in a film festival environment. Probably, the most frustrating experience is the art fair when you present a new video on which you spent a year or two and it's presented on a twenty-inch panel…

MC: Sundance has an installation section now. Its organizers see that they need to expand cinema. Maybe because of the art world, maybe because of the internet, but they see that they can't be a closed system anymore.

CR: Even the experience of time is maybe different. You know it's very different to see a film by an artist and a film by a filmmaker.

KMcC: Speaking of Sundance, we were there a couple of festivals ago. Sharon Lockhart was showing these films in their experimental section. We saw them in the movie theater and then a couple of months later, we saw them at the Barbara Gladstone Gallery in New York. In the movie theater it was so tied back to a tradition of experimental filmmaking from a kind of '70s structural filmmaking way, while in the gallery it was a really different kind of experience: having the viewer be mobile and doing the editing by walking from one screen to the other just seemed more contemporary, more vital.

DB: Another aspect of the moving-image art that Sarah and I have observed is the difference in training—people who are trained in filmmaking techniques versus those who are really self-taught. Animation is open enough that it can accept and allow for different trainings and experiences that people have. So a question would be, is there a difference, do you think, between those who have training in animation, who went to school for it, versus those who came to it on their own?

JM: Who's going to speak up for the academy?

FS: Personally, I never had any formal classes or training so...at the beginning it was very frustrating because I had to discover everything. I feel very lucky that I never had people telling me you have to do this and that—that freedom has shaped my vision.

AK: I think to get to it yourself you need to experiment but if you go to school you get a lot of knowledge which is good—but too much knowledge is intimidating.

MC: I think the artistic process is about so many other things, it's about reading history and reading philosophy and reading poetry and doing this and seeing that.

KMcC: And school is really good at packing all of that together. The upside about school is that density of information. I think film education, and film schools are pretty traditional, they've internalized the industry, segmented and compartmentalized it. The skills taught are a reflection of industrial ways of working with Photoshop and Illustrator, and Final Cut Pro—a studio editing model. Of course it's tweakable and can be personalized, but at the same time these modes of working that reflect industry practice constantly confront you, and may not be relevant to what you're doing, unless you're trying to be a designer or an editor.

MC: I work with a lot of people just out of school and they're really frustrated because no one would ever teach them any film technique.

GG: Joshua and I are on the curriculum committee at the University of the Arts so we went over this whole issue. Do we teach the technique or not? Where do we start? Where do we stop? Personally, I got a BA in Political Science and never took an art course myself, but I always drew.

JM: I basically agree with everyone, but I want to say something that's the opposite—that it's incredibly difficult to animate well in terms of making things, make the movement expressive in a particular way so that it's a component of the piece. When I show my animation to my former students who work in the industry, they can give me a pointed list of forty things that are wrong, and half of those are stylistic issues where they tell me to "Make the expression larger" or "Make the reaction stronger." Those are things they have learned from the nature of the industry. But the other half of the list is actually right-on, in terms of making the animation more naturalistic. But I'm concerned with a different kind of animation; I love animation made by artists. It's not that they capture that essence, it's that they're dealing with more complex issues or subject matter.

CR: A lot of the subjects I am dealing with are about failure. Because I'm not trained as an animator, and for me it's the perfect medium to fail in and to show the essence of humanity.

JM: I think a lot of artists are interested in that threshold of failure in the sense that it's an interesting approximation—"looking at the threshold of a frame rate." Whereas, my former students weren't interested in the threshold, they were interested in very strong key frames, very strong poses, and the best way to get to them.

CR: It's funny. Though it seems that although you use movement, it's not the excellence of movement and it's not the sublime, but more the abject. It's interesting that we all twist this, because you need to twist it.

KMcC: It seems like animation now is so driven by 3-D and photorealism and this sort of...

JMcC: Pixar style you mean.

KMcC: Uncritical verisimilitude and naturalism.

GG: That's a big danger I think. And I think that the problem with Pixar is, "Well, we're gonna reform Disney," and then Disney is part of their DNA. So, they just sort of perfected it. But I think the problem with that kind of animation, I hope I'm not offending anyone here, but it's too slick, it's too smooth, and there's a need for jerky angular movement.

AK: That's why it looks too mechanical or too industrial I think.

SL: Before we stop, can we address animated painting again?

JM: [To GG] One of the things that I was hoping would come up again was Guston. Can you expand on that?

SL: This is actually the point about painting I was interested in—if there were actually moments in which influences came from the realm of painting...

GG: It's just that Guston was cartooning. He amazed and depressed many people who thought he was an Abstract Expressionist when he went back to the figure and back to the hoods and the boots and the cigarettes. And for me he just came alive at that point. So I claim him as an inspiration.

DB: Well, thanks.

SL: This has been wonderful. Thank you.

[1] Transcribed and edited in Robert Motherwell and Ad Reinhardt, eds., *Modern Artists in America*, New York: Wittenborn Schultz, 1951.

[2] Nafiseh Rahi was a leading Iranian animator in the 1970s and '80s. She died in 1990.

[3] Animators call the most dramatic and decisive poses "extremes" or "key frames" and the drawings that link them are called "in-betweens."—Ed.

[4] Della Francesca was trying to suggest sequential movement in this painting by a small figure of Christ in the background taking off his shirt while a larger depiction of Christ, in the act of being baptized, appears in the foreground.—Ed

artists' biographies

ROBERT BREER

Avant-garde multimedia artist Robert Breer was born in 1926 in Detroit, Michigan. Breer studied painting at Stanford University and after moving to Paris in 1949, he began to explore hand-drawn animation. Using stop-motion techniques and 4 x 6 index cards as his signature medium, Breer pioneered the revived interest in experimental animation and attracted international acclaim. His work, which incorporates both geometric abstractions and mundane images from daily life, explores color, form, rhythm, and motion with sharp wit and humor. Breer's career includes solo exhibitions at the Centre Georges Pompidou, Musée d'art moderne national in Paris; The Museum of Modern Art, New York; and the Whitney Museum of American Art, New York. His work was included in the 2004/2005 Carnegie International, Pittsburgh. Breer lives and works in Tucson, Arizona.

PAUL CHAN

Paul Chan was born in Hong Kong in 1973 and grew up in Omaha, Nebraska. In 1996, he graduated from The School of the Art Institute of Chicago with a BFA in Video/Digital Arts and went on to receive an MFA in Film, Video, and New Media from Bard College in 2002. With his drawings, installations, and animations, Chan conjures fantasy realms rife with philosophical complexities. Chan is also a political activist, selectively integrating that passion with his artistic practice. His work has been presented in solo exhibitions at the New Museum in New York; the Institute of Contemporary Art, Boston; the Hammer Museum in Los Angeles; and the Stedelijk Museum in Amsterdam. Notable group exhibitions include the 2008 Torino Triennale, the 2007 Istanbul Biennial, and the 53rd Venice Biennale in 2009. Chan lives and works in New York.

MARTHA COLBURN

Martha Colburn was born in 1971 in Gettysburg, Pennsylvania and she lives and works in Amsterdam and New York. She studied art at the Maryland Institute College of Art and the Rijksakademie van Beeldende Kunsten in Amsterdam. Colburn began filmmaking in 1994 and since then has developed a dynamic aesthetic combining collage, puppetry, and paint-on-glass techniques in stop-action animations. In her pursuit to examine issues of history, politics, sexuality, consumerism, and popular culture, Colburn presents narratives propelled with frenetic urgency. Her work has been exhibited internationally at museums such as the Centre Pompidou in Paris; P.S.1 Contemporary Art Center in New York; and The Museum of Modern Art. Colburn participated in the 2006 Whitney Biennial in New York.

THOMAS DEMAND

Born in Munich in 1964, Thomas Demand lives and works in Berlin. Demand studied art the Staatliche Kunstakademie Düsseldorf and received an MFA from Goldsmiths College, London, in 1994. The artist is best known for photographs and films based on commonplace scenes often pulled from the mass media. Demand meticulously restages each scene in three dimensions using paper, cardboard, and cellophane. The result is recorded on camera, presenting an illusion of reality. Demand's work has been exhibited in solo shows at the Hamburger Kunsthalle, The Museum of Modern Art; SITE Santa Fe; and the Neue Nationalgalerie in Berlin. His work has also been included in group exhibitions at the Guggenheim Museum, New York; the Musée d'Art Moderne de la Ville de Paris; the Shanghai Art Museum; and The Museum of Contemporary Art, Los Angeles. Demand participated in the 50th Venice Biennale in 2003.

BRENT GREEN

Born in Baltimore, Maryland, in 1978, Brent Green is a self-taught filmmaker. The artist transforms autobiographical narratives into haunting animations that he narrates himself. Each story takes shape with an elaborate handmade set and puppets built by Green in his home. The animations often bear evidence of the process by which they were created with scotch tape marks, dust, and scratches visible throughout the films. Solo shows of Green's work have been mounted at SITE Santa Fe and the Sculpture Center in Cleveland, Ohio. His work has also been shown at the Hammer Museum; the Walker Art Center in Minneapolis; the J. Paul Getty Museum in Los Angeles; and the 2009 Sundance Film Festival. Green lives and works in Cressona, Pennsylvania.

GEORGE GRIFFIN

George Griffin was born in 1943 in Atlanta, Georgia. He studied political science as an undergraduate at Dartmouth where he created a cartoon strip for a university literary magazine. In 1968, Griffin began to pursue a full time career in animation. Studying the works of filmmakers Stan Brakhage and Robert Breer as his guiding influences, he developed experimental animation techniques that placed him at the forefront of the 1970s avant-garde movement. Griffin's irreverent and self-referential animations feature series of vignettes that combine drawing, film, and photography. Griffin's work has been shown at museums such as the Kunsthalle Düsseldorf and The Museum of Modern Art. His films have also been shown at international film festivals such as the Tribeca Film Festival, New York; the Cannes Film Festival; and the Strasbourg International Film Festival. Griffin lives and works in New York.

EZRA JOHNSON

Ezra Johnson was born in 1975 in Wenatchee, Washington. He received an MFA in painting from Hunter College, New York, in 2006 after earning a BFA in painting from the California College of Arts and Craft, San Francisco, in 2000. Johnson's animations are based on his practice as an oil painter; each frame in his films is taken from a canvas and collage elements that are continuously repainted as the narrative progresses. With heavy brushstrokes and lush colors, Johnson's work firmly roots itself in the realm of figurative painting. Johnson's work has been shown at the Hammer Museum; the 55th International Short Film Festival in Oberhausen, Germany; and numerous galleries in the U.S. and Italy. He lives and works in New York.

BILL T. JONES AND OPENENDED GROUP

Bill T. Jones was born in Bunnell, Florida, in 1952, and later moved to upstate New York. He began his dance training at the State University of New York at Binghamton, studying classical ballet and modern dance. In 1982, Jones formed the Bill T. Jones/Arnie Zane Dance Company with his long time partner, Arnie Zane. Throughout his prolific career, Jones has explored the integration of the visual arts and dance choreography. He collaborated with new media artists Shelley Eshkar and Paul Kaiser to produce *Ghostcatching*, which opened at the Cooper Union, New York, in 1999. In this virtual dance installation, Jones's movements were digitally captured and manipulated, poetically fusing dance and technology. The OpenEnded Group—Marc Downie, Eshkar, and Kaiser—created a new 3-D-version of *Ghostcatching* for *The Dissolve* Biennial. In 1994, Jones was a recipient of a MacArthur Fellowship. He and the members of OpenEnded Group live and work in New York.

WILLIAM KENTRIDGE

William Kentridge was born in 1955 in Johannesburg, South Africa, where he continues to live and work today. He graduated from the University of the Witwatersrand with a degree in politics and African studies and studied at the Johannesburg Art Foundation. Combining disciplines including film, drawing, puppetry, and theater, Kentridge uses his personal experiences of South Africa's turbulent history as a basis for his work. The artist examines the psychological impact from having witnessed political and racial turmoil and social conflict, speaking to events particular to his native country and to more universal experiences. Major solo exhibitions of Kentridge's work have been mounted at the San Francisco Museum of Modern Art; the Philadelphia Museum of Art; the Moderna Museet in Stockholm; The Metropolitan Museum of Art in New York; and the Museum of Modern Art in New York. His work has also been included in notable group exhibitions such as Prospect. 1 New Orleans in 2008; the Sydney Biennale in 1996 and 2008; Documenta X in 1997 and XI in 2002, Kassel, Germany; and the 1999/2000 Carnegie International.

AVISH KHEBREHZADEH

Born in Tehran, Iran in 1969, Avish Khebrehzadeh lives and works in Washington, D.C. and Rome. Khebrehzadeh studied photography at the Corcoran College of Art and philosophy at the University of the District of Columbia. Khebrehzadeh's animations, lightly drawn and sparingly painted, are compelling in their poetic ambiguity. Solo exhibitions of her work have appeared at the Museum of Contemporary Art, Rome, and the Rhode Island School of Design Museum in Providence. Khebrehzadeh was included in the 2008 Liverpool Biennial and was also a participant in the 50th Venice Biennale in 2003, where she received the Golden Lion Award for the best Young Italian Artist.

LALEH KHORRAMIAN

Laleh Khorramian was born in Tehran, Iran in 1974. She lives and works in New York. In 1997, Khorramian received a BFA from The School of the Art Institute of Chicago and went on to earn an MFA from Columbia University, New York, in 2004. Khorramian's animations resemble paintings that are experienced temporally. With each piece, a story unfolds in an elaborate fantasy realm that is at once as theatrical and cinematic as it is painterly. Khorramian's work has been exhibited internationally, including a solo exhibition at the Mills College Art Museum in Oakland, California, in 2007; the 2nd Moscow Biennial in 2007; and the group exhibition *Greater New York 2005* at P.S.1. Contemporary Art Center. Her short animation, *I Without End,* was screened at the Sundance Film Festival in 2010 in the New Frontier Shorts section. She is a recipient of a Pollock-Krasner Foundation Grant and the Agnes Martin Award.

MARIA LASSNIG

Maria Lassnig was born in Austria in 1919. She studied at the Academy for Applied Arts in Vienna and the New York School of Visual Arts. For over sixty years, Lassnig has produced remarkable works of painting, film, drawing, and sculpture. She has developed a singular voice by challenging conventions of portraiture with profoundly introspective work. Through both abstract and figurative methods, Lassnig creates visual manifestations of complex emotion and physical sensation. In film, the artist expands her interest in self-representation with poignant and humorous narratives drawn from her life experiences. Solo exhibitions of Lassnig's work have been shown at the Kunstmuseum Düsseldorf; the Stedelijk Museum; the Centre Pompidou in Paris; and the Kunsthaus in Zurich. Lassnig also participated in the 39th Venice Biennale in 1980; Documenta VII in 1982; and Documenta X in 1997. She lives and works in Vienna.

JENNIFER AND KEVIN McCOY

Born in Sacramento, California in 1968, Jennifer McCoy received a BA in Theater Arts with a concentration in Film Studies from Cornell University in 1990. Born in Seattle, Washington in 1967, Kevin McCoy earned a BA in Philosophy from Whitman College in 1989. Both artists received an MFA in Electronic Arts from Rensselaer Polytechnic Institute in 1994. Since they initiated their artistic partnership in 1990, Jennifer and Kevin McCoy have produced multimedia works combining film, animation, and kinetic sculpture that examine the relationship between technology and the construction of narratives. Their projects have been exhibited internationally in venues including The Museum of Modern Art; The Metropolitan Museum of Art; P.S.1 Contemporary Art Center; The New Museum; and the Center for Media and Art (ZKM) in Karlsruhe, Germany. The McCoys live and work in New York.

JOSHUA MOSLEY

Joshua Mosley was born in 1974 in Dallas, Texas. He received an MFA in Art and Technology from The School of the Art Institute of Chicago in 1998. Employing diverse methods from computer animation to hand-drawn and stop-motion techniques, Mosley's films explore elemental themes in human existence such as confrontation with nature, the complexities of communication, and journeys into the unknown. Mosley's work has been exhibited in solo shows at the Institute of Contemporary Art, Philadelphia, and the Museum of Contemporary Art, San Diego. His work was also included in the 52nd Venice Biennale in 2007. Mosley lives and works in Philadelphia.

OSCAR MUÑOZ

Oscar Muñoz was born in Popayan, Colombia, in 1951. Producing conceptual pieces in film, photography, and sculpture, Muñoz's work explores the limits of memory, human loss, and the impermanence of the image. A recurring pattern in his practice is the attempt to capture a portrait in evanescent mediums such as human breath, water, and dust. Muñoz's work has been exhibited in solo shows in galleries throughout the world and has also been included in group exhibitions at the Museum of Fine Arts in Houston; El Museo del Barrio in New York; and the San Diego Museum of Art. Muñoz was also a participant in the 52nd Venice Biennale in 2007. He lives and works in Cali, Colombia.

JACCO OLIVIER

Born in 1972 in Goes, the Netherlands, Jacco Olivier studied at the Rijksakademie van Beeldende Kunsten in Amsterdam and continues to live and work there today. Combining painting and film, Olivier photographs a painting in progress as it evolves. The separate phases of his painting are then animated, recording a series of moments that, like fragments of memory, are evocative of stories but ultimately defy resolution. Olivier's work has been exhibited internationally at venues such as the Museum of Contemporary Art in Denver; the Istanbul Modern; and the Centre pour L'image Contemporaine in Geneva. His work was included in the 2005 Prague Biennial.

RAYMOND PETTIBON

Raymond Pettibon was born in Tucson, Arizona, in 1957. As an undergraduate at the University of California, Los Angeles, Pettibon studied economics but soon after graduating, decided to become a professional artist. In his early career, Pettibon was a member of the California punk rock scene, producing illustrations and graphic work for bands and magazines. Over time, his artistic practice evolved, with drawing as his primary discipline. In his drawings and animated works, Pettibon combines language and visual imagery in an ambiguously suggestive manner, as if recording remnants of narratives and half-formed thoughts. Solo exhibitions of his work have been shown at the Philadelphia Museum of Art; the Whitney Museum of American Art; and the Kestner Gesellschaft in Hannover, Germany. Pettibon also participated in Documenta XI in 2002. He lives and works in Southern California.

ROBERT PRUITT

Robert Pruitt was born in Houston, Texas, in 1975. He received his BFA from Texas Southern University and an MFA from the University of Texas at Austin. Pruitt produces drawings, film, sculptures, and installations that draw on his dichotomous experiences working in the contemporary art world and living in the African American community. With stark wit and powerful juxtapositions, his work illuminates the construction of cultural identity and elements of shared experience. Pruitt's work has been exhibited in the 2005 group exhibition *Frequency* at the Studio Museum in Harlem; in a solo exhibition at the Contemporary Arts Museum in Houston in 2006; and in the 2006 Whitney Biennial. He lives and works in Chicago.

CHRISTINE REBET

Christine Rebet was born in 1971 in Lyon, France. She studied painting and scenography at the Art Academy in Venice and theater design at Central Saint Martins College of Art and Design in London. Rebet's hand-drawn, enigmatic animations serve as a stage for her unfettered imagination. Surreal vignettes featuring characters rendered in cartoon-like forms reveal a world that is magical, bizarre, and subtly unnerving. Rebet's work has been exhibited at the Shanghai Art Museum; the Musée d'Art Contemporain in Lyon; and the Moderna Museet. Rebet lives and works in New York.

MARY REID KELLEY

Born in Greenville, South Carolina, in 1979, Mary Reid Kelley received her BA from St. Olaf College, Minnesota, in 2001 and an MFA from Yale University in painting in 2009. Reid Kelley uses painting, video, animation, and performance as vehicles to examine the construction of historical war narratives culled from archive-based research. While Reid Kelley's work is grounded in the told and untold experiences of World War I, her animations unfold in a dreamlike cartoon world where characters—played by the artist herself—speak according to strict rules of rhyme and repetition. The result is an exploration of the political and symbolic weight of language. Reid Kelley recently had her first solo exhibition at the Fredericks & Freiser Gallery in New York. She lives and works in Saratoga Springs, New York.

ROBIN RHODE

Robin Rhode was born in Cape Town, South Africa, in 1976. In 1998, he earned a National Diploma in Fine Art from the Witwatersrand Technikon and received a degree in Television and Dramatic Arts from the South African School of Film in 2000. The artist is known for his serial photographs and films depicting a figure—typically Rhode himself—interacting with drawn images or objects on walls or concrete. These playful pieces allude to aspects of

South African urban youth culture. Solo shows of Rhode's work have been shown at the Los Angeles County Museum of Art; the Hayward Gallery in London; and the Rose Art Museum at Brandeis University, Waltham, Massachusetts. Other exhibitions that have featured Rhode's work include Prospect.1 New Orleans in 2008, and the 51st Venice Biennale in 2005. Rhode lives and works in Berlin.

HIRAKI SAWA

Hiraki Sawa was born in Ishikawa, Japan, in 1977 and lives and works in London. In 2003, he earned an MA in sculpture from the Slade School of Fine Art in London after receiving a BFA in sculpture from the University of East London in 2000. Well known for creating his films in his own apartment, Sawa transforms domestic interiors into settings for musings on the mechanics of motion and fantastically surreal events. Using hand-drawn and digital animation techniques, Sawa amplifies the mundane, breathing life into static objects. Solo exhibitions and screenings of Sawa's work have been shown at the Hirshhorn Museum and Sculpture Garden, Washington DC; the Hammer Museum; the Frist Center for the Arts, Nashville; and the Hayward Gallery in London.

BERNI SEARLE

Berni Searle was born in Cape Town, South Africa in 1964, where she lives and works. Searle earned an MFA from the University of Cape Town after receiving a BFA from the same institution. Exploring South Africa's complex history, Searle creates photos, films, and multimedia installations in which her own body and identity figure prominently. Though her works are aesthetically alluring in their quiet simplicity, they are politically strong in their address to a nation still coping with its past. Searle's work has appeared in exhibitions at The Museum of Modern Art; the Brooklyn Museum; the Kunsthalle Vienna; the Istanbul Modern; and the Smithsonian National Museum of African Art in Washington DC. Her work was included in the 49th and the 51st Venice Biennale in 2001 and 2005; and the Dakar Biennale in 2000, where she won the DAK'ART 2000 Minister of Culture Prize.

CINDY SHERMAN

Cindy Sherman was born in 1954 in Glen Ridge, New Jersey. In 1976, Sherman received a BA from State University College in Buffalo, New York. Known foremost as a photographer, Sherman's body of work comprises staged photographs in which she dons a myriad of costumes, embodying characters whose stories are left untold. Solo exhibitions of Sherman's work have been mounted at the Museum of Contemporary Art, Los Angeles; the Whitney Museum of American Art; The Museum of Modern Art; the Hirshhorn Museum and Sculpture Center; and the Basel Kunsthalle in Switzerland. Sherman has received numerous awards throughout her career including the American Academy of Arts and Sciences Award in 2003 and a MacArthur Fellowship in 1995. She lives and works in New York.

FEDERICO SOLMI

Self-taught New York based artist Federico Solmi was born in Bologna, Italy in 1973. The artist produces humorous, crude, and absurd dystopian narratives that serve as derisive critiques of contemporary society. Borrowing images from pop culture and combining them with various historical references, Solmi satirizes religion, the pornography industry, wall street, and the art world. His work has been shown at institutions such as the Centre Pompidou in Paris; Reina Sofĺa National Musem in Madrid; Haus der Kulturen der Welt, Berlin; the National Center for Contemporary Art in Moscow; and The Drawing Center in New York. Solmi's work was also featured in the 26th Kassel Documentary Film & Video Festival in 2009 and he received a John Simon Guggenheim Memorial Fellowship in that year.

KARA WALKER

Kara Walker was born in Stockton, California, in 1969. She received a BFA from the Atlanta College of Art in 1991 and an MFA from the Rhode Island School of Design in 1994. Walker is known for her work with paper silhouettes that explores complex issues of race, violence, gender, and sexuality. In her film work, Walker's silhouetted figures become puppets, interacting with one another and their surroundings in ways that create new potential for narrative development and the interrogation of American history. Solo exhibitions of Walker's work have appeared at the Walker Art Center; the Whitney Museum of American Art; The Metropolitan Museum of Art; the San Francisco Museum of Modern Art; and the Studio Museum in Harlem. Walker was a 1997 recipient of a MacArthur Fellowship. She lives and works in New York.

HISTORICAL ANIMATIONS

EDISON MANUFACTURING COMPANY

Owned by Thomas Edison, the Edison Manufacturing Company was America's first commercial film studio and the industry leader from 1894 to 1918. Its earliest films were shown on the Edison-invented kinetoscope, a freestanding device with a peephole through which individual viewers watched small moving pictures. While their first productions were typically short films documenting current events, modern marvels, and comedic acts, the studio eventually developed large format, longer films that were projected in theaters. This included their 1903 production *The Great Train Robbery*. One of the first narrative films ever produced, it employed groundbreaking editing techniques such as cross-cutting to show simultaneous action in different locations. The studio also developed early stop-motion trick film methods to make objects appear to move on their own.

FLEISCHER STUDIOS

Fleischer Studios, Inc. was a pioneering American animation studio founded in 1921 by brothers Max and Dave Fleischer. The company was Walt Disney Productions' leading competitor in the 1920s and 30s, producing successful cartoons such as *Koko the Clown*, *Betty Boop*, *Popeye the Sailor*, and *Superman*. While most famous cartoon characters of the early twentieth century were animals, Fleischer Studios' most popular characters were humans. In 1914, Max Fleischer developed a machine called the rotoscope, which allowed animators to trace over live-action film movement for use in hand-drawn animations. The technique was used in the production of the *Koko the Clown* cartoons, with Dave Fleischer, dressed in a clown costume, serving as Koko's live model. Rotoscoping was a significant contribution to the advancement of animation and was adopted by Walt Disney Productions as well.

LOTTE REINIGER

Lotte Reiniger was born in 1899 in Berlin, Germany and was among the first women to achieve a successful career in animation and film direction. In her youth, Reiniger was captivated by silhouette puppetry and adapted the laborious technique for use in her full-length films. Her most notable film, *The Adventures of Prince Achmed*, 1926, is the oldest surviving animated feature and is based on tales from *The Arabian Nights*. After producing nearly seventy films throughout her career, Reiniger passed away in 1981.

DZIGA VERTOV

Born in 1896 in Bialystok, Poland, Dziga Vertov moved with his family to Moscow in 1915. He became an avant-garde filmmaker and cinema theorist primarily known for his documentaries on Soviet life in the 1920s and early '30s. Vertov valued the camera over the human eye for its ability to objectively capture reality, leading a group of filmmakers called the Kinoki (the Film-Eye Group) in an effort to challenge theatricalism in film. He ventured into animation with films such as the political cartoon *Soviet Toys*, originally shown in conjunction with Vertov's newsreels. Vertov's animated work, truncated by the rise of Social Realism in 1934, is often overlooked in accounts of his career. He died in 1954.

the dissolve

exhibition checklist

ROBERT BREER

Bang!, 1986

16mm film transferred to DVD; sound; 10 minutes 17 seconds

Courtesy of the artist and gb agency, Paris

PAUL CHAN

4th ~~Light~~, 2006

Digital projection; computer; 14 minutes

Courtesy of the artist and Greene Naftali Gallery, New York

MARTHA COLBURN

Myth Labs, 2008

16mm film transferred to DVD; sound; 7 minutes 40 seconds

Courtesy of the artist and James Cohan Gallery, New York

THOMAS DEMAND

Rain, 2008

35mm film transferred to HD Video; sound; 4 minutes

Courtesy of the artist and Matthew Marks Gallery, New York

BRENT GREEN

Paulina Hollers, 2006

Video; sound; 12 minutes 35 seconds

Courtesy of the artist and Andrew Edlin Gallery, New York

GEORGE GRIFFIN

Viewmaster, a digital mutoscope, 1976/2007

35mm film original, digitally re-animated, computer, MDF case, LCD monitor, continuous loop

32 x 20 x 20 inches overall

Courtesy of the artist

EZRA JOHNSON

What Visions Burn, 2006

Video; sound; 22 minutes 27 seconds

Courtesy the artist and Nicole Klagsbrun Gallery, New York

BILL T. JONES AND OPENENDED GROUP

After Ghostcatching, 2010

Virtual Dance for Stereoscopic Display

Visual and sound design: Marc Downie, Shelley Eshkar, and Paul Kaiser

Choreography, movement, and voice: Bill T. Jones

Sound recording studio: Harvestworks, New York

Special thanks to Michael Girard

Original version commissioned by The Cooper Union for the Advancement of Science and Art, New York

Courtesy of OpenEnded Group

SITE Santa Fe Commission

WILLIAM KENTRIDGE

History of the Main Complaint, 1996

35mm film transferred to DVD; sound; 5 minutes 50 seconds

Edition: No. 5 of 10

Collection of Ilene and Michael Salcman

AVISH KHEBREHZADEH

Theater III, 2010

Oil on gesso and wood, 90 x 135 inches

Edgar, 2010

Video; sound; approx. 3 minutes

Courtesy of the artist

the dissolve

LALEH KHORRAMIAN

Water Panics in the Sea, 2010

Digital animation; sound; approx. 10 minutes

Courtesy of the artist and Salon 94, New York

MARIA LASSNIG

Maria Lassnig Kantate, 1992

35mm film transferred to DVD; sound; 8 minutes

Courtesy of the artist and Friedrich Petzel Gallery, New York

JENNIFER AND KEVIN McCOY

Traffic #1: Our Second Date, 2004

Tabletop installation with plastic figures, plastic and metal model vehicles, LCD monitor, electronics, lights, video cameras, and video projection; sound

Tabletop dimensions: 37 x 50 x 40 inches, video projection dimensions variable

Collection of Bill Paxton, Ojai, CA

JOSHUA MOSLEY

A Vue, 2004

Mixed-media animation transferred to DVD; sound; 7 minutes 30 seconds

Courtesy of the artist and Donald Young Gallery, Chicago, IL

OSCAR MUÑOZ

Re/trato, 2003

Video; 28 minutes

Courtesy of the artist and Sicardi Gallery, Houston, TX

JACCO OLIVIER

Almost, 2009

Video; sound; 1 minute 35 seconds

Artist's Proof, Edition of 5

Courtesy of the artist, Marianne Boesky Gallery, New York, and Victoria Miro Gallery, London

RAYMOND PETTIBON

Sunday Night and Saturday Morning, 2005

Video; sound; 16 minutes 45 seconds

Courtesy of Regen Projects, Los Angeles, CA

ROBERT PRUITT

Black Stuntman (Volumes 1 and 2), 2004

Video; sound; 8 minutes

Courtesy of the artist

CHRISTINE REBET

The Black Cabinet, 2007

35mm film transferred to DVD; two-channel video installation; sound; 3 minutes 4 seconds

Courtesy of the artist and Galerie Kamel Mennour, Paris

MARY REID KELLEY

You Make Me Iliad, 2010

HD video; sound; 7 minutes 22 seconds

Courtesy of the artist

SITE Santa Fe Commission

ROBIN RHODE

Kid Candle from "Memories of Childhood," 2009

Super 8mm film transferred to DVD; 1 minute 3 seconds

Courtesy of the artist and Perry Rubenstein Gallery, New York

HIRAKI SAWA

Airliner, 2003

Video; 3 minutes

Courtesy of the artist and James Cohan Gallery, New York

the dissolve

BERNI SEARLE

About to Forget, 2005

35mm cinemascope film transferred to three-channel video projection; sound; 3 minutes

Courtesy of the artist and Michael Stevenson Gallery, Cape Town

CINDY SHERMAN

Doll Clothes, 1975

16mm film transferred to DVD; 2 minutes 22 seconds

Courtesy of the artist and Metro Pictures, New York

FEDERICO SOLMI

Douche Bag City, 2010

15 video animations, LCD panels, custom-made frames; continuous loop

Dimensions Variable

Collaborator: Russell Lowe

Courtesy of the artist, LMAK Projects, New York, and ADN Gallery, Barcelona

KARA WALKER

National Archives Microfilm Publications M999 Roll 34: Bureau of Refugees, Freedmen and Abandoned Lands:

1) *Six Miles from Springfield on the Franklin Road,* 2009

2) *Lucy of Pulaski*, 2009

Video; sound; 25 minutes 30 seconds

Original music by Jason Moran

Courtesy of the artist and Sikkema Jenkins & Co., New York

HISTORICAL ANIMATIONS

EDISON MANUFACTURING COMPANY

The Enchanted Drawing, 1900

35mm film transferred to DVD; 1 minute 26 seconds

Producer: J. Stuart Blackton; Camera: Albert E. Smith

The Library of Congress, Paper Print Collection, Washington DC

FLEISCHER STUDIOS

"Big Chief" Ko-Ko, 1924

35mm film transferred to DVD; 7 minutes

Courtesy of Inkwell Images, Morley, MI

LOTTE REINIGER

The Adventures of Prince Achmed, 1926

35mm film, black and white/tinted, transferred to DVD; 65 minutes

Courtesy of Milestone Films, Harrington Park, NJ

DZIGA VERTOV

Soviet Toys, 1924

35mm film transferred to DVD; 10 minutes 45 seconds

Courtesy of the Yale Film Studies Program

the dissolve

THE ABSTRACT DISSOLVE
Curated by Sarah Lewis and Daniel Belasco,
in collaboration with Josh Kline, Director of Public Programs, Electronic Arts Intermix, New York

Stories and plotlines dominate the works selected for *The Dissolve* exhibition at SITE Santa Fe. *The Abstract Dissolve*, a program of historical and contemporary works presented at the Santa Fe Lensic Performing Arts Center on Sunday, June 20, 2010, aimed to connect the aesthetics of abstraction with the premise behind the Biennial itself.

NORMAN McLAREN AND EVELYN LAMBART
Begone Dull Care, 1949
Painted film; color; music by Oscar Peterson Trio; 7 minutes 52 seconds
Courtesy of the National Film Board of Canada, Montreal

STAN BRAKHAGE
Garden of Earthly Delights, 1981
Splicing tape with flowers and grass; 16mm film; 1 minute 44 seconds
Courtesy of Marilyn Brakhage

STEINA
Warp, 2000
Video; sound; 4 minutes 30 seconds
Courtesy of the artist and Electronic Arts Intermix, New York

FORCEFIELD
Tunnel Vision, 2001
16mm film and video; sound; 11 minutes 43 seconds
Courtesy of the artists and Electronic Arts Intermix, New York

ALEX HUBBARD
Collapse of the Expanded Field I-III, 2007
Video; 4 minutes 29 seconds
Courtesy of the artist and Macarone Inc., New York

TAKESHI MURATA

Untitled (Pink Dot), 2007

Video; sound; 5 minutes

Courtesy of the artist and Electronic Arts Intermix, New York

CAROLEE SCHNEEMANN

Carl Ruggles Christmas Breakfast, 1963/2007

16mm film transferred to video; sound; 9 minutes 4 seconds

Courtesy of the artist and Electronic Arts Intermix, New York

KEN JACOBS

His Favorite Wife Improved, 2008

Video; sound; 2 minutes

Courtesy of the artist and Electronic Arts Intermix, New York

AMY GRANAT

Tablecloth Jump, 2008

16mm film; 1 minute

Courtesy of the artist

CLIFFORD ROSS

Harmonium Mountain, 2010

Video; sound; 5 minutes

Courtesy of the artist

the dissolve

director's acknowledgments

SITE SANTA FE'S EIGHTH INTERNATIONAL BIENNIAL *The Dissolve* is a large and complex undertaking that relies on the hard work, good will, and generosity of many people, all of whom have been inspired by the ideas and works of art that Sarah Lewis and Daniel Belasco have brought together in this exhibition. SITE's Board of Directors, excited by the exhibition's experimental nature, has been supportive since the outset, making it especially fitting to be honoring one of their own trustees Michael L. Klein, and his wife Jeanne. Early funding from the Andy Warhol Foundation for the Visual Arts and the National Endowment for the Arts buoyed us up in a difficult economic climate, as did the support from Agnes Gund, the Biennial's Honorary Chair. We are indebted, as well, to the substantial and ongoing generosity of The Burnett Foundation. We are grateful for these expressions of support, as we are for all the donors and sponsors of this Biennial.

SITE's staff never ceases to amaze me with their dedication, intelligence, and passion. They honor the artists and curators by their hard work. Curators Sarah Lewis and Daniel Belasco have demonstrated an extraordinary level of professionalism, range of knowledge, and creativity in the making of the exhibition. David Adjaye and his indefatigable associate Brandon Padron have created an exhibition design unlike any other for a biennial that is wholly unique. The works in *The Dissolve,* all sharing the use of an innovative medium, have provided us with levels of artistry and trenchant insights into society that are deeply needed and appreciated; I am grateful to each of the artists for allowing us into their worlds.

— LAURA STEWARD
Phillips Director, SITE Santa Fe

curators' acknowledgments

THE DISSOLVE IS THE CULMINATION OF A SIX-YEAR JOURNEY that began while we pondered the magical attraction of two animated works—Raymond Pettibon's *Repeater Pencil* and Kara Walker's *Testimony*. At that time, we were curatorial assistants working on Robert Storr's SITE Santa Fe's Fifth International Biennial: *Disparities and Deformations: Our Grotesque* in 2004. Since that moment in the galleries, we have been steadfast in our quest to understand that moment of inspiration—to track its iterations in other examples of contemporary art; to trace its antecedents in the history of the moving image; and to devise a curatorial schema that would best express our discoveries. In that vein, we wish to acknowledge Nancy Mowll Mathews, whose historical exhibition and insightful essay for this catalogue bring together the moving image with a variety of other media and helped inspire this Biennial exhibition. We thank Laura Steward, Phillips Director at SITE Santa Fe, for her forward thinking in accepting an unusual proposal for this Biennial venture, and for her support as we expanded and refined its concepts in the realms of the animated image and in the realization of its commissions. David Adjaye, the internationally noted architect, in outstanding fashion, has brought to fruition our vision for the Biennial, for which we remain enormously grateful. Through his passion for this project and his care in creating this design, he offers us all an experience that far transcends the typical viewing environment for video in contemporary art shows. We also extend our gratitude to his colleague, Brandon Padron, for working closely with David on the plans and for his assiduous attention to every last detail. Countless other people have helped us along the way and it has been a privilege to work with and learn from all of them.

At SITE Santa Fe, our gratitude extends to the Board of Directors and to its entire hard-working staff. Special thanks go to Tyler Auwarter, former Director of Exhibitions, David Benner, Operations Manager, and David Merrill, Operations Assistant, for their smooth and unruffled approach to implementing an ambitious exhibition design and for their ability to remain undaunted by any request. Janet Dees, Thaw Curatorial Fellow, for overseeing the myriad logistical details in organizing an international exhibition, and for writing precise catalogue entries on all the works; Anne Wrinkle, Director of External Affairs, for her diligence and attention to the exhibition's marketing and communications aspects, particularly in her capacity to present this Biennial with a comprehensive and substantive online presence; Joanne Lefrak, for overseeing the production of this extraordinary catalogue and for her consistent sunny spirit throughout; Marc Dorfman and Jo-Anne Skinner for their tireless development efforts; Juliet Myers, Director of Education, for her innovative ideas and lining up of talent for the Biennial's Arts and Culture programs; Candice Jernigan, for welcoming us at every turn as well as handling all of the intricate machinations of the exhibition's special events, and Casey Stojka-Larson for her grace and kind assistance in countless ways; Brian Bixby and Mike Root for a wonderful website; finally, to Marlene Meyerson, on SITE's Board of Directors, for introducing us to the work of a number of contemporary artists and for her warm support of our show.

Our appreciation goes out as well to the extended Biennial team, including: Allison Jones, curatorial assistant, whom we thank for her artful handling of countless details, helping the entire operation to meet deadlines, for her compilation of the catalogue timeline, writing the spot-on bios, and inviting us to speak at the Sotheby's Institute; Scott Sinkler for recording the Artists' Roundtable Discussion in New York in October 2009; S. Zelda Roland for her expert eye trained on the show in its final stages and for her on the ground help during the installation; and to Herbert Lotz, for donating our striking photographic portraits.

Thanks are also due to the collaborators of the *The Dissolve*'s opening weekend: Jean Davidson, Executive Director, Bob Bursey, Producing Director, and Janet Wong, Associate Artistic Director, Bill T. Jones/Arnie Zane Dance Company, for shaping the opening weekend performance and kick-starting the commission of *After Ghostcatching* with OpenEnded Group (Marc Downie, Shelley Eshkar, and Paul Kaiser); to Josh Kline, Public Programs Director at Electronic Arts Intermix, New York, for helping to curate *The Abstract Dissolve*, a fantastic film program; Marilyn Brakhage for her support, as well as to Bob Martin, Director, of the Lensic Theater, where the festival took place.

We also wish to acknowledge Sarah S. King and Diane Armitage of SNAP Editions for a fantastic job editing the catalogue, particularly for the painstaking work of transforming the roundtable transcript into a landmark document; and David Chickey and his colleague Masumi Shibata at Skolkin + Chickey for the striking design of the catalogue that captures the concept of the exhibition.

For their curatorial counsel, we would like to thank John Hanhardt, for his knowledgeable suggestions about the contents of the catalogue; Andrew Lampert at Anthology Film Archives and Lauren Sorensen of Canyon Cinema, for providing curatorial advice on experimental film; and Barbara London, for helping solidify the interpretations within the history of video.

We extend our gratitude for the extraordinary generosity of the lenders from both private and public collections, for parting with their art works for the length of this exhibition as well as to the following individuals at these institutions who have been invaluable in the facilitation of the loans. These include: Ilene and Michael Salcman; Bill Paxton, Ojai, CA; Stacy Bengtson at Regen Projects, Los Angeles; Fabienne Stephan at Salon 94, New York; Jessica Lin Cox at James Cohan Gallery, New York; Tom Heman and James Woodward at Metro Pictures, New York; Annie Rana at Marianne Boesky Gallery, New York; Nathalie Boutin at gb Agency, Paris; Ruth Phaneuf at Nicole Klagsbrun, New York; Marie-Sophie Eiché at Galerie Kamel Mennour, Paris; Annie Ochmanek at Greene Naftali, New York; Andrea Teschke at Friedrich Petzel Gallery, New York; Maria Ines Sicardi at Sicardi Gallery, Houston; Caroline Dowling and Molly Klais Springer at Perry Rubenstein Gallery, New York; Louky Keijsers Koning at LMAK Projects, New York; Dennis Doros at Milestone Pictures, New Jersey; Ray Pointer at Inkwell Image, Morley, MI; Andrew Edlin at Andrew Edlin Gallery, New York; Library of Congress, Washington, D.C.; Adrian Rosenfeld at Matthew Marks Gallery, New York; Emily Letourneau at Donald Young Gallery, Chicago; Michael Stevenson Gallery, Cape Town; and Brent Sikkema of Sikkema Jenkins & Co., New York. Our appreciation as well goes to those who have opened doors to important loans: Ann Wolfe, Curator of Exhibitions and Collections, Nevada Art Museum; Leigh Conner at Conner Contemporary, Washington D.C.; Mirielle Mosler at Mirielle Mosler, New York; Magda Sawon at Postmasters Gallery, New York; Catherine Belloy at Marian Goodman Gallery, New York; Norman Kleeblatt, Susan and Elihu Rose Chief Curator of The Jewish Museum; and John MacKay, Chair of the Film Department at Yale University, for assisting with the loan of Dziga Vertov's work.

Above all, we owe a debt of gratitude to all the artists who have so graciously agreed to participate in the exhibition and play along with our unorthodox vision for a contemporary art Biennial. We have benefited greatly from our ongoing dialogues with them. We also wish to thank those artists who shared their work and ideas with us but were not ultimately selected for the exhibition.

It is a rare and unusual opportunity in life to be able to come full circle and this Biennial does just that in its encapsulation of the history of moving images, while advancing new ideas on the direction of international contemporary art.

— SARAH LEWIS AND DANIEL BELASCO

In addition to all the above mentioned, I would like to personally acknowledge my colleagues at The Jewish Museum, particularly Joan Rosenbaum, Helen Goldsmith Menschel Director; Ruth Beesch, Deputy Director for Programs; Susan L. Braunstein, Curator of Archaeology and Judaica; and Karen Levitov, Associate Curator of Fine Arts for supporting my work on this Biennial, and Curators Norman Kleeblatt and Andrew Ingall for enlightening conversations on animation. I heartily thank Robert Storr for his steadfast encouragement of this biennial from the beginning; and Linda Nochlin and Natasha Staller for their crucial support of my scholarship. My deepest gratitude to my wife Risa Kaufman and children Frieda and Reuben for making life beautiful, and the rest of my family for sharing in a wonderful time in Santa Fe.

— DANIEL BELASCO

In addition, I would like to acknowledge Robert Storr, Dean of Yale University School of Art, for his support of this show from the moment Daniel and I articulated its vision, and for his encouragement of me personally at every possible turn, my gratitude is immeasurable; Agnes Gund for her care, boundless embrace, and insightful advice; Toby Lewis and Marlene Meyerson for their staunch support and joie de vivre; the wonderfully sensitive writer and curator, Bill Kelly, CUNY Graduate Center President, and Gabriella de Ferrari and Amie James for their steadfast commitment to my work and willingness to invite conversation about the Biennial at the CUNY Graduate Center institution; George King, Director, and Maura Reilly, Senior Curator, American Federation of Arts for their support; dear Dodie Kazanjian for recognizing the power of the artistic vision on display in this show, her eloquent and insightful writing on this exhibition, and bringing awareness of its subject to a broader audience; Kianga Ellis for her brilliant engagement with the premise of the show and for the inspiration I derive from her pioneering vision; Dena Muller, Executive Director of ArtTable for her thoughtfulness; and *cara* Francesca Pietropaolo for *un abbraccio* always.

Over the course of six years, this show has also benefitted from conversations with Naomi Beckwith, Assistant Curator, The Studio Museum in Harlem; Donna De Salvo, Chief Curator and Associate Director for Programs, The Whitney Museum of American Art; Jodie Hauptman, Associate Curator, Department of Drawings, The Museum of Modern Art; Curator Linda Norden and Valerie Cassel Oliver, Curator, the Contemporary Arts Museum, Houston; Franklin Sirmans, Chief Curator of Contemporary Art, Los Angeles County Museum; Ann Temkin, The Marie-Josée and Henry Kravis Chief Curator of Painting and Sculpture, The Museum of Modern Art; and Deborah Willis, University Professor and Chair, Department of Photography & Imaging, New York University.

For their invaluable wisdom, grounding observations about contemporary art practice, and for their support during this Biennial process, my thanks go to Dr. Mehret Mandefro, Wynton Marsalis, Salamishah Tillet and Kweli Washington for believing in the vision of the Biennial and for involving Bill T. Jones, Jean Davidson, Janet Wong, and Bob Bursey; I would also like to thank my dissertation committee Professors Daphne Brooks, Matthew Frye Jacobson, Alexander Nemerov, and Robert Farris Thompson; Sarah and George King for welcoming me to Santa Fe so warmly years ago and for their belief in this Biennial from the start; Johannes DeYoung, Sam Messer, Max Saltonstall, and Anahita Vossoughi at Yale School of Art for going above and beyond the call to duty in order to get our Biennial into fantastic digital working order; and most importantly, thanks to my family for their loving support and for making life swing…!

— SARAH LEWIS

SITE SANTA FE IS GRATEFUL TO THE FOLLOWING FOR THEIR SUPPORT:

HONORARY CHAIR
Agnes Gund

HONORING
Jeanne & Michael L. Klein

LEAD UNDERWRITER
The Andy Warhol Foundation
The Burnett Foundation
National Endowment for the Arts

NATIONAL ENDOWMENT FOR THE ARTS

EXHIBITION PATRON
Agnes Gund
Jeanne & Michael L. Klein

CURATORS' PATRON
Toby Devan Lewis
Marlene Nathan Meyerson

CATALOGUE SPONSOR
Rosina Lee Yue & Dr. Bert A. Lies

EXHIBITION SUPPORTER
Karen & Steve Berkowitz
Cornelia Bryer & Herman Siegelaar
Katherine & James Gentry
Jeanne & Jim Manning
Millstream Fund

EXHIBITION FRIEND
Terry K. & Richard C. Albright
Dottie & Dick Barrett
Gay Block & Rabbi Malka Drucker
Suzanne Deal Booth
Carmel & Tom Borders
Century Bank
Susan Foote & Stephen Feinberg
Christopher Hill & Rodolfo Chopoena
Rita & Kent Norton
JoAnn & Steve Ruppert
Courtney Finch Taylor & Scott Taylor
Ann Tenenbaum & Thomas H. Lee
Kathy & Charles Webster
Zane Bennett Gallery

PREVIEW COCKTAIL RECEPTION SPONSOR
UBS Financial Services, Houston

BIENNIAL WEBSITE SPONSOR
Avalon Trust

PANEL DISCUSSION SPONSOR
TAI Gallery
Alicia & Bill Miller
Nancy Ziegler Nodelman & Dwight Strong

SITE GUIDE SPONSOR
Marcellin Simard, MD/Santa Fe Cardiology

WINE SPONSOR
Frederick Wildman & Sons

BIENNIAL GALA CO-CHAIRS
Fay & Donald Kirby
Wendy & Peter Trevisani

BENEFIT COMMITTEE
Joyce Buford
Lori & Joel Dunlap
Linda Durham
Fay & Donald Kirby
Rick Liberto
Robin Merlo & Michael Lescander
Lorlee & Arnold Tenenbaum
Fabene Welch
Mildred Witte
Bebe Woolley & Daniel Gorski

IN HONOR OF JEANNE AND MICHAEL L. KLEIN
Marion Barthelme & Jeff Fort
Karen & Steve Berkowitz
Cornelia Bryer & Herman Siegelaar
Marian & Chris Casey
Susan Emerling & A. Thomas Torres, AIA
Sandy & Jim Fitzpatrick
Katherine & James Gentry
Will Halm & Marcellin Simard
Christopher Hill & Rodolfo Chopoena
Mihail S. Lari & Scott E. Murray
Rick Liberto
Jeanne & Jim Manning
Marlene N. Meyerson
Alicia & Bill Miller
Rita & Kent Norton
Linda Pace Foundation
Joann & Gifford Phillips
Lyn & Pete Selig
Mary Sloane & Andrew Wallerstein
Lorlee & Arnold Tenenbaum

SITE SANTA FE STAFF (listed alphabetically)

David Benner
Operations Manager

Brian Bixby
Webmaster

Monica Butler
Curatorial Assistant

Brittny Dayes
Visitor Services and Education Coordinator

Janet Dees
Thaw Curatorial Fellow

Marc Dorfman
Director of Development

Bill Hinsvark
Visitor Services and Publications Associate

Candice Jernigan
Events Manager

Joanne Lefrak
Education and Catalogue Manager

David Merrill
Operations Assistant

Juliet Myers
Director of Education and Public Programs

Catherine Putnam
Deputy Director and Chief Financial Officer

Michelle Ryals
Accountant and Human Resources Administrator

Jo-Anne Skinner
Membership and Travel Program Manager

Sage Sommer
Exhibition Assistant

Bill Stengel
Exhibition Assistant

Laura Steward
Phillips Director

Casey Stojka-Larson
Development Associate

Anne Wrinkle
Director of External Affairs

SITE GUIDES

Zoe Blackwell
Monica Butler
Zoila Cleaver
Carol Canfield
Vienne Felix
Elizabeth Mesh
Tim Scott

PREPARATORS

Julia Benjamin
Pam Ellison
Alexis Elton
Michael Gurule
Sage Sommer
Bill Stengel

IMAGE CREDITS

for Inventing the In-Between:

page 14: Le praxinoscope à projection d'Émile Reynaud pour La Nature, revue des sciences – 1882, n°492, page 357

page 14: Trade advertisement for the mutoscope, 1999 from the Mutoscope American Manufacturing Studios

page 14: Thomas Edison, Kinetoscope, from La Nature, Paris, 1894. Photo credit: Image Select/Art Resource, NY

page 14: A portrait of J. Stuart Blackton from 1912. Credit: Stacy, N.Y., "J. Stuart Blackton, head-and-shoulders portrait, facing left, resting head on hand." 1912; Prints and Photographs Division, Library of Congress

page 15: Georges Méliès, screenshot from *Le Voyage dans la lune* (*A Trip to the Moon*) (1902)

page 15: Émile Cohl, *Fantasmagorie*, 1908

page 15: *The Sculptor's Nightmare* / American Mutoscope and Biograph Company, 1908; Director Wallace McCutcheon, Camera, G.W. Bitzer. Filmed on April 18 and 20, 1908, in New York City studio. Library of Congress Paper Print Collection

page 15: Winsor McCay, image of Little Nemo, from *Little Nemo in Slumberland* (1905-1914)

page 16: Dziga Vertov, still from *Soviet Toys*, 1924; 35mm film transferred to DVD; 10 minutes 45 seconds. Courtesy of the Yale Film Studies Program

page 16: Marcel Duchamp (1887-1968) © ARS, NY, Anémic Cinema. 1925, 35mm black & white film, silent, 7 minutes long. Technical assistance: Man Ray and Marc Allégret. Musée National d'Art Moderne, Centre Georges Pompidou, Paris, France. Photo credit: CNAC / MNAM / Dist. Réunion des Musées Nationaux / Art Resource, NY © 2010 Artists Rights Society (ARS), New York / ADAGP, Paris / Succession Marcel Duchamp

page 17: Lotte Reiniger, *The Adventures of Prince Achmed*, 1926; 35mm film, black and white/tinted, transferred to DVD; 65 minutes. Image courtesy of Milestone Film

page 17: Len Lye, *A Colour Box*, 1935; 4 minutes, 35mm Dufaycolour. Courtesy Len Lye Foundation / Govett-Brewster Art Gallery / New Zealand Film Archive / The British Post Office

page 18: Jiří Trnka, *The Czech Year* (Špalí ek, 1947). Image courtesy of KRÁTKY FILM PRAHA

page 18: John Whitney, visual music *Digital Harmony*, 1959

page 19: Robert Breer, *Homage to John Cage*, 1963; Folioscope, plastic, metal, acrylic painting; 112 x 25 cm; unique piece. Courtesy of the artist and gp agency, Paris

page 19: Sol LeWitt, *Muybridge II*, 1964 (schematic presentation). Painted wood with ten compartments, each containing a photograph by Barbara Brown, Los Angeles, and flashing lights; 9 ½ x 96 x 10 ½ inches. Collection of SF MoMA, Purchase through the Shirley Ross Davis Fund and the gifts of Mimi and Peter Haas, Helen and Charles Schwab, Phyllis Wattis, and Pat and Bill Wilson. © 2010 The LeWitt Estate / Artists Rights Society (ARS), New York

for *The Dissolve* essay:

page 23: Edison Manufacturing Company, still from *The Enchanted Drawing*, 1900; 35mm film transferred to DVD;1 minute 26 seconds; Producer: J. Stuart Blackton; Camera: Albert E. Smith. Image courtesy of the Library of Congress, Paper Print Collection, Washington DC

page 23: Oscar Muñoz, still from *Re/trato*, 2003; video; 28 minutes. Image courtesy of the artist and Sicardi Gallery, Houston, TX

page 24: Patent drawing for Fleischer's original rotoscope, 1914

page 24: Fleischer Studios, still from *"Big Chief" Ko-Ko*, 1924; 35mm film transferred to DVD; 7 minutes. Image courtesy of Inkwell Images, Morley, MI

page 25: Bill T. Jones and OpenEnded Group, still from *Ghostcatching*, 1999; digital art installation; visuals and sound design: Marc Downie, Shelley Eshkar, and Paul Kaiser; choreography: Bill T. Jones; installation architect: Marco Steinberg; Motion Capture: Futurelight, Modern Uprising; Software Support: Michael Girard and Susan Amkraut. Image courtesy of Bill T. Jones, Shelley Eshkar, and Paul Kaiser

page 25: Isaiah West Taber (1830 -1912), *Loie Fuller Dancing*; photograph; 22.6 x 18.4 cm.; Inv. Pho1984-18-6. Repro Photo:Jean-Gilles Berizzi. Photo credit: Réunion des Musées Nationaux / Art Resource, NY; Musée d'Orsay, Paris, France

page 26: Eadweard Muybridge (1830-1904), *The Transverse-Gallop: one stride,* from "Animals in Motion"; photograph, 1887. Photo credit: Image Select / Art Resource, NY

page 26: Mary Reid Kelley, still from *You Make Me Iliad,* 2010; HD video; 7 minutes 22 seconds. Image courtesy of the artist;

page 27: Jasper Johns, *Study For "Skin" 1,* 1962; charcoal and oil on drafting paper; 22 x 34 inches. Photo: Dorothy Zeidman; Art © Jasper Johns/Licensed by VAGA, New York, NY

page 27: Berni Searle, still from *About to Forget,* 2005; 35mm cinemascope film transferred to three-channel video projection; 3 minutes. Image courtesy of the artist

page 28: Lotte Reiniger, still from *The Adventures of Prince Achmed,* 1926; 35mm film, black and white/tinted, transferred to DVD; 65 minutes. Image courtesy of Milestone Films, Harrington Park, NJ

page 28: Winsor McCay, Gertie the Dinosaur carrying animated version of Winsor McCay, 1913

page 29: Raymond Pettibon, drawing from *Sunday Night and Saturday Morning,* 2005 ; Video; 16 minutes 45 seconds. Image courtesy of the artist and Regen Projects, Los Angeles, CA

page 30: William Kentridge, still from *History of the Main Complaint,* 1996; 35mm film transferred to DVD; 5 minutes 50 seconds. Image courtesy of the artist and Marian Goodman Gallery, New York

page 30: Jacco Olivier, still from *Almost,* 2009; video; 1 minute 35 seconds. Image courtesy of the artist and Marianne Boesky Gallery, New York

page 31: Ezra Johnson, still from *What Visions Burn,* 2006; video; 22 minutes 27 seconds. Image courtesy the artist and Nicole Klagsbrun Gallery, New York

page 31: Maria Lassnig, still from *Maria Lassnig Kantate,* 1992; 35mm film transferred to DVD; 8 minutes. Image courtesy of the artist and Friedrich Petzel Gallery, New York

page 32: Joshua Mosley, still from *A Vue,* 2004; mixed-media animation transferred to DVD; 7 minutes 30 seconds. Image courtesy of the artist and Donald Young Gallery, Chicago, IL

page 33: Brent Green, still from *Paulina Hollers,* 2006; video;12 minutes 35 seconds. Image courtesy of the artist and Andrew Edlin Gallery, New York

page 33: Richard Serra, still from *Hand Catching Lead,* 1968; video, 3 minutes

page 34: Dziga Vertov, still from *Soviet Toys,* 1924; 35mm film transferred to DVD; 10 minutes 45 seconds. Courtesy of the Yale Film Studies Program

page 34: Robert Pruitt; still from *Black Stuntman (Volumes 1 and 2),* 2004; video; 8 minutes. Image courtesy of the artist

page 35: Martha Colburn, still from *Myth Labs,* 2008; 16mm film transferred to DVD; 7 minutes 40 seconds. Image courtesy of the artist and James Cohan Gallery, New York

page 35: Diagram of how Cinerama is projected

page 36: Jennifer and Kevin McCoy; *Traffic #1: Our Second Date,* 2004; tabletop installation with plastic figures, plastic and metal model vehicles, LCD monitor, electronics, lights, video cameras, and video projection; tabletop dimensions: 37 x 50 x 40 inches, video projection dimensions variable. Image courtesy of the artists

page 36: Image from David Adjaye's design proposal for SITE Santa Fe's Eighth International Biennial, 2009. Courtesy of Adjaye Associates

page 37: Christine Rebet; *The Black Cabinet,* 2007; still from 35mm film transferred to DVD; two-channel video installation; 3 minutes 4 seconds. Image courtesy of the artist and Galerie Kamel Mennour, Paris

page 37: George Griffin, *Viewmaster, a digital mutoscope,* 1976/2007; still from 35mm film re-animated, computer, MDF case, LCD monitor; continuous loop; 32 x 20 x 20 inches. Image courtesy of the artist

This catalogue has been published on the occasion of SITE Santa Fe's Eighth International Biennial:

the dissolve
SARAH LEWIS AND **DANIEL BELASCO**, CURATORS

JUNE 20, 2010–JANUARY 2, 2011

ISBN: 978-0-9764492-9-4
Library of Congress Control Number: 2010926110

SITE SANTA FE
1606 Paseo de Peralta, Santa Fe, New Mexico 87501
Tel: 505.989.1199 Fax: 505.989.1188
www.sitesantafe.org

Design: Skolkin + Chickey
Managing Editor: Joanne Lefrak
Editor: Sarah S. King, SNAP Editions
Associate Editor: Diane Armitage, SNAP Editions
Transcription for the Artists' Roundtable Discussion: Keryn Sovella

Printed and bound by Imago Inc., China

Distributed by D.A.P./ Distributed Art Publishers
155 Sixth Avenue, Second Floor, New York, NY 10013-1507